Gothic Vision

The Gothic Vision

Three Centuries of Horror, Terror and Fear

DANI CAVALLARO

continuum

LONDON • NEW YORK

CONTINUUM
The Tower Building, 11 York Road, London, SE1 7NX
370 Lexington Avenue, New York, NY 10017-6503

First published 2002

© 2002 Dani Cavallaro

British Library Cataloguing-in-Publication Data
A catalogue record for this book is available from the British Library.

ISBN 0-8264-5601-4 (hardback)
    0-8264-5602-2 (paperback)

Library of Congress Cataloging-in-Publication Data
Cavallaro, Dani.
    The gothic vision: three centuries of horror, terror and fear / Dani Cavallaro.
        p. cm
    Includes bibliographical references and index.
    ISBN 0-8264-5601-4 — ISBN 0-8264-5602-2 (pbk.)
        1. Horror tales—History and criticism. I. Title.

    PN3435 .C33 2002
    809.3´8738—dc21   2001047149

Typeset by Kenneth Burnley, Wirral, Cheshire
Printed and bound in Great Britain by MPG Books Ltd, Bodmin, Cornwall

Contents

It has been said that we only fear that which we do not know.
Yet perhaps what we fear most is not the possibility of the unknown,
but all the horrors that we know to be true.

Andrew Pyper, *Lost Girls*

Introduction

HE GOTHIC VISION investigates narratives of darkness – the textual constellations of the phenomenon of fear – that represent violent desecrations of common sense and logic. My central argument proceeds from three interrelated premises. First, that terror and horror, the concepts around which assessments of dark fiction have traditionally revolved, are not antithetical, as it has often been contended, but complementary. Terror has conventionally been linked to fear triggered by indeterminate agents, and horror to fear occasioned by visible gore. Although feelings of disorientation and anxiety indubitably alter according to the degree to which their causes may be related to material or incorporeal occurrences, these do not constitute fixed and self-contained categories for they incessantly collude and metamorphose into each other as fear's interdependent affects.

Second, *The Gothic Vision* maintains that fear is not a sporadic event but an ongoing condition endowed with eminently ambivalent powers. Though blinding and numbing, it concurrently operates as a function of consciousness insofar as it offers illuminating insights into the experience of being human as fractured and chaotic. Fear is not disturbing because it intimates that the fabric of our lives, an apparently orderly weave, is being disrupted or is about to be disrupted, but because it shows us that the fabric has always been laddered and frayed. What is aberrant is not the disconcerting sensation of dread but rather the fantasies of order superimposed upon life to make it look seamless and safe.

The third premise is that the representational field where the interaction of terror and horror is most patent is that of the Gothic. This term is here employed to refer to a cultural discourse that utilizes images of disorder, obsession, psychological disarray and physical distortion for the purposes of both entertainment and ideological speculation. I argue that it is vital to acknowledge that the tropes of mental, bodily and ethical disintegration fostered by the Gothic are inextricably linked to specific ideological, historical and political circumstances. Thus, while fear is approached as a widespread and immensely resilient phenomenon, it is also stressed that particular structures of fear obtain in particular times and places, and that their fictional correlatives cannot, therefore, be explained away as escapist flights from social reality. My argument can be summarized as follows: terror and horror are not binary opposites but constantly interacting phenomena; the field where they interact is that of fear as a pervasive condition; the omnipresence of fear is paralleled by the ubiquity of dark tales of Gothic orientation.

The Gothic Vision aims to show that the ideas outlined in the preceding paragraphs can be documented by recourse to both synchronic and diachronic modalities. Representations of horror, terror and fear can be explored synchronically – in terms of their situation at any one point in time. Concurrently, given that those representations are not immutable but rather alter according to social and ideological factors, it is possible to study them diachronically – as part of a historical trajectory. In examining a broad historical range of dark narratives with reference to the articulation of recurrent themes in various contexts, the book seeks to demonstrate that historical analysis and cultural analysis are interwoven and that their specific aims and methods should be viewed not in terms of opposition and duality but in those of complementarity and collusion.

'The Frame of Reference: Theoretical Debates on Horror, Terror and Fear', develops these ideas by evaluating existing approaches to terror and horror, by arguing for their interdependence as the coordinates within which fear unfolds, and by examining their narrative encoding by the Gothic.

Part 1, 'Darkness', examines mythological, historical and psychological approaches to darkness as germane to fear due to its pervasiveness and its fusion of positive and negative connotations: darkness is an ambivalent phenomenon, associated, on the one hand, with chaos and deception, and on the other with illumination and truth. It is linked both to intangible threats likely to induce terror and to tangibly frightening forms likely to evoke horror: in both cases, it is important to recognize the cultural specificity of the contexts in which darkness manifests itself, and of the psychological effects which those contexts tend to produce.

Part 2, 'Haunting', explores the merging of the material and immaterial sources of fear with a focus on the figure of the ghost and its language. Like darkness, the discourse of spectrality holds constructive potential for it is implicated in an ongoing quest for otherworldly dimensions that are capable of providing illuminating insights at the same time as they threaten to destroy us. The rhetoric of haunting invites us to reassess culturally prescribed modes of perception and to suspend our disbelief in the face of what we have been trained to consider impossible.

Part 3, 'Narrative and the Self', suggests that there is a correspondence between the themes treated by dark fiction and the processes through which such stories are constructed. The most salient affinity lies in the sense of uncertainty that looms over both the unfolding of the plot and the author's or narrator's creative endeavour, and is often rendered especially prominent by an unresolved tension between visual and verbal discourses. Uncertainty relates the narrative to terror as an experience of fear conjured by impalpable forces. However, there is also a material component at work: the story is a troubling body in its own right, carrying traces of its teller's attempts to come to terms with both inveterate fears and contingent historical predicaments.

Part 4, 'Child and Adult', assesses the interplay of horror and terror with reference to various forms of abuse inflicted upon young protagonists of dark fiction in a range of socio-historical circumstances. Literal children and adolescents, Gothic heroines, illegitimate relations, ethnic minorities, subcultures and marginalized sexualities constitute the principal categories alternately construed as passive and innocent on the one hand, and criminally disruptive on the other. Their shared ongoing fear stems from their subjection to a cruel ideological imperative: producing an identity out of the reality of having been abandoned.

Part 5, 'Monstrosity', examines the confluence of terror as a potent yet indistinct apprehension of sublime dread and horror as a physical manifestation of the inexplicable and the abnormal. Vampirism is discussed as one of the most enduring kinds of physiological and psychological deviance, capable of eliciting both revulsion and fascination. The ideological specificity of various vampire figures, created according to the desires and concerns of different generations, is stressed. A gallery of hybrid, grotesque and abject creatures is then examined so as to illustrate the idea that what simultaneously scares and cheers us most is the recognition of everyone's more or less latent monstrosity.

For Paddy

The Frame of Reference:
Theoretical Debates on Horror, Terror and Fear

> Normally, we shun what causes distress; most of us don't play in traffic to
> entertain ourselves, nor do we attend autopsies to while away the hours. So why
> do we subject ourselves to fictions that will horrify us?
>
> (Noel Carroll, *The Philosophy of Horror*)

Dark fiction ushers in what could be termed an 'aesthetic of the unwelcome', a
discourse concerned with the ways in which we react to, conceptualize and
represent the murkier facets of our bodies and psyches. Relatedly, it foregrounds the inconclusiveness of any action, attitude or belief by evoking
enveloping histories of pleasure and strife where no experience leads unproblematically to either reward or punishment. Moreover, many dark texts are often
as funny as they are scary: their mood is frequently one of grotesque humour
and jocular tenebrism. The comic dimension is reinforced by elements of
theatricality that range from the operatic to the burlesque and hint at Goya's
famous image of human life as a deceptive performance: 'The world is a mas-
querade; face, dress, voice, everything is feigned. Everybody wants to appear
what he is not; everybody deceives, and nobody knows anybody' (caption to
Plate 6 of *Los Caprichos*, 1799; Gassier and Wilson 1971). People are players
bound to be crushed by the preposterous illusion of their condition unless they
recognize that they are caught in a play directed by the hypocritical and the
insane. In this treacherous world, rational speculation rapidly metamorphoses
into frantic ranting, logic into monstrous irrationality. This is epitomized by
Goya's Plate 43 of *Los Caprichos*, where conflicting interpretations of the relationship between the rational mind and the figments of the imagination are
encapsulated in a single, distressingly laconic, text: 'The Sleep of Reason
Produces Monsters' (1799; Gassier and Wilson 1971). One reading suggests that
the relaxation of conscious vigilance unleashes monsters; another reading
indicates that the rationalist dreams fostered by the Enlightenment are likely
to spawn monstrous aberrations. (The historical and cultural significance of
monstrosity is the subject of **Part 5**.)

The dark brew of fear and pleasure, nightmare and comedy, is, according to Angela Carter, what helps narratives of darkness retain 'a singular moral function – that of provoking unease' (1996:459). The damnation of lecherous monks, the collapse of degenerate fathers and illegitimate sons, the burning of vampires, and indeed death itself do not put a definitive seal on these narratives, for even these ostensibly final events, as Fred Botting stresses, are 'the prelude to other spectral returns' (1996:180). Even narratives which round off their plots by declaring one party triumphant over another are inconclusive. They leave readers adrift in their aftermath by inducing them to wonder what it might be like to be the loser. Often, even after all loose ends have apparently been tied, one is left with the feeling that a pervasive malice rules the world through ruthless self-preservation.

There have been many attempts throughout Western literary and critical history to define viable coordinates within which narratives of darkness could be read and explained. The theoretical model based on the opposition between terror and horror has proved especially influential, terror deemed intangible and resistant to definition, horror definable by virtue of its material nature. David Punter outlines the opposition as follows: terror denotes the 'trembling, the liminal, the sense of waiting' as well as 'a limitless implication of the self in a series of actions which persuade us of their inexorability', whereas horror 'is a stark transfixed staring' which 'provides us with shock and surprise' (1998:236–7). According to this model, the unsettling powers of horror are linked to identifiable objects, most notably the body, and to visible disruptions of the natural order which cause intensely physical reactions. The very etymology of horror points to the corporeal dimension, for the Latin *horrere* actually means 'to shiver' or 'to bristle'. James B. Twitchell states:

> the shiver we associate with horror is the result of the constriction of the skin
> that firms up the subcutaneous hair follicles and thus accounts for the rippling
> sensation, almost as if a tremor were fluttering down our back. From this comes
> the most appropriate trope for horror – creeping flesh or, more simply, the
> 'creeps'. (1988:10–11)

He then adds: 'The word "horripilation" . . . is still used in zoology to describe the condition commonly known as gooseflesh'. Noel Carroll likewise associates the experience of horror with feelings of nausea, revulsion, disgust and visceral abhorrence: the 'recurring sensations' which accompany it include 'muscular contractions, tension, cringing, shrinking, shuddering, recoiling, tingling, frozenness, momentary arrests, chilling' (1990:24).

Terror, conversely, disturbs because of its indeterminateness: it cannot be connected with an identifiable physical object and the factors that determine it accordingly elude classification and naming. Thus, if horror makes people shiver, terror undermines the foundations of their worlds. The Latin root of terror, *terrere*, indeed means 'to shake up'. The opposition just outlined originates in eighteenth-century aesthetics. Ann Radcliffe, in particular, observes: 'Terror and horror are so far opposite, that the first expands the soul, and awakens the faculties to a high degree of life; the other contracts, freezes, and nearly annihilates them' (1826:145–52). While the causes of terror are uncertain and obscure, those of horror lack the dimension of mystery. It follows, according to Radcliffe, that terror has a tendency to stimulate the mind and the senses, whereas horror does nothing to arouse the reader's or viewer's imaginative faculties. This opposition is corroborated by Devendra P. Varma: 'The difference between Terror and Horror is the difference between awful apprehension and sickening realization: between the smell of death and stumbling against a corpse . . . Terror thus creates an intangible atmosphere of spiritual psychic dread . . . Horror resorts to a cruder presentation of the macabre' (1988:16). Robert Hume subscribes to the notion that terror partakes of the mysterious and horror of the corporeal by contrasting the terrifying writings of Horace Walpole and Ann Radcliffe, which are said to hinge on 'suspense and dread', with the horrifying works of Matthew Lewis, William Beckford, Charles Maturin and Mary Shelley, described as inclined to 'attack [the reader] frontally with events that shock or disturb him' (1969:289). The tendency to associate terror with relatively positive sensations and thus elevate it above horror is also borne out by everyday language, where words such as *terribly* or *terrific*, for example, often carry complimentary connotations. The same applies to adverbs and adjectives that hark back to terror's presumed kinship to the sublime: *awful/awfully*, *incredible/incredibly*, *fearful/fearfully*. Of course, language is open to manipulation. Yet, it is likely that most people would take the statement 'you look terrific in your new outfit' as more obviously appreciative than the uncommon alternative 'you look horrific in your new outfit'.

An interesting reversal of the binary opposition between horror/materiality and terror/intangibility is proposed by Twitchell's theoretical model: 'The etiology of horror is *always* in dreams, while the basis of terror is in actuality . . . The distinction between horror and terror has nothing to do with violence and grue; it has everything to do with the psychological resonance of sequence and imagery' (1988:19–20). Twitchell also argues that horror has less to do with fear than with enculturement, which would seem to make it a stabilizing agent: horror has 'to do with laying down the rules of socialization and extrapolating a hidden code of sexual behaviour. Once we learn these rules, as we do in adolescence, horror dissipates' (66). The notion that horror is part of a learning curve of cultural adjustment is corroborated by the popularity of horror amongst adolescents. Though intriguing, this theory is not without problems. Indeed, it would be arduous to demonstrate that socialization is definitively accomplished in one single phase of psychosexual development, as though it were a case of potty-training. Horror may well be one of the vehicles through which the young are exposed to the dark and required to cope with it. Yet, taboos and forbidden fantasies do not evaporate in direct proportion to aging. As Twitchell himself concedes, 'horror monsters . . . are acting out those desires that we fear' (68) and there is no reason to assume that such desires do not play as vital a role in adult life as they do in adolescence. (The issues of age, socialization and generational conflict are addressed in detail in **Part 4**.)

Psychoanalytically, the experiences of terror and horror are comparable to the phenomenon of the *uncanny* as theorized by Sigmund Freud. Uncanny effects arise when familiar circumstances unexpectedly acquire unfamiliar connotations without our being able to ascertain how or why this has happened. They may be generated by 'doubts whether an apparently animate being is really alive; or conversely, whether a lifeless object might not be in fact animate' (Freud 1919:226) or by a failure to differentiate between 'image and reality' (244). Produced through the collusion of familiarity and strangeness, they evoke correspondingly ambivalent emotions: excitement, jouissance and exhilaration on the one hand, and revulsion, dread and disgust on the other. As Victor Sage and Allan Lloyd Smith argue, by creating pockets of non-meaning in ostensibly ordinary worlds, the uncanny operates as 'a kind of gap between codes, a point at which representation itself appears to fail, displace, or diffuse itself' (1996:2). If the uncanny is akin to terror by virtue of its largely undefinable nature, it is also, however, related to horror insofar as it compels us to confront our material nature. As David B. Morris points out, the uncanny is a 'vertiginous and plunging' sensation 'which takes us deep within rather than far beyond the human sphere'. It 'is released as we encounter the disguised and distorted but inalienable images of our own repressed desire' (1985:299–319).

Aesthetically, the opposition between horror and terror is related to that between the *beautiful* and the *sublime*. A beautiful object has a material form and clear contours, while the sublime defies definition due to its tendency to exceed acceptable levels of either magnitude or energy. The most illustrious contribution to the theorization of the sublime in the English-speaking world is Edmund Burke's *A Philosophical Enquiry into the Origin of Our Ideas of the Sublime and the Beautiful* [1757], where he argues that sublime emotions are engendered by anything capable of conveying ideas of terror and pain to the mind without actually endangering the physical self. Vast, dark and towering objects, mighty torrents, vertiginous precipices, erupting volcanoes, impervious mountains and roaring oceans rank as plausible sources of the sublime. Above all, the Burkean sublime has a propensity to immobilize the self into a state in which the mind is totally absorbed by one irresistibly powerful object. In their essay 'On the pleasure derived from objects of terror' (1773), Anna and John Aikin echo Burke's views by focusing on supernatural occurrences. They emphasize that the taste for unsettling images derives from the mind's reluctance to give in to the monotony of everyday reality, what Burke himself terms 'stale unaffecting familiarity' (Burke 1987:136). The Aikins state:

> A strange and unexpected event awakens the mind, and keeps it on the stretch; and where the agency of invisible beings is introduced, of 'forms unseen, and mightier far than we', our imagination, darting forth, explores with rapture the new world which is laid open to its view, and rejoices in the expansion of its powers. (Aikin and Aikin 1773:125)

The sublime is thus endowed with cathartic powers.

In his *Critique of Judgment* [1790], Immanuel Kant defines the sublime as the property of the infinitely great (mathematical sublime) or of the infinitely active (dynamic sublime). For the sake of simplification, it could be argued that an imposing mountain exemplifies the former and a tempestuous sea the latter. The sublime is undefinable and unrepresentable: we may only apprehend it insofar as we may be able to grasp its incomprehensibility. This happens when reason fleetingly gives way to the imagination. As a result, Jean-François Lyotard observes, 'the sublime sentiment' is 'a strong and equivocal emotion: it carries with it both pleasure and pain. Better still, in it pleasure derives from pain' (1984:77).

Binary oppositions, Lyotard's argument suggests, are ultimately bound to prove reductive rationalizations. What is here proposed, in an attempt to avert the dangers implicit in binary thought, is that terror and horror are closely interconnected and that each is capable of metamorphosing into the other. In response to the Radcliffean model, it could be argued that terror may well be incorporeal per se (as intimations of danger and malevolence are often impalpable), but acquires vibrant bodies through the psychological and physical reactions of those exposed to terror and through the material settings of its occurrences. Horror, for its part, may well be tied to corporeal phenomena, yet our inability to classify its sources renders it elusive, as does the sensation that the motives leading to brutal spectacles are ultimately unfathomable. Twitchell's model can be questioned by pointing out that there is no real evidence to back up the assertion that terror is more directly anchored to reality than horror. Twitchell attempts to defend this argument by maintaining that the agents of terror are grounded in a contingent cultural domain while horror's tropes transcend time and space. However, this position is, to say the least, highly subjective; as will be argued in some depth at a later stage, even fantastic monsters gain different connotations from diverse cultural and historical contexts. It would be very hard to prove that terror ensues from what people happen to fear in a particular epoch and that horror, by contrast, transcends time.

The interaction of terror and horror is most explicitly conveyed by stories that articulate the experience of fear as an ongoing condition. Such narratives intimate that fear is not triggered by a single disturbing moment or occurrence but is actually a permanent, albeit multi-faceted, aspect of being-in-the-world. Concrete and intangible phenomena contribute equally to its dynamics. We oscillate constantly between terror and horror because we may only endure the pervasiveness of fear to the extent that we may be willing to acquaint ourselves with its more or less subtle modulations and transformations. Saying that we cannot avoid or escape it, however, would be missing the point, for we actually seek fear, consciously or unconsciously. This is because we cannot resist the attraction of an unnameable something that insistently eludes us. Narratives of darkness nourish our attraction to the unknown by presenting us with charac- ters and situations that point to something beyond the human, and hence beyond interpretation – a nexus of primeval feelings and apprehensions which rationality can never conclusively eradicate. According to H. P. Lovecraft, dark narratives are capable of evoking a sense of quasi-religious awe which puts the reader in 'contact with unknown spheres and powers . . . the beating of black wings or the scratching of outside shapes on the unknown universe's outermost rim' (1973:16). This experience is described as cosmic fear, a sensation that provides intuitive insights into primordial aspects of reality which materialist cultures shun. The cosmic fear theorized by Lovecraft is something of a visionary event tinged with mystical overtones that reaches back towards humankind's dawn and thus constitutes a transgenerational phenomenon. Lafcadio Hearn [1900] embraces a germane approach in maintaining that the individual experience of fear is inextricable from the experience of a whole 'race': 'Elements of primeval fears – fears older than humanity – doubtless enter into the child-terror of darkness' and 'fears of ghosts may very possibly be composed with inherited results of . . . ancestral experience of nightmare' (quoted in Bloom 1998:44).

Entering the circle of fear does not mean relinquishing reality in pursuit of an imaginary world. In fact, it means confronting what threatens us most acutely, and the reasons for which we perceive it as a threat. Fear, to paraphrase Alfred Hitchcock, wakes us up. Proceeding from the assumption that fear is 'one of the most everyday yet least examined of human feelings', Marina Warner likewise highlights the positive potentialities of fear: the 'condition of being scared is becoming increasingly sought after not only as a source of pleasure but as a means of strengthening the sense of being alive, of having a command over self'. People are forced by horrific images 'to stare at the possibility of their non-being, at death itself, but they then discover that they are still alive, outside the tale' (2000:4, 6). Fear does not anaesthetize consciousness but actually sharpens it. It makes us aware that reality contains many more layers than common sense would have us recognize, and that some of these layers are enticing, though also menacing, precisely because we do not understand them. In experiencing dread, we are often torn between curiosity and anger: a consuming desire to know who or what is unsettling us, and a sense of irritation produced by the impossibility of final knowledge. Both emotions alert us to the submerged reality of ancestral appetites.

According to Clive Barker, narratives of darkness can help us understand the power and legitimacy of our wildest drives by 'valuing our appetite for the forbidden rather than suppressing it, comprehending that our taste for the strange, or the morbid, or the paradoxical, is contrary to what we're brought up to believe, a sign of our good health' (1986; quoted in Bloom 1998:100). Darkness may scare us into hiding under the bedclothes but it is also, more importantly, capable of reminding us that what we most often cower beneath is the burden of self-imposed limitations resulting from the internalization of cultural norms that only hypocritically claim to protect the self.

Moreover, dark fiction may enable us to negotiate solitude as a primary ingredient of the experience of fear which, in Stephen King's words, haunts us relentlessly as we 'pass between grinning babyhood and grunting senility': 'Alone. Yes, that's the key word, the most awful word in the English tongue. Murder doesn't hold a candle to it and hell is only a poor synonym' (1977:236). Although many of King's own tales may seem to offer reparative conclusions, they do not finally exorcize the awareness of certain loneliness any more than they could ever repress the knowledge of certain death. In *Danse Macabre*, King describes the collusion of horror and solitude thus: 'Horror in real life is an emotion that one grapples with . . . all alone. It is a combat waged in the secret recesses of the heart . . . What do you see when you turn out the light? the Beatles asked; their answer: I can't tell you, but I know that it's mine' (1993:27).

If, at the level of everyday lived experience, terror and horror merge in the domain of fear as a pervasive condition, at the level of representation they are drawn together by Gothicity as a cultural discourse that provides the underpinning of disparate narratives of darkness of which terror and horror are the recurring affects. The terms *goth* and *gothic* have been invested with several not always clearly related meanings. Historically, they are associated with the Germanic tribes, such as the Visigoths, responsible for overthrowing the Roman Empire and, in this respect, connote barbarity in contrast to classical civilization. However, many Gothic tales are staged not in Northern but in Southern settings, often Italian, the barbarous being equated to Catholicism and its ceremonial excesses, in contrast with Protestant propriety and self-restraint. Goth and gothic also refer to an architectural style popular in Western Europe from the twelfth century to the sixteenth century, and subsequently revived in the eighteenth and nineteenth centuries. In architecture, as in historiography, goth and gothic are often used contemptuously to describe a style that contravenes classical rules of harmony, stability and decorum through its emphasis on dynamic lines, elaborate and soaring structures, and an intricate profusion of detail. As a modern trend, goth and gothic denote a component of the punk and post-punk music scene that has gradually come to constitute an independent and polyphonic subculture with repercussions in various areas of fashion, literature and the arts generally.

In relation to narratives of darkness, Gothicity primarily refers to tales of obsession and haunting which employ images of disorder, alienation and monstrosity for the purposes of both entertainment and ideological reflection. The fascination with the violation of cultural boundaries combines with anxieties bred by the possibly dire repercussions of transgression. In schematic form, Gothicity can be mapped as follows:

Geographical connotations
- Northern barbarity versus English civilization
- Mediterranean depravity versus Anglican rectitude

Ideological connotations
- archaic disorder versus modern discipline
- medieval darkness versus enlightenment
- anti-classical leanings versus (neo)classical ethos
- crudeness versus elegance
- savage paganism versus refined morality
- aristocracy/feudalism versus bourgeoisie/capitalism
- landed classes versus cosmopolitan gentry

Psychological connotations
- terror
- horror
- the sublime
- the uncanny
- spectrality
- secretiveness
- obsession
- paranoia
- psychosis
- melancholia
- persecution
- claustrophobia

Physical connotations
- bestiality
- monstrosity

- the hybrid
- the grotesque
- revulsion
- pollution
- disease

Stylistic connotations
- exaggeration
- ornamental excess
- surrealist effects
- dream language
- tenebrous comedy

The Gothic has repeatedly been codified in relation to and in contrast with dominant genres and forms. In both the eighteenth century and the nineteenth century, for example, it was common to associate Gothicity with tastelessness, and with the consumption of pulp fiction by a supposedly unrefined, albeit economically ascendant, middle-class market and particularly with women. However, the Gothic's ideological function was implicitly recognized, insofar as the experience of fear was frequently endowed with purging powers. Thus, the Gothic was considered capable of facilitating the reconstitution of a sense of normality, equilibrium and order by provoking extreme fear and hence encouraging the expulsion of the fearful object. Yet this potentially cathartic function was also regarded with suspicion, since many Gothic narratives, equipped with a moral, reparative finale, could by no means be deemed morally correct in their entirety. The guardians of taste and propriety felt that stabilizing endings might be simply paying lip service to canonical ethics without really purging the main body of the story of immoral or amoral messages.

It is vital to realize, therefore, that although the Gothic has time and again been branded as escapist, its tales are culturally, historically and economically relevant to a very tangible social reality. E. J. Clery persuasively documents the Gothic's relevance by examining the emergence of tales of darkness and the supernatural in relation to their socio-political contexts. She argues that an 'intimate connection' exists 'between fictions of the supernatural and the growth of consumerism' and that so-called works of fantasy do not 'escape into a never-never Gothic past' but actually 'engage with issues of the present' (1999:Foreword). Dark tales are linked to the operations of consumer culture because their circulation was made possible by the emergence, in the early industrial era, of novel technologies for the production, distribution and marketing of fiction. More importantly, Clery maintains, both those tales and consumerism were seen by many – especially within the traditional landed classes – to pander to the 'escalation of "unreal needs"' and accordingly demonized. The consumption of fantasies and the consumption of 'luxury commodities' (7) were thus drawn together as twin instances of cultural degeneration.

It is against this background that tales of the marvellous and the supernatural were resisted and derided over a protracted period of time. The scornful dismissal of Gothic fiction, moreover, is intimately bound up with gender politics. Indeed, the reading of fantasies was associated primarily with women, their unwholesome susceptibility to imaginary threats and whims, and their openness to romantically extravagant and licentious images. Thus, disparaging the Gothic as a second-rate genre was concurrently a means of denigrating female readers as members of a second-rate sex. It could also be argued that women were associated with novels on the basis of cultural stereotypes that inscribed both the female body and the body of a mass-consumed fiction as trashy and tainted. It remains to be proved that women were indeed the principal consumers of Gothic novels, and that men would only deign to peruse them if they could consider them allegorically redeeming. However, as Clery shows, the coupling of implausible and possibly corrupting tales and femininity has produced an intriguing myth:

> The library books pass through many hands: held cheap by their temporary
> owners, they are soiled, marked and defaced, manhandled until they fall apart.
> It represents a prostitution of print, a commercial promiscuity, irresistibly sug-
> gesting a parallel fate for the (*de jure*) female readers who devour and
> internalize the stories. (97)

(This idea is discussed further in **Chapter 8.**)

In the light of this reading, it is hardly surprising that, in spite of women's prominence on the Gothic scene, quite a few of them should have entertained ambivalent feelings towards the world of darkness: 'The Gothic marketplace would seem to be one in which women would hold equal sway. Many Gothic authors were women; even a printer of Gothic romances, Ann Lemoine, was a woman'. However, 'author Charlotte Smith, whose life of domestic violence resembled a Gothic novel, was singled out for unique public humiliation by her publisher. Ann Ward Radcliffe preferred to be thought dead or insane than an authoress' ('Women and the Gothic'). According to Eve Kosofsky Sedgwick, 'the Gothic makes a teasing proffer of insight into important historical questions. Within the historical frame of the Industrial Revolution, the Gothic is preoccupied with dramatizing versions of the mutual reappraisal of the middle and upper classes', as well as 'the position of women in relation to changing shapes of patriarchal domination' (1985:83). (See also **Chapter 10.**)

David Punter corroborates the idea that Gothicity is culturally relevant despite its frequent relegation to the sphere of escapist fiction. Indeed, it sustains, albeit tangentially, a social critique of the Age of Reason by dramatizing the unchartable incursions of chaos into order:

> Gothic, precisely insofar as because of its historical and geographical distancing it does not appear to represent a "real" world, may in fact be delivering that world in an inverted form, or representing those areas of the world and of consciousness which are, for one reason or another, not available to the normal processes of representation. (1996:15)

Furthermore, it could be argued that the Gothic has assumed different guises over the centuries in conjunction with broader cultural shifts. Clive Bloom observes that 'the gothic speaks to the dark side of domestic fiction: erotic, violent, perverse, bizarre and obsessionally connected with contemporary fears' (1998:2). The 'decisive break between the gothic of *Otranto* and the psychological horror of the late nineteenth century', he argues, is marked by Edgar Allan Poe's 'The Fall of the House of Usher' [1839], where the internal realm of the psyche becomes the principal threat and, within it, 'the ineffable demands of the will' (1998:3). Indirectly echoing Schopenhauer's and Nietzsche's theories, Poe posits the *will* as an indomitable force, generally indifferent to the destinies of individuals: 'an innate and primitive principle of human action, a paradoxical something, which we may call *perverseness*'. This 'unconquerable force' coincides with a 'tendency to do wrong for wrong's sake', to the point that 'the desire to be well is not only not aroused, but a strongly antagonistic sentiment exists'. According to Poe, we perform certain actions 'merely because we feel that we should *not*' (1845; quoted in Bloom 1998:24–5, 27). This is precisely what the human character in Poe's poem 'The Raven' (1845) masochistically pursues: he asks increasingly unanswerable questions of his ominous visitor out of a perverse desire to be denied acceptable explanations for his abysmal sorrow.

An important development, in the history of narratives of darkness, is also the popular demand, from the mid-nineteenth century onwards, for 'supernaturalism, "spiritism", mysticism and theology' (Bloom 1998:6) resulting in some of the most famous ghost stories ever written, by M. R. James, Henry James and Algernon Blackwood, for example. (This genre is examined in depth in **Part 2**.) The next crucial event is the appearance of the magazine *Weird Tales* in 1920, as a novel site for the articulation of the dark, the fantastic and the supernatural. As Bloom points out, one of its major contributors and editors, H. P. Lovecraft, 'created a whole "horror lifestyle" and culture around "Arkham" and the mythos of Cthulhu' (1998:7). This, incidentally, is attested to by the existence of rather massive Web rings devoted to Lovecraft and his followers, the mythos itself, and both literary and visual interpretations. Fantasy, the supernatural, horror and the grotesque have concurrently been gaining growing popularity in tandem with science fictional themes. Bloom also talks of a '"revival" of horror in the late 1970s' with authors such as King, Herbert, Blatty and Campbell at the forefront, and of an 'extraordinary increase in horror fiction sales' in the 1980s, linked to the incremental popularity of a variety of interrelated motifs – including supernatural manifestations, graphic violence and sexual violation.

The enduring hold of Gothicity may be attributed, to a considerable extent, to its inclination to draw us into tabooed universes – today, no less that in the eighteenth century. It exposes areas of otherwise inhibited expression, the *non-things* that insistently fill up the interstices between one accepted cultural compartment and the next. The taboos confronted by both twentieth-century and post-millennial audiences revolve around the awareness of a radical disjuncture between the self's aspirations and the dehumanizing requirements of its environment. Not surprisingly, perhaps, a major manifestation of Gothicity in recent history comes from disaffected subcultures.

The terms *goth* and *gothic* were first used in the context of late twentieth-century popular culture in the late 1970s and early 1980s to designate an offshoot of the punk movement and the music styles of bands such as Bauhaus, The Damned, The Cure, Siouxsie and the Banshees, and Sisters of Mercy. However, what helped the tag Gothic to stick had primarily to do with apparel and body images indicative of a dark aesthetic: black clothes and hair, black and white makeup, a profusion of silver jewellery, bondage and fetish garments and accessories, velvet, fishnet tights and shirts, opera-style gloves and cloaks, lace, pointy shoes, high heels, combat boots, chains, studs, spikes, crosses and chokers. If Goth is a fashion, it is also, however, a mind set: according to the *Goth Primer*, it 'celebrates the dark recesses of the human psyche' and 'makes depression and angst a lifestyle choice'. Just as early Gothic fiction was jeered at and farcicalized, Gothic subcultures have often been the butt of hilarious disdain. As Alicia Porter points out, it has often been ridiculed as a stereotypical attitude ultimately amounting to 'sitting around in circles on the floor of pubs . . . smoking a lot and talking about being a bat' (Porter:website). Moreover, this subculture has often been criticized on the basis of its lack of commitment to pressing cultural issues. James Hannaham, for example, argues that its invariably theatrical expression of an awareness of grief renders it untrustworthy, since 'the requisite adornment that goes hand in hand with a "Gothic" aesthetic . . . calls the sincerity of the wearer into question' (1997:96). Other critics, conversely, have stressed the countercultural validity of Gothic artists. Csaba Toth, for instance, argues that

> They remark on the postindustrial disappearance of the labouring body against
> the backdrop of vacant factory yards, deserted farms, bleak downtowns, a
> polluted environment, and ever-present television screens. In this Gothic land

of the end of the long cycle (of the post-war boom), boundaries between the 'normal' and the pathologized 'other' collapse, and the 'normal' is often more dreadful than its 'unnatural' opposite. (1997:89–8)

Richard Davenport-Hines associates the emergence of Gothic subcultures in Britain and the US with a reaction against 'fundamentalist groups' fighting 'to ban from museum displays, gallery exhibitions, television, the Internet, magazines, CD lyrics and videos' (1998:9–10) anything representing or even simply alluding to cultural darkness. Tabooed materials of this kind are described by Cristoph Grunenberg as 'everything that disturbs the uncompromising doctrine of an imaginary nuclear family, the dream of a caring, non-violent society, the Puritan repugnance of sex . . . and an obsessive preoccupation with physical and mental cleanliness' (1997:205). The resurgence of Gothicity, in this respect, may well signify a reaction against enforced sanitation. In Gothic subcultures, as in their narrative antecedents, the emphasis repeatedly falls on images of transgression and disintegration that symbolize the undoing of both personal and collective identities. Drawn to the *ruin* as the epitome of psychological, bodily, linguistic and aesthetic breakdown, Gothicity pursues a death-wish that could be read either as an invitation to confront humanity's most inveterate fears or as a morbid obsession with decay. It is largely as a result of this ambiguity that it lends itself to contrasting interpretations as both a serious cultural phenomenon and a ludic spectacle.

Just as fear is a pervasive phenomenon rather than a sporadic emotion, so the narratives of darkness that articulate it are not limited and somehow aberrant genres on the periphery of literary fiction but actually a crucial dimension of creativeness. Tales of terror, horror, the uncanny, haunting, suspense and monstrosity have indeed been treated as genre fiction, arguably in an attempt to tame their troubling messages by relegating them to the margins of art. The distrust of fantasy and of the imagination so insistently exhibited by Western thinkers has served to buttress this strategy of exclusion. As Rosemary Jackson maintains, 'the fantastic has constantly been dismissed by critics as being an embrace of madness, irrationality, or barbarism and it has been opposed to the humane and more civilized practices of "realistic" literature'. This has led to a 'repeated neutralization of its images of impossibility and of desire' (1981:172–3). However, darkness is a stubborn constant in the making of fiction which exceeds generic boundaries. This pervasiveness may at least partly be explained with reference to the ideological significance of darkness. It may well be the case, as many critics contend, that dark narratives play a normative role, that their function is to serve as agents of stability. Yet it is undeniable that the damage done on the way to restoration leaves hardly any stone unturned.

As Jackson argues, there have been assiduous attempts to domesticate fantasies, especially those veering towards the marvellous, as *'compensatory'* discourses promising the triumph of 'goodness' and 'order' (174). Fantasies can be enlisted in the preservation of the myth of cultural harmony. Nevertheless, tales of the marvellous, such as fairy tales and utopias, will ultimately evince gaps and aporias that undermine their reparative function. (See also **Part 4** for a discussion of the cultural function of fantasy.) This is corroborated by their openness to transgressive interpretations, as shown, for example, by Angela Carter's reformulation of 'Little Red Riding-Hood' in 'The Company of Wolves' (1993) or Poppy Z. Brite's articulation of the 'Puss-in-Boots' theme in 'King of the Cats' (1999). The taming of fantasy has often been accomplished by sublimating its dark undercurrents. According to Freud, sublimation is at the very roots of creativity, insofar as the '"phantasizing" activity . . . provides man with compensation for having renounced instinctive gratification' (Jackson 1981:174). Gothic fiction could be regarded as a paradigmatic case of compensatory sublimation that aimed at consolidating, as Jackson maintains, 'a dominant, bourgeois ideology, by vicarious wish fulfilment through fantasies of incest, rape, murder, parricide, social disorder. Like pornography, it functioned to supply an object of desire, to imagine social and sexual transgression' (175). Yet, sublimation and recuperation are concurrently denied by an insatiable longing for dark otherness, the dissolution of ethical restraints and the chaos of non-meaning. If this yearning appears to negate reason, it could also be seen as an invitation to expand reason's territory to include a recognition of the unrecognizable.

Stephen King's endorsement of Clive Barker's *Books of Blood* reads: 'What Barker does makes the rest of us look like we've been asleep for the past ten years.' Whether or not one agrees with King's evaluation of Barker's achievements, his words usefully imply that horrific images have the power to revive consciousness. They are capable of waking us up or at least reminding us that we have been asleep without necessarily knowing that this was the case. The revitalizing properties of fear are central to the orchestration of narratives of darkness. Any reader of terror, horror, the Gothic and related tales of fantasy and the supernatural is likely to remember at least one moment of exposure to an unsettling image capable of jarring perception out of its habitual operations. Such moments are comparable to those uncanny situations in which, having become absorbed in a routine activity, we suddenly become aware of an unfamiliar thought or feeling uncoiling through our minds and bodies. The awareness pricks the sensorium and shakes the conscious self. It compels us to look at ourselves from the outside, to become spectators of our actions and reactions. There is something simultaneously unnerving and energizing about such situations. We feel displaced but, at the same time, we catch a glimpse of potent, submerged forces.

Narratives of darkness give shape to the disorienting sensations described above by intensifying their power and frequency through an emphasis on the irreducible hold of the inexplicable. They seldom allow us to forget that hidden energies are indefatigably at work all the time, that they are hidden because human beings have made them so, and that what has been secreted is always on the verge of erupting. Although this alerting function is common, in varying degrees, to all dark fiction, it is important to recognize that the shapes given by individual tales to unsettling exeriences are quite diverse. It is also important, in this respect, to realize that the relationship between those narratives and generic classification is ambiguous, for they often exhibit an inclination to combine several genres, hence making genre criticism itself a precarious and unreliable endeavour. Dark textuality eludes the keenest attempts to ghettoize its themes by enclosing them within academic genres and, indeed, consistently overspills the structures it adopts. There have indubitably been sustained attempts to force fictional articulations of darkness into generic categories, and these have often led to their marginalization as pulp unworthy of scholarly scrutiny. Indeed, even when they feature on academic syllabuses, they are not, by and large, dealt with in a systematic fashion. The devaluation of dark fiction has proceeded largely from its association with popular culture and mass culture and its concomitant labelling by recourse to generic tags that emphasize its cheapness: thriller, chiller, splatterpunk, romance, fantasy, family saga, Gothic horror and suspense are among the most widely employed earmarks.

The critical tendency to view popular and mass cultures as devoid of authentic value can be traced at least as far back as the Frankfurt School. Particularly influential has been the position, propounded by Theodor Adorno and Max Horkheimer, that popular works are mere commodities which lack the distinctive qualities of art, products of a 'pleasure industry' consisting of nothing more than 'the automatic succession of standardized operations' (1986:137), denying any real 'fulfilment' (140) and hence intent on 'perpetually cheat[ing] its consumers of what it perpetually promises' (139). More recently, the presumed inferiority of popular culture has been proclaimed by Walter Nash in *The Language of Popular Fiction*, who states bluntly that 'popfiction' has no 'merit' for it 'is committed to the simplest moralities, the crudest psychologies, and has few philosophical pretensions' (1990:3). Scott McCracken has opposed this argument by proposing that 'popular fiction can only be easily dismissed if it is treated in isolation and not as part of [a] larger dynamic' (1998:5). It could be argued that a central factor in this larger dynamic is precisely the phenomenon of fear as an ongoing condition. Indeed, attempts to brand narratives of darkness as second-rate popular commodities and accordingly classify them with reference to devaluing labels have served not only to push them to the periphery of creative endeavour, but also to assist the desire to sublimate and tame the experience of fear by arbitrarily framing its representations. This colonizing programme should be thoroughly questioned. Genres and subgenres are designed to contain and delimit. They ask us to approach stories as clones based on accepted formulae, to cherish them if they feature expected signifiers and to reject them if they do not.

Two main strategies may be deployed to interrogate the domesticating approach: a contextualization of the narratives themselves and a recognition of their contribution to the development of a sense of identity. As Marina Warner argues, even traditional narrative forms, such as the fairy tale, which may seem wholly familiar and formulaic and hence impervious to change, actually alter over time in relation to the circumstances of their narration and reception: the 'meanings they generate are themselves magical shape-shifters, dancing to the needs of their audiences' (1995:xx). Scott McCracken stresses the need for contextualization by maintaining that we cannot appeal to universal, timeless notions of 'cultural value' and that we should therefore 'refuse the abstract categories of high and low, good and bad' by focusing instead on 'the kinds of values a particular audience has a vested interest in creating and sustaining'. Accordingly, generic classifications 'are best understood . . . not in terms of basic elements, but as historical and relational' (1998:5, 12). Where the issue of identity is concerned, it is vital to realize that narratives of darkness do not merely allow us to toy with alternative selves by inviting us to identify with fictional characters and experience emotions vicariously. They actually encourage us to resituate ourselves, to foster the extension of the self and indeed its dispersion into a plethora of selves that are always implicated with specific cultural structures. Anthony Giddens argues that the 'project of the self . . . consists in the sustaining of coherent yet continuously revised biographical narratives' (1982:5). Narratives of darkness could be said to provide some of the materials through which such biographies can be endlessly created and edited by compelling us to address the provisional status of identity in the face of nonrational forces that threaten insistently to pulverize its mythical continuity and fullness. Thus, both fictional narratives and the stories through which identities may be fashioned are caught in processes of constant reinvention and historical reinscription.

What I seek to emphasize is that fictions concerned, in disparate fashions, with the realm of the Beyond are likely to be disrespectful of conceptual cages used to delimit either the text or the self. In other words, tales of horror, terror and fear resist categorization by cultivating an eerie dialectic between anxiety and desire that often manifests itself as a commitment to 'the unsaid and the unseen . . . that which has been silenced, made invisible, covered over and made "absent"' (Jackson 1981:4). It is by allowing repressed materials to surface, often abruptly, and by articulating them in ways which defy conservative compartments, that those stories enable dread to operate as a psychodynamic awakener. Consciousness is sharpened by its exposure to the

Beyond and by intimations that its maps inevitably exceed the scope of any generic atlas. Many critics associate reality with consciousness and narratives of darkness with soporific escapism. Whether or not this position is accepted will depend on what is meant by consciousness. If it is associated merely with the physiological state of being awake, then much dark fiction could indeed be said to have a sedative effect by transporting its readers into the oneiric sphere of nightmares. If, however, the notion of consciousness is refined to designate not simply the state of being awake but also an awareness of being awake, then tales of darkness have much to contribute to the attainment of this condition.

— Part 1—
Darkness

Introduction

It is always dark. Light only hides the darkness.

Daniel Kian McKiernan, 'Darkness'

Darkness is the basic ingredient that all narratives discussed in this book share. There is the gloom of stereotypical Gothic settings and props: ruined castles and abbeys, murky crypts and fungoid dungeons, clammy cellars, dank passages and stairwells echoing with howls, groans and tapping fingers, dripping charnel houses and ivy-clad monasteries, secret cabinets, storms, bleak forests and treacherous marshes. These becreepered places take on especially dark connotations at particular times of the day, night, season and year. Lonely spots in the grip of forbidding northern winters, preferably in the dead of night, are elements of a well-known matrix. No less spooky, however, are those times of transition, from day into night, from summer into winter, that disturb due to their indeterminateness, to their blurring of neat distinctions. The darkest times are often disorientingly crepuscular rather than pitch black. Beside the hardware of places and times of darkness one has to take into account the software of dark psyches: Gothic mentalities tinged with neurotic, psychotic and paranoid proclivities. In this mental realm, the night is always dark regardless of the amount of moonlight shed upon it since the moon is itself cold, stabbing, unable to supply any real sense of comfort. As landscape and architecture, climate and seasons, thoughts and emotions collude to evoke a tenebrous universe, paradoxically light ultimately proves as impenetrable as darkness itself.

Darkness has been invested with negative connotations by many mythologies and religions. Frequently, it is associated with the baser instincts, lack of clarity and order, a pervasive sense of fear and a fate of unrelieved sorrow. It is also linked to the concept of the Absurd, as the condition created by impotent minds seeking meaning in a meaningless universe. Christianity damns it by positing the Devil, the Prince of Darkness, as the enemy of God's Logos. In Hindu mythology, darkness symbolizes Time the Destroyer; in Iranian mythology, it is the power connected with Ahriman, Lord of Lies; in Islam, it epitomizes indiscretion.

Derogatory assessments of darkness traditionally go hand in hand with the conventional tendency to conceive of it as black. Both colonial and patriarchal myths have been intent on demonizing it as the mysterious and savage province of either literally or metaphorically black people: putatively primitive races in the context of ethnic discrimination, and feminine psychology and non-heterosexual sexualities in the realm of gender politics. The proclivity to regard racial blackness as symptomatic of feral and base urges is a sinister constant in Western history, as is the inclination to construe sexual preferences and activities likely to question patriarchal norms as *blackened* by prospects of moral and physical degeneration. However, such myths are context-bound and open to reversal. For example, while in the West it has been common, as Marina Warner points out, to 'scare the young into obedience' by recourse to aliens such as 'Gypsies, Jews, Turks, blacks' – as borne out by the Italian appellation of the bogeyman as 'l'omo nero' (literally, the black man) – a 'lullaby from the plantations of Gran Canaria' describes the enemy ready to devour the child as 'the white devil' (2000:161–3). Questioning the blackness of darkness is a means of interrogating a whole collection of stereotypes. If darkness alludes to menace and fear, it must be stressed that the images are not inevitably black. At the same time, blackness cannot be universally assumed to connote evil since much that is threatening is evoked by its very opposite.

In the context of gender-related definitions of darkness, inversions also obtain. It is routine, for instance, to portray witches as nefariously black, misshapen, hunchbacked and warty female monsters. Yet, even so-called good fairies, fashioned as caring figures bathed in radiance and beauty, may prove cruel and ungenerous. The Blue-Haired Fairy in Carlo Collodi's *Pinocchio* [1883] is a case in point. (See also **Chapter 11.**) Far from embodying the notion of sweetness and light, the Fairy is capable of acting as quite a callous mother, and of decreeing sadistically dark punishments with a good deal of self-righteous smugness. In Robert Coover's carnivalesque reworking of Collodi's classic, the Blue-Haired Fairy is even more overtly tinged with negative nuances than in the nineteenth-century narrative. (See also **Chapter 1.**) Painfully sought after by Pinocchio – 'an aging emeritus professor from an American university' (Coover 1997:15) – through Venice's disconcerting labyrinth, the Fairy is here conceived of as a prismatic character: the fabulous creature supposed to have put flesh on a wooden puppet's limbs; a lost and very possibly fickle lover; an unattainable object of desire comparable to the Petrarchan angelic ladies of the courtly love tradition, once forsaken by the unruly Pinocchio himself; and an authoritarian and possessive mother. Partly as a result of his own sense of guilt and partly as a result of her puzzling ambiguity, Pinocchio sees her alternately as his 'dearest playmate' (321), a seductive nymphet reminiscent of 'a Hollywood starlet he once knew' (322); a 'deceitful ogress'; a 'poor lonely fairy' (323); a concerned parent and a bawdy slut: 'She is grotesque. Hideous. Beautiful' (329). What ultimately makes the Fairy monstrous and what Pinocchio resents most are her impossibly lofty standards, her determination to eradicate from his being the 'idleness' that she describes as 'a dreadful disease': 'Oh, yes, yes, I've heard all that before! You always were the *good* little fairy, weren't you? Society's little helper! Civilization's drill sergeant! But I was free! I was happy! And you, with your terrifying heartbreaking parade of tombstones and canon, put strings on me where there were none'.

George Eliot's novella *The Lifted Veil* [1878] also problematizes the ethical value of darkness by intimating that we may be seriously mistaken in interpreting other people's enigmatic behaviour as the product of a complex magnetic personality likely to yield, upon the disclosure of their darkest secrets, fascinating depths. When the psychic narrator finally gains access to his wife's inner being, he discovers that her charismatic elusiveness is merely a facade. Once lifted, the veil reveals a void: 'The terrible moment of complete illumination had come to me, and I saw that the darkness had hidden no landscape from me, but only a blank prosaic wall' (1985:49). Darkness does not necessarily mask an alluring mystery. It may also, in fact, conceal the absence of anything more interesting than shallow glamour and greed.

Figures of light, then, are not always benevolent. Many popular spectres are not rendered any less malicious by their paleness, luminescence or pearly-white translucence. The 'Jack-o'-lantern' (also known as 'will-o'-the-wisp' in England and 'fairy light' or 'foxfire' in Ireland) is a potentially beautiful phosphorescent light but it is also associated with witches, vengeful lost souls and death omens. Likewise, light is the far-from-comforting hallmark of bewitching, glimmering mirages such as those evoked by the mermaid-like Breton Morganes and the Italian Fate Morgane, all descendants of the baleful apparitions contrived by the Arthurian Morgan le Fay. The idea that light cannot be unproblematically linked to propitious situations is confirmed by the fact that black itself is not uniformly recorded by anthropological research and the study of folklore as the scariest hue for, as Warner observes, the 'most frightening colour of all . . . is the absence of colour: the whiteness of negation, found in night-flyers such as barn owls and certain moths . . . The owl that hunts and screeches, gleaming ghostly in the shadows . . . has a paralysing effect on its prey' (2000:180–1).

Moreover, the idea of darkness as negative and destructive is counterbalanced by a recognition of its positive aspects. In several traditions, it is associated with primordial chaos and its powers. This does not make darkness fundamentally evil, for an inchoate and prenatal universe is the precondition of form and of the light that grows out of it. After all, embryos develop in the darkness of the womb and germination takes place in the dark earth. Darkness is also linked to spiritual initiation and rites of passage, as in the trope of the 'dark night of the soul' posited by St John of the Cross.

In psychoanalytical terms, darkness is related to the realm of the *shadow*: the receptacle of all things dreaded and disowned by consciousness. In Jungian psychoanalysis it is described as the repository of emotions that civilized and enlightened society shuns. What is most menacing about the shadow is that it has an autonomous energy that tends to express itself through terrifying and monstrous forms. Paradoxically, the more intensely the shadow is repressed, the more powerful and energetic it becomes. Thus, although darkness is associated with a regressive state, it vibrates with vitality and creativity. It is imperative to acknowledge these qualities, since what is commonly demonized as evil may actually open our eyes to valuable experiences and submerged levels of reality. Darkness can be enlightening. The shadow's energy is most likely to affect those who, like the narrator in Susan Hill's *The Woman in Black*, deliberately avoid 'all contemplation of any remotely non-material matters' and cling to 'the prosaic, the visible and tangible' (1998:13). As Stephen King suggests in *Salem's Lot*, attempts to explain darkness and its shadows tend to come across as naive incantations when compared with appalling and incontrovertible, albeit unquantifiable, evidence of supernatural malice. Faced with the possibility of vampiric attacks in the community, one of the central characters endeavours to hold on to the down-to-earth convictions that 'things like Coleridge's "Cristabel" or Bram Stoker's evil fairy tale' are 'only the warp and woof of fantasy', that the 'mark of the devil on a woman's breast is only a mole' and that 'the man who came back from the dead and stood at his wife's door dressed in the cerements of the grave was only suffering from locomotor ataxia'. Yet, these apparent proofs of the rule of reason disintegrate against a basic knowledge, which rationalization can neither mollify nor deride: *'I'm frightened'* (1977:194–5).

Moreover, darkness is inevitably perceived as a punishment by those who, like Neil Gaiman's Master of Yin-Yang, are possessed by fear and refuse to recognize its illuminating potentialities: 'It was fear that drove him, and fear that pushed him into the darkness . . . And the fear stole the joy . . . leeched the pleasure from his life' (1999:42). A viable alternative is to embrace darkness and to grapple with the crepuscular limbo to which reason and systematic knowledge are so insistently relegated by fear. Arguably, it is by accepting the omnipresence of darkness that we may also begin to acknowledge the inevitable pervasiveness of dread. Much of the time, people strive to localize the experience of fear by associating it with extraordinary entities and phenomena. Creatures of the Beyond such as demons and spooks serve a consolatory purpose, for they enable us to nourish the illusion that the ordinary world, putatively immune to the influence of those entities and occurrences, may not be constitutionally burdened by fear.

Yet, the real 'challenge', as the character of Terry Dare states sardonically in William Peter Blatty's 'Elsewhere', actually stems from being in the world, *this* world. By resorting to supernatural threats, human beings seek to exorcize the terrors and horrors of the everyday and the mundane, acting 'as if living on a spinning rock hurtling through the void dodging asteroids and comets weren't challenge enough, not to mention tornadoes, death and disease as well as Vlad the Impaler and earthquakes and war' (1999:576). Unwittingly echoing Dare's words, the psychic expert Anna Trawley later observes: 'To exist in the limitless dark of this universe, bruised and unknowing whence we came and where to go, to take breath on this hurtling piece of rock in the void – these alone are a terror in themselves, are they not?'. The corollary of Trawley's rhetorical question, regardless of the effects on her mentality of the regular use of *Ouija* boards, is a frank recognition of fear as intrinsic to human existence: 'Fear, if we correctly observe our situation, is our ordinary way, like feeding, like dying' (628–9).

The approaches cited in the preceding paragraphs variously intimate that if darkness is an ambiguous adversary, light is no unequivocal saviour either. Ramsey Campbell's delineation of this idea, based on a comparison between shapes rendered spooky by darkness and their appearance in daylight, is particularly evocative, in this respect:

> Some of it may look like a big city at night, but is it only litter we see scuttling away from the streetlamps? Why is that bin liner grinning as it swoops towards us on the wind? You might hope daylight would drive such presences away, but here light only makes the shadows darker and shows us things that would have done better to stay in the dark. (2000)

Thomas Ligotti's 'The Shadow, the Darkness' dramatizes the paradoxical status of darkness as simultaneously obfuscating and illuminating through the ambivalent character of Grossvogel – prophet, charlatan, inspired artist and ruthless businessman. Grossvogel preaches about a 'pervasive shadow that causes things to be what they would not be' and an 'all-moving darkness that makes things do what they would not do' (1999:275–6). This leads him to believe that the only reliable reality is a densely corporeal construct, a nexus of indomitable forces comparable to Schopenhauer's will and Nietzsche's will-to-power (though Ligotti's character does not take the time to speculate this far), and that abstract notions like 'soul' and 'self' are 'nonsense and dreams', in contrast with the 'physical body' that stubbornly endures thanks to is reliance on the '*activating*' forces of shadow and darkness (283).

In Dennis L. McKiernan's 'Darkness', light and darkness join forces as equally ruthless enemies. The protagonist, Harlow, inherits from a great-uncle a mansion wired so that by activating any one switch, all the rooms will be flooded by glaring brightness. Convinced that this electric peculiarity has to do with his ancestor's pathological fear of the dark, Harlow turns the house back 'into a normal one' (1999:552). At first, the return to a proper balance of light and darkness seems salutary. Before long, however, the protagonist too becomes prey to a 'fear of the dark' which, much as he tries to conceptualize it as 'a primitive reaction. Coded in the genes. A holdover from cavemen days' (554), ends up destroying him, the antidote to darkness supplied by 'night-vision goggles' (559) finally benefiting his opponent in its relentless pursuit.

What the discourse of darkness requires us to address is the apparently unfathomable chain of reasons for which we feel drawn to what scares us, and thus begin to grasp the significance of our urge, however subliminal this may be, to go on confronting the ubiquity of fear. Julia Briggs may be quite right in proposing that what takes us into frightening areas of darkness is an admixture of cockiness and inquisitiveness. In her study of ghost stories, for instance, she observes:

> there is nearly always a distinct moment when the hero commits some error, perhaps a form of hubris, by taking a wrong decision, or by choosing against advice to prosecute some scheme . . . There is no apparent folly in such under-takings and the act of hubris then lies in not heeding warnings or signs. But perhaps the emotion that most frequently lures the unwitting hero on is curiosity . . . the innocent curiosity of Bluebeard's wife . . . Faust's hunger for forbidden knowledge. (1977; quoted in Bloom 1998:114)

Concurrently, the journey into darkness has been described as an effect of the longing to transgress the rules of both safety and sanity. Poe, most memorably, states: 'We stand upon the brink of a precipice. We peer into the abyss – we grow sick and dizzy. Our first impulse is to shrink from the danger. Unaccount-ably we remain . . . Examine these and similar actions as we will, we shall find them resulting solely from the spirit of the Perverse. We perpetrate them merely because we feel that we should *not*' (1845; quoted in Bloom 1998:26–7). According to Georges Bataille, there is something intrinsically erotic about this state of affairs, insofar as the erotic experience epitomizes the spirit of the perverse as a quasi-diabolical urge to violate the most inveterate boundaries: physical, psychological, ethical, aesthetic, philosophical and religious. Indeed, as Bataille argues in *The Tears of Eros*, eroticism asserts itself simultaneously as 'the most moving of realities' and as 'the most ignoble' – as 'horrible' and yet 'divine' (quoted in Straub 1999:8). Relatedly, according to Bataille, the horror evoked by perverseness and eroticism alike is capable of drawing us into 'a state of bliss bordering on delirium' (1987:267). It is spurious, in this scenario, to think in terms of barriers and limitations, for 'the limit is only there to be over-reached. Fear and horror are not the real and final reaction; on the contrary, they are a temptation to overstep the bounds' (144).

— 1 —

𝔇𝔞𝔯𝔨 𝔓𝔩𝔞𝔠𝔢𝔰

DARK PLACES are multi-faceted phenomena since darkness, as a space in its own right, has an uncanny proclivity to spawn a variety of settings and environments. Throughout these disparate locations, however, one can detect traces of a Gothic vision devoted to exposing the pervasiveness, across various topographies and geographies, of tropes of displacement and disorientation that are linked to the ongoing interplay of terror and horror. Much as Gothicity appears in different constellations predicated upon contingent cultural circumstances, its underlying affects feature with striking regularity. (The relationship between darkness and space is also examined in **Chapter 6**, with a focus on the discourse of spectrality, and in **Chapter 10**, with reference to the link between dark dwellings and dynastic or generational crises.)

In much early Gothic fiction, darkness is the locus of torment, punishment, mystery, corruption and insanity – the place in which, as in Matthew Lewis's *The Monk* [1796], defenceless victims are trapped, often in the unwelcome company of dismal apparitions and abject creatures. This topos has endured over the centuries and is still prominent today amongst writers as diverse as Anne Rice and Stephen King, Clive Barker and Peter Straub. Not infrequently, darkness denotes the forbidden. From Bluebeard to Daphne du Maurier's *Rebecca* [1938], dark places are associated with locked rooms which hide not only taboo objects but also unutterable secrets and crimes. Gothic buildings have, of course, altered substantially over the centuries in relation to a number of social and economic changes. However, the intrinsic spirit of Gothicity has managed, thanks to its metamorphic resilience, to perpetuate and express itself through different visual and architectural forms. Even by focusing on one particular historical moment, we are likely to find evidence for the Gothic's ability to infiltrate diverse spatial situations. The eighteenth century would seem an especially apposite period for the purpose of illustration, for it is at this point in history that Gothic architecture and decoration enjoy their most sensational revival through works that range from the sombre to the frivolous.

Some of the most memorable dark places are products of apocalyptic sensibilities keen on giving shape to the murkiest aspects of human existence. The
etchings of Giambattista Piranesi (1720–78) epitomize this trend. His
imaginary prisons ('carceri d'invenzione') repeatedly depict a nightmarish proliferation of endless staircases and interlocking galleries, populated by
captives, lunatics and damned souls in the grip of agony and despair. The staircases lead nowhere, as though to suggest that there is no purpose or
destination in Piranesi's world and that his faceless characters have nothing to
expect, except, possibly, the suffering intimated by the hideous machinery,
ropes, pulleys and wheels that surround them as so many torture engines.
Piranesi's work could indeed be said to embody the darkness conventionally
associated with the Middle Ages, which is precisely where Gothic architecture
originates, and with the savage tenebrism of the barbarian tribes, ascendant in
that epoch in conflict with the imperial legacy of Rome, from whose appellations the term Gothic derives.

The collusion of dark places and dark emotions is not always as explicit as it
is in Piranesi. In fact, in the case of the two best known authors committed to
the construction of Gothic locations in both fiction and architecture, Horace
Walpole and William Beckford, darkness is linked not so much to either horror
or terror as to the absurd. The metaphorical darkness underlying Beckford's and
Walpole's pursuits is most obviously conveyed by their architectural creations:
Fonthill Abbey and Strawberry Hill. While the abbey was supposed to be darkly
grandiose, Strawberry Hill admitted ornamentation to the extreme of frivolity.
Both, however, can be regarded simultaneously as objects of humour and as dis-
turbing reminders of their creators' obsessions.

Fonthill Abbey, the 276-foot tower erected by William Beckford with the
assistance of the neo-Gothic enthusiast James Wyatt, typifies one of the most
distinctive features of Gothic architecture – a drastic suspension of gravity and
logic. The abbey was indubitably an imaginative project but also an impossibility on the practical plane. As Victor Sage points out, 'Its structure was insecure,
the mason, who confessed the fact to Wyatt on his deathbed, having neglected
to put in the foundations the architect had specified under the tower. The
octagonal tower duly collapsed in 1825' (1998:94). Yet, Fonthill's collapse may
have been less an accident than an intended component of its destiny.
Beckford, contemptuous of the classical style and captivated by ruins, is likely
to have *wished* Fonthill to be a crumbling structure able to provide an appropriate setting for his Ossianic passions. Thus, while associated with the sublime,
the abbey also partakes of the jocular. This point is emphasized by William
Hazlitt, who maintains that Beckford and Wyatt's project is 'a cathedral turned
into a toyshop' (quoted in Franklin 1998:23). Kenneth Clark calls it a 'sudden
outburst of romantic rhetoric' (1995:89). Fonthill is also, of course, a telling
commentary on the flaws of that architectural phallocentrism dubbed by Marie

Mulvey-Roberts 'Toweromania' (1998:xvi). The fate of Beckford's hero/villain Vathek, notorious designer of preposterously soaring towers, confirms this reading.

Strawberry Hill, Walpole's villa, brings together a bewildering variety of motifs and forms into an extravagant assemblage that irreverently flouts the distinction between reality and illusion. Walpole's construct is intrinsically surreal. Indeed, while legion architectural and decorative details from disparate sources are accurately replicated to make Strawberry Hill quintessentially Gothic, the villa's overall structure is like no Gothic building ever erected or planned. Eclectic juxtaposition is its priority. Walpole himself was well aware of the villa's jocose attributes and keen to enhance their impact through his own conduct. As Richard Davenport-Hines observes, 'His posture in his toy castle, with its towers, galleries and cloisters, were jokes through which he drew visitors into complicity . . . "Strawberry Hill is the puppet-show of the times," he declared in 1755' (1998:132).

The Gothic's penchant for assuming a variety of spatial forms is further cor-roborated by the fact that Gothic plots unfold in changing architectural structures. Transformations in the character of the narrative setting cannot be attributed merely to individual preferences. In fact, they mirror shifts in the social and ideological fabric. Early Gothic fictions elect the castle as the setting most overtly evocative of the sins which the developing middle classes, the most avid consumers of Gothic fiction, wish to associate with the aristocracy. Castles embody their inhabitants' dark desires, most conspicuously a desire for power that invariably carries sexual connotations. This is clearly the case in *The Castle of Otranto* [1764], where individual longings are rendered dark by their sexual nature and by their ideological encoding as illicit and perverse. Indeed, the novel teems with sexual yearnings taboo on either ethical or economic grounds: incestuous drives, adultery and attraction between socially incompat-ible people. Moreover, the castle's ability to introject such desires and project them back in visible form is so intense that the building itself acquires autonomous life, an energy more vibrant and tantalizing than that evinced by any of the animate beings enclosed within its walls. One of the most intriguing aspects of *The Castle of Otranto* is precisely the fact that the castle's architec-ture, with its battlements, closets, vaults and trapdoors, is so alive as to suggest that the dwelling is Walpole's actual protagonist and controlling force.

In Victorian fiction, castles are gradually superseded by less archaic locations. However, as Manuel Aguirre observes, 'The Victorian age does not forsake the Gothic findings. Dracula's castle is a true heir of Otranto and Udolpho.' Rather, it aims at 'adapting the fantastic to the bourgeois and replacing the castle by mansions, houses, apartments' (1990; quoted in Bloom 1998:199). These changes do not simply bear witness to a democratization of built space. They also, more importantly, indicate a recognition, however subliminal, of the pervasiveness of the darkness, secretiveness, madness and corruption once presented as defining traits of the traditional gentry. The dark Other can no longer be contained within the boundaries of the castle, for otherness courses through society. This recognition has steadily been gaining momentum since the Victorian age and has culminated, in recent years, in the insistent desecration of the apparently safest places. In contemporary articulations of the Gothic vision, most notably in film, the suburban bourgeois dwelling has come to play a prominent role as a site of fear and violence. This is clearly demonstrated by films such as John Carpenter's *Halloween* (1978), Wes Craven's *A Nightmare on Elm Street* (1984), and their various sequels and spoofs such as Craven's own *Scream* series (1996–99) and Keenen Ivory Wayans's *Scary Movie* (2000). According to Aguirre, the notion that darkness cannot be confined to discrete enclosures is confirmed by the increasingly maze-like character of perceived and lived space: 'Not just one particular locus, but the world itself of some specific individual is tainted, has a labyrinthic nature . . . The haunter is no longer contained by a mere castle, the ghost walks; and man cannot successfully escape it because his whole world is its labyrinth' (1990; quoted in Bloom 1998:205–6).

Over the centuries, spatial darkness has consistently been related to the labyrinthine character of troubling locations. This idea will be taken up again later in this chapter in the context of a discussion of the urban environment. What should be stressed at this juncture is that the labyrinth operates simultaneously as a space of punishment symbolic of unresolved fears and as an implicit invitation to understand and accept a view of the human condition as one of perpetual wandering and entrapment. Thus, like fear itself, the labyrinth may work as a function of consciousness. According to Italo Calvino, the willingness to confront the labyrinth is a prerequisite of the ability to grapple with the puzzling intricacy of reality as a whole and hence the ability to produce narrative constructs that do justice to that intricacy without pandering to the desire for consolatory simplifications:

> On the one hand, there is the attitude now necessary to confront the complexity of the real . . . what we need today is a map of the labyrinth as detailed as possible. On the other hand, there is the attraction of the labyrinth itself, of losing oneself in the labyrinth, of representing the absence of escape routes as humankind's true condition . . . Left out are those who believe they may defeat labyrinths by escaping their difficulty; it is therefore scarcely appropriate to require literature, given a labyrinth, to provide the key to get out of it. What literature can do is to define the best attitude needed to find an exit point, even though this will be no more than a passage from one labyrinth to another. (1980:96)

With the explosion of traditional enclosures and their replacement by sprawling labyrinths, several conventional distinctions become obsolete. A forerunner of this trend is R. L. Stevenson's *The Strange Case of Dr Jekyll and Mr Hyde* [1886], where the inside and the outside, the private sphere of the home and the public urban environment meet and merge in mutual suffusion. The late Victorian London depicted by Stevenson is a sinister maze of crime-infested night-time streets that mirror the darkness of the houses associated with Jekyll and Hyde. In earlier Gothic narratives, both castles and mansions, as receptacles of mystery and evil, are often contrasted with the outside world as the daylight domain of rationality and order. Stevenson departs from this formula by making inner and outer worlds mirror images of each other. Relatedly, while earlier Gothic characters might wish, if not actually manage, to escape violence by breaking out of the oppressive home into the outside, Stevenson's characters are unlikely to find solace or sanctuary in the urban darkness haunted by the like of Jack the Ripper. At the same time as it erodes the idea of the outside as a space of potential freedom, *Jekyll and Hyde* reinforces the darkly Gothic connotations of the domestic interior as a locus of both physical and psychological confinement. Jekyll's house reflects both the visible and the inchoate threats seething throughout the surrounding city. Something of an unholy union of home and 'laboratory or . . . dissecting-rooms' (1979:51), the dwelling epitomizes spatial darkness in the guise of the monstrous hybrid. As Lucie Armitt observes, 'severance and disunity are written into its very foundations. As the more homely portions of the interior are elaborated upon . . . these *heimlich* elements [are] shown to be in a state of dissolution' (1996:121). The interface between the dark outside and the dark inside is provided by the facade of Hyde's dwelling: 'Two doors from one corner . . . a certain sinister block of building thrust forward its gable on the street. It . . . showed no window, nothing but . . . a blind forehead of discoloured wall . . . The door . . . was blistered and distained' (Stevenson 1979:30). Stevenson's story construes spatial darkness as the product of a concurrently confrontational and symbiotic relationship between internal and external dimensions, between self and non-self, between architectural disorder and psychological turbulence.

Emma Tennant's reworking of *Jekyll and Hyde* in *Two Women of London* capitalizes on this motif and highlights the social, economic and sexual signifiers defining both domestic and public spaces. The monstrosity of Mrs Hyde's dwelling is related to the aberrant topography that makes Notting Hill and Ladbroke Grove simultaneously contiguous and worlds apart. It is 'the tatterdemalion house that shouldn't be part of the gardens at all, butting as it does the thronging, littered thoroughfare of Ladbroke Grove' (1990:1). Stevenson's narrative posits sexual urges and, more specifically, homosexual drives as places of darkness to be conquered or denied. Jekyll tells Utterson that he 'will never set eyes on [Hyde] again', that he is 'done with him' (Stevenson 1979:52).

Lanyon likewise tells Utterson that he is 'quite done with that person [Jekyll]' (57). These disclaimers point to the wish to eradicate all memory of personal connections which dominant ideologies would deem suspicious or downright intolerable. Tennant, writing a century later, deals with gender issues more explicitly. However, a strain of prohibition is still noticeable. Mrs Hyde's impropriety, in particular, does not simply consist of her daring to roam the spaces of the Notting Hill gardens but is also associated with a violation of both aesthetic and sexual mores that encapsulates the experience of the uncanny:

> There was certainly nothing homely about the sight of Mrs Hyde that evening. Disgusted, possibly, by an unwelcome combination of the familiar and the unknown – for the 'thing' wore nothing more alarming than a white mac, one of those plastic, half-transparent coats with a hood that sell in millions – Jean Hastie commented that 'it was odious that a woman should disport herself in a respectable area such as this' . . . For Jean, the sartorial appearance of Mrs Hyde – for she wore nothing, it was true, under the diaphanous white plastic – was alarming and all-important. (1990:31)

Cities, both ancient and modern, repeatedly stand out as some of the most intriguing of dark places. This is largely due to their contradictory status: they are constructs and, to this extent, foster the illusion that their planners and builders can control their growth; at the same time, they have an almost organic way of developing according to their own rhythms and of creating pockets of mystery and invisibility which are well beyond the control of their inhabitants. The darkness of autonomously and mischievously developing cities is highlighted by texts which, like Jeanette Winterson's *The Passion* (1988) and Robert Coover's *Pinocchio in Venice* (1991), posit the urban environment as the setting of undisciplined pleasures and hideous assaults on the self in a pervasive atmosphere of geographical anarchy. The proverbially loose character of Venice's history and fabric makes it an ideal candidate for the representation of a Gothic vision of endless metamorphosis. As the character Villanelle points out in *The Passion*, its spatial coordinates are quintessentially protean, flexible and therefore resistant to notions of linear progression and predictable destinations: Venice is 'the city of mazes . . . Although wherever you are going is always in front of you, there is no such thing as straight ahead' (1988:49). 'The city I come from,' Villanelle later observes, 'is a changeable city. It is not always the same size. Streets appear and disappear overnight, new waterways force themselves over dry land. There are days when you cannot walk from one end to the other, so far is the journey, and there are days when a stroll will take you round your kingdom like a tin-pot Prince' (97). Venice defies mapping. This results both from the fluidity of its urban growth and from the conflicting images associated with the city over time. On the one hand, Venice has been considered dreamy, romantic and vaporous, and on the other, hard-headed, sceptical and pragmatic.

In *Pinocchio in Venice*, the city is primarily a fairground of carnivalesque exuberance, Babylonian excess and tumultuous desire, whose gleaming surfaces are consistently darkened by the ominous shadows of ubiquitous puppets, masked creatures and riotous festive crowds. Above all, Venice, for Coover as for Winterson, epitomizes spatial darkness by virtue of its labyrinthian topography – 'magical, dazzling, and exquisitely perplexing' (1997:40) when contemplated from afar with an art historian's detachment but infinitely menacing when experienced directly. Thus, Coover's Pinocchio is soon forced to relinquish his idealized image of the Serenissima and the initial sense that everything about the city is 'enchanting' and that he himself is the object of its 'benediction' (25). The first pang of panic makes itself felt when he realizes that his guide is taking him around 'in circles' and 'his old childhood terror of the dark' is by no means alleviated by the guide's matter-of-fact assertion that 'Venice is not like other cities' since 'To reach some places you must cross a bridge twice' (26). Pinocchio's fear escalates when, pursued by invisible killers, he finds himself stranded in the freezing Venetian night. Vainly reaching for comforting images of light, especially, 'the luminous spectacle of Venice' immortalized by the like of 'Giorgione, Titian and Tintoretto' (41), he has no choice but to acknowledge that he is becoming both physically and mentally lost, the sense of dislocation induced by an environment that is 'weirdly white and pitch black at the same time' being replicated by the fact that, concurrently, 'his mind has gone blank and his spirits horribly dark'. The sensation that the bridges and squares are pervaded by the 'terrible flutter' of 'a thousand assassins' echoes a tormented self-haunting bred by shame and guilt, circular and ongoing as Venice's own 'mazy turnings' (42–4).

Both Winterson and Coover use the dark – though, paradoxically, often radiant – labyrinth of Venice to parody the classic topos of the journey through darkness as one of self-discovery. Winterson's Henri loses his mind, while Coover's old professor finally discovers just one barely uplifting thing: that, flesh or no flesh, he has been 'nothing but a puppet' all along (320). The epiphanic element and its critique hark back to an earlier narrative also set in Venice, Daphne du Maurier's story 'Don't Look Now'. Here Venice is employed as a setting for the exploration of the relationship between the experience of space and notions of discovery and truth. Laura and John get lost in the maze of narrow canals, twisting alleyways and 'the slippery steps of cellar entrances' reminiscent of 'coffins' (1973:19) shortly after the amazing revelation proffered by some mysterious twin sisters that their dead child Christine has not actually departed the world. Laura longs to believe the story while John categorically dismisses it. Both, however, are deeply unsettled, and their meandering through dark streets which they cannot recognize symbolizes that sense of confusion. Ultimately, the tale blatantly undermines the rationalist approach championed by John and suggests that if the journey through darkness leads to any discovery, this amounts to the realization that it is impossible to grapple with forces which, like 'the maze of back streets' (53) through which John unknowingly rushes towards death, tolerate no mapping.

The city may be the source, not merely the setting, of dislocating and distressing experiences. Christopher Fowler has contributed to this theme by making London the protagonist of his books and by stressing the connection between crime, horror and terror and the city's hidden dimension. In *Roofworld* (1995), tribal gangs live and fight on the rooftops, the principal threat represented by the evil Chymes and the occult worshippers who support them. London is the final prize for the possession of which the opposing parties struggle with one another. In *Disturbia* (1997), the journalist Vincent Reynolds is forced to rely on his knowledge of London's history and mythology in order to survive a lethal journey through its principal landmarks.

In contemporary representations of the city as a space of darkness, the sense of isolation associated with conventional Gothic locations often gives way, as Giles Menegaldo points out, to 'a complex framework of buildings and houses and streets' that 'supposes proximity and even promiscuity' (1996:189). This does not necessarily entail that traditional Gothic motifs are totally abandoned, for they can actually participate in an imaginative dialogue with contemporary settings and plots. This idea is exemplified by a number of Ramsey Campbell's stories, where Gothic locations such as haunted houses, dark caves and underground worlds combine with real scenarios, often inspired by his native Liverpool, to portray the urban environment as a generator of anxiety and fear. Moreover, as was already the case with Stevenson, the fusion of old and new fostered by Campbell facilitates a 'subtle blending of interiority and exteriority' (196). This is harrowingly demonstrated by 'The Entertainment'. The foreboding sense of helplessness conveyed right from the start by the desolate seaside town, with its 'waving isolated trees that looked too young to be out by themselves' (Campbell 1999:225) is replicated by the eerie atmosphere of the hotel in which the protagonist, Shone, seeks shelter when prevented by stormy weather from reaching his destination. The place turns out to be an unorthodox asylum, where a motley crew of varyingly senile or deranged guests requires him to perform a series of grotesque acts out of a frenzied lust for brutality and violence. As the 'entertainment' reaches its insane climax, Shone is faced with an appalling scene: 'The room was either too dark or not quite dark enough . . . A restless mass crouched in it – a body with too many limbs, or a huddle of bodies that had grown inexplicably entangled by the process of withering' (243). Having managed to flee, Shone is soon forced back into the spooky hotel by a police patrol who mistake him for one of its inmates. At this point, he discovers that he has aged unaccountably in the space of just a few hours and is ominously informed by a ghostly voice 'like an escape of gas' (245) that he will 'be plenty of fun yet'. He is destined to be engulfed by a darkness far more oppressive than the one he has hitherto experienced – a darkness 'worse than the first sticky unseen touch of the web of the house in his face' (246).

If the urban environment repeatedly lends itself to the articulation of images of darkness, whole geographical regions may also stand out as embodiments of a distinctively Gothic vision. The American South is a case in point. For William Faulkner, in particular, southern history is permeated by eminently Gothic tropes and emotions. The vision offered by Faulkner is to a considerable extent a product of a deep cultural rift that posits the South as ravaged by social fragmentation, poverty, racial violence and blocked opportunities, in contrast with the affluence and politically progressive attitudes of the North. Although the South's fundamentally agricultural economy and attendant alienation from the industrialized world have often been given as explanations for its distinctiveness, it is nonetheless crucial to realize that what sets it apart from the rest of America is primarily a set of mentalities and traditions. Not all southerners despised the technologized North, as indicated by substantial migration from the South to the North in a quest for better prospects. However, it is undeniable that the white families who remained in their original regions were stubbornly entrenched behind their conventional mores and the appalling legacy of a plantation economy historically inseparable from the horrors of slavery. Moreover, connotations of difference and alterity have traditionally been reinforced by the picture of a mysterious and foreboding environment – associated with rich and engulfing vegetation, insect-infested swamps and hence disease – that could indeed be regarded as a Gothic space of darkness and decay.

Central to the traditional communities depicted by Faulkner is the notion of the family: a structure supposed to inspire undying respect and loyalty which almost invariably turns out to be, as is often the case in Gothic fiction, a sick and fragmented institution. In *As I Lay Dying* [1930], for example, the various members of the Bundren family are driven by conflicting interests and oppressive secrets that inevitably set them apart from one another. What Faulkner offers is a Gothic vision in which alienation is lived constantly as a concurrently personal and social reality. Pivotal to that vision is an incurable fatalism that stresses the implausibility of self-development and, ultimately, the undesirability of life itself: 'The reason for living,' Addie Bundren maintains, 'was to get ready to stay dead a long time' (1996:157). In Addie's tormented conscience, death is the only conceivable form of transcendence, for it is through physical dissolution that she may distance herself from a darkly ungenerous environment and, by extension, shed the 'I' that is finally as useless and arbitrary as any other word: 'I knew that motherhood was invented by someone who had to have a word for it because the ones that had the children didn't care whether there was a word for it or not. I knew that fear was invented by someone that had never had the fear; pride, who never had the pride' (159–60).

The association of the American South with Gothic darkness also plays a prominent role in several contemporary writers. Nancy A. Collins associates the South with a distinctive type of 'dark fantasy' capitalizing on the 'tall tale' as 'a genuinely American form of story-telling, one that lends itself to the Southern American voice' (Snyder 1999). (Further reference to Nancy A. Collins is made in **Chapter 14**.) Elements of dark fantasy feature prominently in a number of stories set in the South. James Lee Burke's *In the Electric Mist with Confederate Dead*, for example, uses a typically Southern environment – 'networks of canals and bayous, sand bogs, willow islands, stilt houses, flooded woods, and stretches of dry land where the mosquitoes swarmed in gray clouds' (1997:117) – as the setting for a tale of dark fantasy wherein the adventures of a contemporary detective, Dave Robicheaux, become intertwined with spectral reconstructions of the American Civil War. Here, the South is unromantically portrayed as a space of historical decay, present day corruption and sadistic crimes echoing the brutality of earlier acts performed in 'the defense of a repellent cause like slavery' (370).

The most heinous sin with which the South is connected is slavery. Toni Morrison in *Beloved*, starkly exposes the horrors of the plantation economy as an admixture of unashamed cruelty and hypocritical attempts to conceal the reality of oppression. The Garners' plantation is called 'Sweet Home', as though to suggest that its inmates live and work harmoniously together. In fact, all spaces are ineluctably dark for the oppressed as long as dark skins are invested with damning connotations. The true identity of 'Sweet Home' is actually encapsulated by the ruthless sexual exploitation of the plantation's sole female slave, Sethe, who, seeking freedom for herself and her offspring, is compelled to perform an unutterably painful act, infanticide. Morrison also stresses the inescapability of spatial darkness: having achieved freedom, Sethe and her family find themselves trapped in a 'spiteful' dwelling – 'full of baby's venom' (1987:3). Darkness can never be left conclusively behind any more than the brutality of slavery can be attenuated or glossed over. This is ironically conveyed by the name 'Beloved' itself: an ostensibly positive word which, however, designates a hungry and potentially destructive force in the present, whilst concurrently harking back to the novel's central horror. 'Beloved' is the one word which Sethe was able to purchase by selling herself to the engraver, and have placed on the murdered baby's tombstone. (*Beloved* is discussed further in **Chapter 4**.)

Both Anne Rice and Poppy Z. Brite frequently resort to Southern locations as ideal backdrops for the exploits of their vampires and other serial killers. Both, moreover, suggest that despite the apparently impenetrable darkness surrounding their characters' actions, the South's Gothic makeup contains elements of colourful excitement. New Orleans is uniquely attractive to Rice's vampires because of its racially hybrid composition and paradoxical coalescence of self-indulgent excess and a superstitious addiction to repentance. On the one hand, it is highly sensuous and fun-loving, and compulsively addicted to the worship of tradition, on the other. In *Interview with the Vampire* (1976), Louis describes the city as a 'dream held intact . . . by a tenacious, though unconscious, collective will' (Rice 1994a:219–20). Brite, similarly, depicts New Orleans as a world of gory crimes, malignant loves, and both physical and mental abuse which is simultaneously terrifying and irresistible. The city is presented as a kaleidoscopic space in which opposites do not merely coexist but actually fuse into unexpected and magical combinations. In *Drawing Blood*, the air itself is described as 'perfume', as 'a heady melange of thousands of odors: seafood and spices, beer and horseshit, oil paints and incense and flowers and garbage and river mud, . . . softly sifting brick, stone trodden by a million feet' (1994b:39). It is noteworthy, however, that even in this bouncy and bustling world of constant movement, the dark phantom of the past is never quite exorcized: 'The Market . . . was probably one of the most culturally and racially diverse spots in the city. Good karma for a place where, not two hundred years ago, slaves had done the morning shopping' (40). (The writings of Rice and Brite are also examined in **Chapter 13**.)

Because of their ability to encapsulate and expose complex historical, ideological and psychological realities, dark places often turn out, paradoxical as this may seem, to be illuminating. The examination of major developments in the spatial representation of darkness – from eighteenth-century art and architecture through configurations of the urban environment in nineteenth-century and contemporary fiction, to the Gothic vision articulated in broader regional terms by narrative interpretations of the American South – corroborates this idea. It is largely because of their enlightening potential that we continue to seek dark places, despite their menacing and frightening connotations, as dimensions capable of activating consciousness and helping us situate the experience of fear in its both individual and collective manifestations.

— 2 —

𝔇𝔞𝔯𝔨 𝔗𝔦𝔪𝔢𝔰

WE ARE CONSISTENTLY DRAWN to dark places as locations capable of epitomizing, by virtue of their overt association with terror and horror, the ubiquity of fear as a primary ingredient of existence. (See **Chapter 1**.) No less compelling is the lure of dark times as moments or events in which otherwise diffuse sensations of dread crystallize within specific historical circumstances. Just as dark spaces can be enlightening thanks to their inclination to situate fearful occurrences in relation to both personal and social geographies, dark times can help us position the experience of fear in relation to both personal and social calendars.

Dark times are undoubtedly associated with private moments of sorrow, anxiety or doubt. It is when we are most acutely aware of being frightened that we are also pointedly conscious of being alone. Most people have some experience, for example, of what Poppy Z. Brite describes as nights 'shaped by an unseen dark hand', nights that 'seem made for plodding through the mind-sludge, poking at swollen and corrupted things'. These private times of darkness may well be considered an affliction, and a recognition of their inevitability is not necessarily any more comforting than the acknowledgement of the pervasiveness of fear. However, they also carry positive connotations for, much as they seem 'made for torture', they also invite 'reflection' and a 'savouring of loneliness' (1994a:234) rather than a recoiling from it.

While the importance of the private dimension must be appreciated in examining the theme of dark times, it is nevertheless crucial to consider the historical situation of narratives of darkness. Horror, terror and Gothicity cannot be explained away as forms of escapism, if what is meant by escapism is a total retreat from society. Indeed, escapism is itself ideologically encoded. In examining the sociohistorical circumstances in which the Gothic finds its inception, it is vital to acknowledge the prominent part played by class tensions, uncertainties about the relation of the present to a nebulous past, and apocalyptic anxieties about the future. Moreover, the fantasy worlds sought by the Gothic's most avid readers were part of a rigidly mapped social calendar – the holiday realm of non-productive indulgence necessary to the preservation of a productive routine of efficiency and thrift. The dream-like journey undertaken by many heroes and heroines as they descend into the Gothic building and hence into its owner's seedy secrets is also a descent into history – an attempt to understand and come to terms with social reality rendered urgently necessary by intimations of crisis and change. The political implications of the discourse of darkness should not be underestimated.

That the Gothic vision is not escapist but historically situated in a complex nexus of social issues is forcefully, albeit not always explicitly, demonstrated by Horace Walpole's *The Castle of Otranto* [1764]. The narrative poses a central question: which is darker, the murky past or an apparently enlightened present which actually thrives on what E. J. Clery describes as the 'inhumane enforcement of patrilineal property laws' and 'the obscure legal status of women' (1999:Foreword)? As Clery persuasively argues, the political significance of Walpole's story is made evident by the writer's shift of perspective from the first preface to the second. The first preface adopts a fundamentally antiquarian approach by attributing the narrative to the author 'Onuphrio Muralto' and by locating the story's events in a distant past: 'The principal incidents are such as were believed in the darkest ages of christianity' (Walpole 1996:5). Moreover, Walpole is eager to point out the story's distance from a putatively rationalist present by stressing its superstitious dimension and its ethically simplistic message. He announces that 'some apology for it is necessary. Miracles, visions, necromancy, dreams, and other preternatural events, are exploded now even from romances' and that he wishes the author 'had grounded his plan on a more useful moral than this; that *the sins of fathers are visited on their children to the third and fourth generation*'. If the book is worth reading it is because of its 'entertainment' value and its commitment to the inculcation of 'lessons of virtue' (6–7).

The second preface, on the other hand, emphasizes the tale's relevance to Walpole's own times. Having 'ask[ed] pardon of his readers for having offered his work to them under the borrowed personage of a translator' due to 'diffidence of his own abilities', Walpole here suggests that his intention was to 'blend the two kinds of romance', namely the 'imagination and improbability' typical of ancient tales of fantasy and the imitation of 'nature' held to be the defining trait of modern novels (9). Walpole is advocating the desirability of establishing a dialogue between the past and the present, old and new systems of belief. 'The second preface,' Clery states, 'alters the meaning of the first by suggesting that the spurious antiquarian account of the work's origins in the late gothic era is a disguised account of its true origins in the present' (1999:61). The temporal displacement effected by the first preface may be considered a way of making the supernatural events dramatized in *Otranto* acceptable to a modern audience. Yet, ultimately, the novel ironically shows that evil and fear are unremittingly at work in the here and now and cannot be relegated to a remote epoch marked by Italian/Catholic greed and corruption. *The Castle of Otranto* evokes a feudal past defined by an iniquitous stratification of legal, economic and sexual rights governed by eminently aristocratic and patriarchal imperatives. However, in doing so, the novel actually foregrounds the persistence of old ideologies in the modern era. As Clery points out,

> the moment when the providential doctrine of kingship was revoked, in 1688, was the point at which aristocratic ownership of land became sacralized in its place, and the following century was to be the scene of a ceaseless struggle to maintain the legitimacy of the aristocracy's continuing political and economic domination of a rapidly changing society on the basis of a mystique of land. (73)

Walpole also stresses the ambiguous role played by the supernatural in the restoration of order. The monstrosity of the unearthly agents presented in the novel graphically intimates that even though they are supposed to serve providential justice, they are concurrently diabolical. The dénouement does not provide any genuine vision of order or harmony. Supernatural phenomena mow down with equal vehemence the evil and the innocent. This is exemplified by Theodore's fate: finally recognized as true heir to the title and property which Manfred has usurped, he is nonetheless deprived of his beloved Matilda, unwittingly slaughtered by her infamous father. Even times of resolution and recuperation can prove unfathomably dark.

The Gothic vision's concern with matters of law, property, inheritance and power is also evinced by the late eighteenth-century writings of Charles Brockden Brown. These lend substantial credence to the proposition that narratives of darkness are implicated in social and ideological issues by making the reality of pre- and post-revolutionary America and related political debates central to their plots. In deploying typically Gothic themes that pivot on violent and preternatural disruptions of both the body and the psyche (from somnambulism to spontaneous combustion), Brockden Brown rarely loses sight of the broader cultural and historical scene. Indeed, those violations of the natural order become ways of commenting on the fragility of the rationalist ethos supposed to sustain America and of exposing the fallibility of human decisions, the unpredictability of human actions and the selfish motives underlying apparently ethical choices.

In *Wieland and Memoirs of Carwin the Biloquist* [1798], in particular, Brockden Brown explores the tension between 'religious evangelism and enlightened rationality' (Botting 1996:116) as a means of showing that the supernatural can never be conclusively accounted for in natural terms. On one level, his narrative belongs to the category described by Montague Summers as explained Gothic (1938), for the mysterious voices which Theodore Wieland takes as emanations of God's will and by which he is thereby led to kill himself and his family turn out to be the product of a ventriloquist's skills. However, at the same time as the emphasis shifts from the domain of the supernatural to empirical reality, the notion of religious faith itself remains cloaked in mystery. What the novel ultimately promulgates is not the triumph of rationalism over darkness but the indelible agency of dark times in which the powers of reason are suspended. Above all, *Wieland* exemplifies a dark phase in American history. In an effort to separate itself from an intrinsically European legacy of prejudices and superstitions, American society as portrayed by Brockden Brown strives to give natural explanations to apparently inexplicable phenomena, yet is forced to confront the destructive drives of religious devotion, untempered by enlightened reflection, as a source of sepulchral gloom.

Unsurprisingly, darkness is most commonly associated with winter as a bleak season suited to the production of dark tales. As the doomed boy Mamilius states in Shakespeare's *The Winter's Tale*, 'A sad tale's best for winter: I have one / Of sprites and goblins'. The connection between Christmas and darkness has a long history. *The Castle of Otranto* itself was first published on 24 December 1764. Charles Dickens strengthened this connection for the modern age. Having already included some spooky tales in *The Pickwick Papers* [1836], Dickens proceeded to make Christmas coterminous with darkness in *A Christmas Carol* [1843]. Soon after, bumper Christmas editions containing multifarious narratives of darkness became a popular feature of the festive season. In her Introduction to *The Virago Book of Victorian Short Stories*, Jennifer Uglow suggests that the popularity of spooky stories at this particular time of the year can be attributed to the fact that 'the yuletide tradition linked the bourgeoisie to an older world of demons and spirits which they thought they had left behind' (1992:x–xi). Following this reading, it could further be argued that, although in Christian cultures Christmas symbolizes a decidedly anti-pagan moment in the history of religions, its link with eerie occurrences and demonic entities draws it close to a pre-Christian heritage. In the 1890s, M. R. James, Provost of King's College Cambridge, contributed significantly to the consolidation of the link between Christmas and chilling and eerie stories, by making Christmas the time for the reading of his ghost tales to disciples and friends (Chitchat Readings). (M. R. James's stories are examined in **Part 2**.)

The connection between Christmas and darkness has retained its hold to the present day, as shown, for example, by Susan Hill's *The Woman in Black* [1983]. The novel opens with a chapter entitled 'Christmas Eve', part of which is filled with kids 'vying with one another to tell the horridest, most spine-chilling tale, with much dramatic effect and mock-terrified shrieking' (1998:18–19). In spite of Jerome K. Jerome's satirical debunking of the Christmas–darkness partnership in 1891 ('Oh, it is a stirring night in Ghostland, the night of

December the twenty-fourth!'), the tradition goes on. In Clive Barker's 'The Yattering and Jack' (1984, *Books of Blood*, vol. 1), for example, the reader is presented with the haunting of Jack Polo, 'gherkin importer' and 'one of nature's blankest little numbers' (1999a, vol. 1:37), by the Yattering, 'a minor demon' (39) forbidden to leave his intended victim's house. The haunting reaches its climax, after months of Jack's thick-skinned indifference to the Yattering's tricks and bland rationalization of mysterious occurrences, in the course of Christmas celebrations in which the protagonist is joined by his daughters. The demon uses his full powers to intimidate the two women to the point of insanity, thereby succeeding, albeit provisionally, in generating fear in the otherwise apathetic Jack: 'Jack was afraid. The house was suddenly a prison. The game was suddenly lethal' (48).

Even when he does not overtly relate his plots to religious festivities, Barker frequently emphasizes the connection between dark times and a sense of ceremony. In 'The Midnight Meat Train' (*Books of Blood*, vol. 1), for instance, Mahogany performs ritual slaughters in the night-time New York subway to supply meat for the degenerate, undying breed of Fathers who survive, locked in eternal darkness, on the edge of the city. Mahogany is driven by eminently aesthetic and artistic priorities: his victims are 'completely stripped', their clothes are folded in a 'neat and systematic way', their bodies are 'meticulously shaved' (1999a, vol. 1:13) and their wounded carcasses carefully bled. Moreover, they must be healthy, sturdy and in their prime, for only the peachiest flesh is 'ideal for slaughter' (19). Mahogany's life becomes entangled with that of the bored and disillusioned Leon Kaufman who, having survived a night of spectacular dissections aboard a blighted carriage and having murdered the Butcher himself, is eventually appointed by the Fathers as his successor. Kaufman's ordeal, replete with horrific visions of pieces of bodies craving human flesh and an encounter with the 'Father of Fathers', a repulsive mass of 'budding, blossoming' (34) forms, marks a paradoxically dark time. Indeed, although Kaufman is condemned to serve the monstrous tribe and to do so in silence (his tongue has been cut out), it is at this point that his life acquires a meaning, a purpose.

Barker has commented on the story's finale thus: 'Kaufman's a real marginal, a disenfranchised accountant whose life doesn't mean anything until he realizes there are greater forces at work than he had ever thought. And there, I think, is a story with a perfect happy ending' (1987a). This reading militates in favour of the notion that dark times may unexpectedly turn out to be epiphanic. The same applies to another story contained in the first volume of the *Books of Blood*, 'In the Hills, the Cities'. (See also **Chapter 14** for a discussion of this story.) Here Barker explores the collusion of darkness and revelation by making an especially monstrous and overwhelming incarnation of darkness the agent of transformation and discovery. Dark moments stand out as paradoxical junctures at which destructive and creative forces are inextricably intertwined, and fear accordingly manifests itself both as a wrenching awareness of loss and as a curious, albeit apprehensive, reaching towards the unknown. 'At the end of "In the Hills, the Cities",' Barker comments,

> both protagonists die, but they gain meaning, extraordinary meaning . . . when they see the beasts in the hills, some new vision is presented to them which hitherto they wouldn't even have been capable of imagining . . . I very much like the ambiguity or the ambivalence of a moment which can be terrible and significant simultaneously, the way that many of the pivotal moments in our lives are very often rites of passage moments in which things are lost which can never be claimed again. Yet the territory ahead is, by virtue of the fact that it is new, also exciting and extraordinary. (1987a)

The link between darkness and times of transition is also at the roots of Hallowe'en, a festival which, like Christmas, now evinces a coalescence of Christian and pre-Christian motifs. The origins of Hallowe'en can be traced back to Celtic Britain, where the 31st of October, officially the end of summer, was a feast day dedicated to Samhain, the Lord of the Dead. Largely inspired by fears connected with the impending winter and with the malevolent demons that might infest its long hours of darkness, the festivity aimed at purifying the earth and driving the wandering dead away from the realm of the living by means of massive fires. Animal immolations were also performed, as this was the time for culling the herds of the animals deemed unsuitable for breeding purposes. No conclusive evidence exists of the practice of human sacrifice.

As a moment of closure, Samhain was suited to the commemoration of the departed, hence its association with death. However, while Samhain signalled an ending, it also denoted the beginning of a new year to the Celts. It was an interstitial moment, ushering in the darkness of winter on the one hand, and fresh, more luminous prospects on the other. It played a prominent part in a belief system that attached great value to 'turning points, such as the time between one day and the next, the meeting of sea and shore, or the turning of one year into the next' since these were perceived as 'magickal times', times when 'the "veil between the worlds" was at its thinnest' (Moonstone 1995). The importance of transitional moments enabling the passage from one world to another is still emphasized today by practitioners of witchcraft. According to Caroline Robertson, for example, 'Witchcraft is about threshold worlds and shifting realities' (McGrath 2000:39). Yet the link between Samhain and witchcraft goes deeper. Witches are among the most prominent figures connected with Hallowe'en and remain sources of unending inspiration for its iconography. More importantly, however, there are correspondences between the ancient Celtic rituals, with their commitment to the recognition and celebration of the rhythms and patterns of the natural world, and widespread forms of witchcraft, including the type of modern witchcraft known as Wicca or the Craft, devoted to the promotion of natural magic (often with the infusion of folk wisdom) for healing and generally beneficial purposes.

As an emblematic turning point, Samhain was also a carnivalesque time in which everyday rules could be suspended and the playful forces of chaos could be given free rein. As Rowan Moonstone observes, 'many humans were abroad on this night, causing mischief' and engaging in 'practical jokes'. They would also play at 'imitating the fairies', believed to 'trick humans into becoming lost in the fairy mounds', sometimes carrying carved turnips and wandering from house to house asking for treats (1995). The Fairy Folk, like the Little People and other creatures of Celtic derivation, are, incidentally, a major influence in Anne Rice's *Witches Chronicles* (*The Witching Hour* 1991), *Lasher* (1994), *Taltos* (1995)) and the vicissitudes of the Mayfair Clan over several generations.

When Christianity took root, it seemed sensible to the elders of the church not to ban the immensely popular pagan festivity but rather hijack it and incorporate it into its own calendar. In 834, All Saints' Day, previously placed on the 13th of May, was moved to the 1st of November and the 31st of October became All Hallows' Eve, Hallowe'en. In 988, a further feast day was instituted for the 2nd of November, All Souls' Day, known in many countries as the Day of the Dead. Despite Christianity's desire to tame the pagan fascination with the dead and the possibility of their return as more or less hungry ghosts, aspects of the old tradition lingered on. Christianity requires its followers to pray *for* the souls of the departed, rather than *to* them as powerful spirits capable of affecting the living. Yet the rituals associated with the commemoration of the dead are still coloured by pre-Christian beliefs. This is most obviously demonstrated by the Mexican festival of the Day of the Dead in which the souls of the deceased are honoured through intriguing customs that vary according to the ethnic traditions of different areas. As Dale Hoyt Palfrey notices, it is common to celebrate the dead through 'colourful adornments and lively reunions at family burial plots, the preparation of special foods, offerings laid out for the departed on commemorative altars and religious rites that are likely to include noisy fireworks' (1995). Ostensibly a time of darkness, the Day of the Dead is also a time for joyful revelry. On one level, the colour and noise with which death is surrounded could be seen as attempts to ritualize the fear death invokes, to fuel the dream that we may control it as long as we are able to stage it. On another level, the Mexican festivities point to a synthesis of Catholic and pre-Hispanic traditions. The idea that if death is to be feared it may nonetheless be also worth seeking and courting harks back, to some extent, to the belief current among the Aztecs that death, especially if incurred in battle or sacrifice, was a reward. The winner of a ceremonial game was offered up to the gods, not the loser.

Today, the tendency to appropriate ancient traditions such as Hallowe'en is a prerogative not so much of the church as of consumer culture. Hallowe'en is a rapidly growing industry providing costumes that enable both children and adults to impersonate an extensive cast of ghoulish, demonic, skeletal and gory creatures derived from both the infernal netherworlds of medieval mythology and the Gothic realm of Frankenstein's creature and Dracula. It also promotes a staggering variety of products ranging from toys, candles, toiletries and pumpkin carvers to electronic postcards, computer clip art and fonts. The large number of websites currently dedicated to Hallowe'en art, fashion, literature and history – with or without links to related topics, such as haunting and haunted houses – bears witness to the festival's ever-expanding commercial potential.

In spite of the traditional association of feast days such as Christmas and Hallowe'en (and of winter generally) with darkness, these are by no means the only murky times. Summer is often a time of darkness. This is exemplified by Joe R. Lansdale's 'Mad Dog Summer', a classic of Southern Gothic (a subgenre discussed in **Chapter 1**) imbued with an oppressive sense of decay and harrowing intimations of nature's hostility: 'summer set in with a vengeance, hot as hell's griddle, and the river receded some and the fish didn't seem to want to bite . . . Most of the crops burned up, and if that wasn't bad enough . . . there was a bad case of the hydrophobia broke out' (1999:484). Similarly, in Stephen King's *Bag of Bones* (1999) summer heat operates as a metaphor for a simmering evil. (See also the introductions to **Part 2** and **Part 3**, and **Chapter 12**.)

Besides Christmas, other key moments in the religious calendar tend to carry ominous connotations. Good Friday is one, not surprisingly perhaps, given its association with the enigmatic events surrounding the mysteries of death and resurrection. To this day, Easter remains insistently disturbing largely because it harks back to pagan rituals revolving around the regeneration of nature in spring through immolations and offerings, by positing Christ as the sacrificial Lamb that must die in order to be everywhere. More importantly still, the pre-requisite of Christ's redeeming omnipresence is his openness to being eaten again and again. Partaking of the blood and body of the Lord is central to Christianity: hopes of regeneration and redemption may only be entertained, paradoxically, by participating in a symbolic act of massacre. (This theme is also discussed in **Chapter 13**.) F. Paul Wilson's 'Good Friday' (1999) magnifies the dark connotations of this time by linking it to epidemics of vampirism, thereby suggesting that certain times of the year seem especially auspicious to the breeding of monsters. The story offers a reinterpretation of the themes of blood-drinking and the relationship between mortals and the undead in the context of economic imperatives. Wilson's vampires are, effectively, unscrupulous entrepreneurs ready to suck other people's souls dry for the sake of profit. As Sister Carole and Sister Bernadette watch them parade down the streets, in the course a dismal night of tumult and woe, from the deserted convent of St Anthony, forsaken by all who believe 'the rumours that the undead might be moving this way', they are described thus: 'Passing on the street below was a cavalcade of shiny new cars – Mercedes Benzes, BMWs, Jaguars, Lincolns, Cadillacs' driven by men with 'lupine faces' acting 'as if they owned the road'. They are 'bands of men who do the vampires' dirty work during the daytime' (1999:135–6). Good Friday is portrayed as a quintessentially dark time in which archaic horrors combine with those spawned by present day nefarious greed.

Staying with the theme of vampirism, it could be argued that certain historical contexts are more readily associated with darkness, and indeed with a cultural yearning for darkness, than others. A case in point is vampire fever, a phenomenon characteristic of early nineteenth-century Paris. 'The magic lantern salons of Paris in the late 1700s,' David Skal observes, had already 'projected bat-winged demons on clouds of smoke to terrify and entertain the ancestors of the modern motion picture audience' (1990:4). Yet, public interest in vampirism and its theatrical potential actually gained obsessional proportions with the appearance of John Polidori's *The Vampyre* [1819] and its almost instantaneous French adaptation as the stage melodrama *Le Vampire* by Charles Nodier. According to Montague Summers, 'Immediately upon the furore created by Nodier's *Le Vampire* . . . vampire plays of every kind from the most luridly sensational to the most farcically ridiculous pressed on to the boards. A contemporary critic cries: "There is not a theatre in Paris without its Vampire!"' (1960:303). Anne Rice uses this historical backdrop in the creation of her *Théâtre des Vampires* in *Interview with the Vampire* [1976]. This venue is situated in the cradle of a distinctively dark geographical and historical sensibility: 'Paris in the days before the grand boulevards and gaslight was a dangerous place full of narrow streets, menace, and shadows. At night, fearful pedestrians carried torches' (Skal 1990:14). Rice's theatre is a place where vampires, acting as marionettes in scenarios which mock human life and any sense of purpose by precipitating all action into a whirlpool of violence and frenzy, concurrently invert the relationship between illusion and reality: while killing on stage, the blood-drinkers induce the spectators to believe that they are merely performing a set piece. Reality is disguised as performance. A dark time to kill, in the most ruthless fashion, masquerades as a bright time of mirth. (See also **Chapter 13.**)

Paradoxically, some of the darkest times grow out of occasions which one could expect to be joyous and light-hearted: feasts, weddings and celebrations. These are frequently used by narratives of darkness as preambles for horrors and terrors to come. Horace Walpole's *The Castle of Otranto* arguably inaugurates this tradition by turning a wedding into a funeral with almost preposterous rapidity. In Matthew Lewis's *The Monk* [1796], a grand religious ceremony presumed to bring spiritual enlightenment becomes the prelude to a chain of horrendous crimes. In Daphne du Maurier's *Rebecca* [1938], to cite a more recent example, a masked ball intended as an affirmation of happiness and vitality ushers in bleak premonitions of death and insanity. Thus, although particular seasons and days are readily associated with darkness, corrosive and debilitating forces may be unexpectedly released by harmless or even apparently promising situations. This suggests that there is no self-evident partition between dark times and occasions, either private or public, in which to rejoice. Death itself partakes of this ambiguous logic.

Indeed, the Gothic vision does not present death as an unequivocally dark time. Often death is lightened by its association with extraordinary or supernatural phenomena. This implicitly suggests that death is something which can only happen in an imaginary realm and cannot really affect ordinary existence. Death as it is represented in several narratives of darkness is theatrical, glamorous, the pinnacle of extreme passions. It is not, in other words, death as most ordinary people have experienced it. To this extent, fictionalizations of death are capable of presenting it not as a dark occurrence but as a polychromatic spectacle, made somewhat attractive by its unreality. At the same time, representations of death, however fantastic or dramatic, force us to acknowledge the reality of mortality as the one undeniable certainty of existence. In the logic of a piece of fiction, death may simply come across as a convenient plot device allowing for a variety of special effects. Yet, by unrelentingly staging death – either literally or metaphorically – as an essential component of their aesthetic, dark narratives concurrently convey the stark certainty of extinction. Reflections upon death are as pervasive as fear itself and, indeed, the most widespread source of dread. Concomitantly, just as fear is in a position to operate as a function of consciousness, so repeated exposure to images of destruction and decay, however sensational these may be, can help us confront our own transience. As readers who, finally, are able to survive the narrative's most violent moments, we may entertain a fantasy of immortality. However, the irrevocable law of mortality is insistently thrown back onto the scene by dark fiction's compulsive return to tropes of physical and mental disintegration. We, the readers, may be the survivors and the characters the victims. Yet in impelling us to confront the omnipresence of death-in-life, the Gothic vision ultimately dissolves the separation between survivor and victim by stressing that survivors are never immune to infiltration by victims.

— 3 —

𝕯𝖆𝖗𝖐 𝕻𝖘𝖞𝖈𝖍𝖊𝖘

NARRATIVES OF DARKNESS evoke a universe of taboos in which the non-things which culture represses are brought to the foreground. In pulling to the surface occluded realms, those stories demonstrate that fantasy is not outside social reality but actually a constellation of social reality in inverted form. This inversion is repeatedly dramatized by recourse to images of psychological dislocation and turmoil. Since it would be far too ambitious, in the present context, to attempt to enumerate all the forms of psychological disturbance presented by the Gothic vision, a cross-section of available interpretations of the theme of dark psychology is offered in the form of illustrative case studies.

What seems to afflict the Gothic psyche most intensely is an overarching sense of uncertainty as to whether the sources of fear lie in the past or in the future. This is vividly exemplified by Henry Fuseli's *The Nightmare* (in both the 1782 and the 1790 versions), where it is unclear whether the climax of the episode referred to by the title has occurred or is about to occur. The prostrate female figure may be unconscious or exhausted as a result of her subjection to some assault, possibly sexual, but may equally be on the verge of becoming the victim of some act of violation or penetration. According to Rebecca Brown (1999), the painting exemplifies the proposition that darkness is inherent in the mind and that it cannot be relegated to a remote context, since it is actually endemic in the here-and-now: 'As Fuseli's painting of *The Nightmare* suggests, our own minds can be as dark and mysterious as any exotic, earthquake-busted landscape. And the identity of the writhing woman on the bed – the one who doesn't know what's happened to her, what's going to happen, or whether or not she wants it – isn't someone from long ago: it's you.' The monstrous shapes that share her space could also be regarded as *you* insofar as they symbolize the dark otherness that inhabits us all. They can be interpreted as malevolent forces or, alternatively, as harbingers of forbidden pleasures. Equally, they may be enacting their culturally sanctioned roles – as incubus, as nightmare – without any further concern for either the tormented woman or her viewer. After all, one of the psyche's darkest aspects is its penchant for indifference to the plight of others. As Tolkien once observed with reference to fairy tales, 'elves are not primarily concerned with us, nor we with them' (1966:9–10).

The most obvious connection between darkness and the mind can be observed at the level of character presentation. Inspecting the long gallery of varyingly evil, deranged and secretive Gothic fiends, one finds recurring signs of obsessional, compulsive or downright psychotic behaviour. This is most starkly exemplified by the figure of the hero–villain as a paradoxical admixture of mental and somatic attributes. William Beckford's Vathek (*Vathek*, 1786) is handsome and imposing but utterly revolting when irate; Ambrosio in Matthew Lewis's *The Monk* [1796] is an awe-inspiring preacher, yet he is governed by perverse passions; Charles Maturin's Melmoth (*Melmoth the Wanderer*, 1820) combines ice and fire; in Emily Brontë's *Wuthering Heights* [1847], Heathcliff is depicted as aristocratically attractive yet darkened by pride and vengefulness; Daphne du Maurier's Maxim de Winter (*Rebecca*, 1938) is presented as sensitive and affectionate but at the same time enveloped by an aura of secrecy and mystery.

The conceptual conflicts personified by the hero–villain parallel the tension between the ego and the id – conscious reason and unconscious fantasies and desires – as theorized by Freudian psychoanalysis. However, while the application of this discipline may be seductive as a means of considering dark texts, it is potentially complicit with precisely the universalizing and hegemonic propositions that the Gothic vision seeks to contest. In the hero–villain's case, in particular, one should not lose sight of the cultural significance of a figure capable of embodying the contradictions ingrained in the society that produces him – an apparently enlightened world coursed through by corruption, despotism and superstition, in which individuals are simultaneously encouraged to transgress moral constraints and stigmatized for doing so. The conflicts on which the characterization of the hero–villain hinges are fundamentally a corollary of one of the defining traits of Western capitalism: the desire, paradoxically coexistent with a pseudo-humanistic glorification of autonomous choice, to police personal aspirations as a means of hindering the eruption of putatively unruly passions. Psychological dissonances also indicate that the fear *of* the individual is no less potent than the fear *in* the individual which this study posits as an ongoing feature of being-in-the-word.

William Godwin's *Things As They Are, or, the Adventures of Caleb Williams* [1794] offers an especially intriguing example of the ways in which the psychological darkness ensuing from a personal conflict can function as an allegory of the darkness underlying broader relations of power and knowledge. The novel revolves around the relationship between Caleb and his master, Falkland. An archetypical Gothic despot, Falkland is concurrently an incarnation of the injustice and malice that pervade the legal system upon which the aristocracy relies for the perpetuation of its iniquitous mastery. The centrality of judicial issues to the plot is confirmed by the fact that, as Maurice Hindle points out, 'Trials and court appearances abound in *Caleb Williams*, and a tense atmosphere of "trial" (mostly Caleb's) pervades the whole' (1988:xi). Falkland is brought to trial twice for the murder of Tyrrel, is acquitted the first time and convicted the second. Caleb himself is tried three times prior to the climactic passage in which he drives his erstwhile mentor to confess his guilt. The psychological and ideological complexity of Godwin's text can be fully appreciated by comparing the narrative's two successive endings.

The original ending emphasized the novel's political dimension as a critique of the abuse of power, making Caleb utterly impotent in the face of the structure of things as they are, his eloquence and integrity carrying no weight in comparison with the credentials of a respected, though felonious, landowner. In having Caleb jailed and poisoned, the Falkland of the first finale is depicted as totally indifferent to any appeal to equanimity. What is here foregrounded is the hegemonic validation of a despot's rights, something to which Caleb ascribes the most nefarious potential earlier in the novel:

> I held my life in jeopardy, because one man was unprincipled enough to assert what he knew to be false! . . . Strange that men from age to age should consent to hold their lives at the breath of another, merely that each in turn may have a power of acting the tyrant according to law! . . . Turn me a prey to the wild beasts of the desert, so I be never again the victim of man, dressed in the gore-dripping robes of authority! (Godwin 1988:218–19)

The revised ending places less obvious emphasis on Falkland's personal villainy so as to stress the criminal darkness inherent in the political system at large. At the same time, as Gary Handwerk (1990) points out, it throws into relief 'the complicated interaction between ideological and ethical concerns' for, although Caleb triumphs by inducing Falkland to confess, he is left with a paralyzing 'sense of the emptiness of that victory'. At the very point when Caleb appears to bypass culturally imposed disparities of authority and status, these reinscribe themselves onto his very being in the guise of an unrelievable sense of guilt: 'No penitence, no anguish, can expiate the folly and the cruelty of this last act I have perpetrated', he ruefully comments (Godwin 1988:331). His own psyche is thus irremediably darkened by his exposure of Falkland's crime and, ultimately, annihilated. In the closing paragraph, he states: 'I began these memoirs with the idea of vindicating my character; I have now no character that I wish to vindicate' (337). Caleb has become Falkland's mirror image, Falkland in inverted form. Insofar as he perceives himself as the culpable persecutor, he is existentially inseparable from his tormentor and hence a nonentity independent of the role models Falkland has fashioned for him throughout the odyssey of pursuit and detection which the narrative traces.

Published just two years after *Caleb Williams*, Matthew Lewis's *The Monk* supplies a further example of the hero–villain's implication with societal issues by focusing on the eruption of violent carnality in the midst of repressive cultural formations. The monastery where the monk Ambrosio, having devoted his existence to an obsessive ethos of abstinence, suddenly grows into a sexually insatiable monster, can be seen as a metaphor for various imprisoning structures ranging from families to political regimes. In his breathless pursuit of forbidden fruit, with each succeeding object of desire becoming an increasingly dangerous and incriminating possession, Ambrosio stands out as an amplified version of the Lacanian subject: a creature doomed to insatiable longing and to the disabling frenzy induced by the inevitability of any one source of partial satisfaction being replaced by an even more ardent desire (Lacan 1977). The monk's psychological darkness is reinforced by the awareness that in spite of his commanding presence, he is a victim, a passive toy in the hands of diabolical deceivers who are both preternatural and culturally specific. His paradoxical position is foregrounded to burlesque extremes by the preposterousness of the ending, a fine example of jocular tenebrism and enforced theatricality. Ambrosio, having been captured by the Inquisition, does not relinquish his recently acquired proclivity for impious behaviour but sells his soul to the Devil in exchange for his release from prison. The reward, alas, is a sadistically protracted death adorned by 'tortures the most exquisite and insupportable' (Lewis 1998:376).

In less spectacular Gothic narratives, darkness is often associated with a psyche unable to perceive where real evil comes from, with the state of false consciousness in which characters like Jane Austen's Catherine Morland (*Northanger Abbey*, 1818) are locked. Austen's narratorial mood is one of trenchant irony and the impressionable heroine's reactions are accordingly described by recourse to stylized Gothic images. (An analogously humorous and parodic treatment of darkness characterizes Thomas Love Peacock's *Nightmare Abbey* [1817–18] and *Crotchet Castle* [1831].) However, the novel does not present Catherine's predicament as undilutedly funny. In fact, it argues that her very susceptibility to nameless terrors is a symptom of a culturally determined malady – the stultifying encoding of women as constitutionally over-emotional and unreflective. Authentic evil is seen to lie not with the stereotypical situations portrayed in romantic fiction but with real social conditions that enslave women to a destiny of ignorance. Behind the glitter of Austen's prose lurks the darkness of vulnerable psyches fed on the vapid promise of sentimental thrills curbed by the threat of unspeakable punishments. *Northanger Abbey* shows that the most fearful facet of the Gothic vision consists of repressive role models which the members of a particular society are systematically, albeit often surreptitiously, required to internalize.

Internalization also plays a key role in Nathaniel Hawthorne's approach to the Gothic within a new world setting. (For a related treatment of the role played by darkness in American literature, see the discussion of Charles Brockden Brown in **Chapter 2**.) Although *The Scarlet Letter* [1850] does not feature overtly Gothic motifs such as the ancient castle symbolic of an imprisoning feudal legacy, it is nevertheless Gothic in an ethical sense. As Robert Miles argues, 'the Puritans are revealed as internalizing these things within themselves. The reformed, "modern", Calvinist theology they optimistically bring to the New World eventually proves to be, in itself, a Mediaeval prison; the bars are the superstitious ones of fanatical faith rather than mouldering stones' (1998:110). Hawthorne ideates the darkest dungeon in the guise of the psyche unable or unwilling to rise above dogmatism and prejudice, and provides an anatomy of the psychological darkness of a whole society sustained by stifling moral standards and shallow notions of respectability. Committed to concealing that this is the case, the Puritan community displaces its own self-doubts onto the character of Hester by condemning her to wear the letter A on her bosom as the index of her adultery. As Fred Botting points out, 'The boundaries and conventions distinguishing good from bad are, in the exclusions they legitimate and the repressions they demand, as much a site of darkness and uncertainty as Hester's "immorality"' (1996:117).

The psyche often exhibits its darkest traits when its hidden drives do not find an outlet in action. In such cases, mental life folds and unfolds in its own interiority, spawning endless fantasies of transgression and morbid desire. The themes of possession, addiction and neurotic repetition play an important role. The quest for levels of experience transcending the strictures of socialized existence is often dramatized by recourse to tropes of hubristic overreaching laden with Faustian connotations. An emblematic example of the Gothic hero–villain driven by boundless ambition is supplied by William Beckford's *Vathek*, the oriental tyrant willing to satisfy the gruesome demands of a whimsical Giaour in exchange for greater and greater power. Vathek's first move towards certain damnation consists, significantly, of the annihilation of innocence itself through the 'direful sacrifice' (1986:170) of 50 children, whose blood the demon uncompromisingly requires. (See also **Chapter 12**.) The darkest facet of Vathek's psyche coincides with his conviction, highlighted by Peter Hyland, that 'his choice is a free one; his final choice at Istakar, where the good genius offers him a last chance for mercy, is certainly an act of will' (1990). The Faust-like Caliph consigns himself to eternal darkness through a typically theatrical flourish of Gothic rhetoric: 'Whoever thou art, withhold thy useless admonitions . . . I have traversed a sea of blood, to acquire a power, which will make thy equals tremble: deem not that I shall retire, when in view of the port . . . . Let the sun appear! let him illumine my career! it matters not where it may end' (Beckford 1986:241–2). As Hyland observes, the entire episode is reminiscent of

> the offer made by the Old Man to Marlowe's Faustus, and in it Vathek performs irrevocably the action which makes him a Faust-figure. To use Fiedler's term, he chooses to be damned, 'whatever damnation is. Not to fall into error out of a passionate loss of self-control, not even to choose to sin at a risk of damnation; but to commit oneself to it with absolute certainty for as long as forever is.' (1990)

Vathek's desire to circumvent mortal limitations is repeatedly frustrated and his freedom of choice consequently exposed as illusory and incompatible with the rules of a deterministic universe from which no escape is allowed. Having 'lost the most precious gift of heaven: – HOPE', the overreacher is 'left to wander in an eternity of unabating anguish' (Beckford 1986:254). Related themes are explored in Charles Maturin's *Melmoth the Wanderer: A Tale*, where the hero–villain, driven by the urge to obtain forbidden knowledge, has the power to inflict pain with impunity as he roams the world in search of a person prepared to trade his own destiny for Melmoth's impending damnation. The story greatly influenced a number of later writers drawn to Faustian motifs, from Goethe and Byron, to Baudelaire, Poe, Hawthorne and Wilde.

The connection between a dark fascination with excess and the Faust theme is still evident in contemporary Gothic fiction. In J. G. Ballard's *Crash* [1973], for example, the trope of Faustian overreaching provides a narrative leitmotif in the guise of Vaughan's obsession with the dramatic engineering of a car crash with Elizabeth Taylor. A car crash may seem rather unpromising as a means of attaining an experience of ultimate sublimity. Yet in Vaughan's world even the most mundane of 'wounds and impacts', 'collisions' and 'fractures' become Gothic symbols of an ideal encounter between chromium and legend. The character repeatedly fantasizes about 'the image of windshield glass frosting around her [Taylor's] face as she broke its tinted surface like a death-born Aphrodite'. Vaughan's compulsion to mythologize the occurrence he dreams of is borne out by the classical reference and further reinforced by an allusion to medieval iconography, as he imagines the film star's 'uterus' being 'pierced by the heraldic beak of the manufacturer's medallion' (1995:8). The theme of fatal excess is ultimately encapsulated by Vaughan's vision of cosmic resolution, where the localized image of the 'identical wounds' which the quintessential crash may inflict on its victims eventually leads to the panoramic image of 'the whole world dying in a simultaneous automobile disaster, millions of vehicles hurled together in a terminal congress of spurting loins and engine coolant' (16). It is only while entertaining these thoughts that Vaughan is able to accord the attributes of shape and motion to a world which he otherwise

considers utterly amorphous and static. Just as Faust is traditionally represented as a scholar dissatisfied with conventional forms of knowledge, so
Vaughan is portrayed as a scientist who feels betrayed by the promises of the
Enlightenment. According to Scott McCracken, *Crash* depicts 'a world in which
the modernist dream of solving social problems through technology no longer
holds'. Within this world, Vaughan's project typifies the 'disillusion with technological utopianism' (1998:112). Moreover, just as in Faust's world reason is
superseded by the dark demands of magic, so in *Crash* the irrational holds sway.
As Jean Baudrillard observes, 'the Accident is everywhere . . . no longer on the
margins . . . no longer the exception to a triumphant rationality', for 'it is the
Accident which gives life its very form' (1991:314–15).

The Faust topos also features prominently in Anne Rice's fiction. Echoing
T. S. Eliot's reflections in his essay on Baudelaire (Eliot 1999), the *Vampire
Chronicles* [1976–98] intimate that any action, however regrettable, is preferable to inaction, for freedom consists of the right to err no less than of the right
to seek out the truth. The vampires' obsession with goodness points to an insatiable passion for extremes. Goodness, claims Louis in *Interview with the
Vampire* [1976], is a 'phantom' (1994a:362) which only becomes comprehensible as a concept when one is adrift in the tide of evil. In *The Queen of the
Damned* [1988], Lestat, for his part, exhibits his own fixation with extremes as
he wallows in melodramatic visions of goodness and claims to be prepared to
'suffer martyrdom' and 'torments unspeakable' in order 'to be someone who was
good' (1994c:304). The self-sacrificial conception of goodness embraced by
Gretchen (significantly named after Goethe's character) in *The Tale of the Body
Thief* [1992] is no less excessive, as she is determined to give up physical
pleasure in the name of abstract notions of virtue which ultimately only cause
her pain. Rice also links the passion for extremes with the theme of derange-
ment. According to Katherine Ramsland, 'Where boundaries break down and
maximum freedom seems possible, insanity can result for those who cannot
face up to the resultant chaos and abyss. As Marlow said in Joseph Conrad's
Heart of Darkness, the spectre of limitlessness for those who are not gods is
madness' (1994:193).

Narratives of darkness not only depict psyches in the grip of obsessions and
delusions, they also dramatize the effects of disruptive occurrences whereby
people are forced to face their own darkness, this often consisting of unacknowledged sexual urges. It is to the relationship between psychological
darkness and sexuality that the final segment of this chapter is devoted. Arthur
Schnitzler's *Dream Story* [1926] and Stanley Kubrick's film based on this novella,
Eyes Wide Shut (1999), explore what may happen when repressed erotic
fantasies come to life and threaten to shatter the smug self-confidence of their
owners. What darkens the psychodynamics of the relationship between Frigolin
and Albertine (Bill and Alice in the movie) is, paradoxically, the apparent

luminosity of their bourgeois existence – the cluster of conventions that prevent them from recognizing that their conjugal life is woven on conflicting impulses, unruly sexual drives and self-restraint, murderous anger and tenderness, mutual desire and revulsion. When, unexpectedly, the characters feel troubled by memories of encounters pregnant with sexual connotations, they have to confront longings that they have repressed and concealed out of principles of reserve and propriety ultimately amounting to hypocrisy and self-deception. The image of the mask plays a crucially symbolic role in the story. It suggests that the disguises adopted by Frigolin and various other characters he associates with in his nocturnal peregrinations do not occlude their identities but rather emphasize that the socialized self is a web of intrigue, distortion and falsehood. The mask does not conceal the psyche but actually gives its darkness visible form. That the mask serves a revelatory function is emphasized in the closing chapter when Frigolin is compelled to disclose his night-time secrets to Albertine by the sight of the mask, which he has hired to attend a satanist celebration and then misplaced; lying on his side of the bed when he finally returns home. He 'became aware of something very close to Albertine's face on the other pillow, on *his* pillow, something dark and quite distinct, like the shadowy outline of a human face. His heart stood still for an instant until he grasped the situation' (Schnitzler 1999:97). As a result of their journey into darkness, Frigolin and Albertine learn to acknowledge the murkiness of their own oppressively encultured psyches and the need to cultivate their erotic drives.

Repression is indubitably one of the principal components of a dark psyche plagued by disavowed sexual desires. No less vital a part is played by perversion, a phenomenon which Angela Carter insistently associates with the urge to conquer anything that threatens to challenge dominant power structures. *Nights at the Circus* (1984), for instance, explores the connection between psychological darkness and perverse sexual desires that hinge on the reification of the female body. As Gina Wisker points out, 'In her examination of sexual politics' Carter 'repeatedly presents scenarios where women are . . . disempowered objects of desire' (1993:163). However, it must be stressed that Carter is not condoning violence against women by making it the recurring theme of her fiction but actually attributing it to the pervasiveness of unsavoury impulses traditionally legitimated by patriarchal dispensations. Carter also aims to expose the stereotypical vacuity of the classic fairy tale model in which oppressed heroines are invariably rescued by brave princes and heterosexual happiness is the narrative's primary aim. The male villains are hardly desirable and Walser, though benevolent, is hardly presented as a saving hero. In fact, there is something quite pathetic about this character. He starts off as a stern rationalizer, unwilling to accept that Fevvers could naturally possess both arms and wings, and ends up 'bamboozled' by a Shaman (1984:294) prior to his rescue by the Cockney Venus.

Nights at the Circus abounds with instances of the perverse domination of women. Madame Schreck's 'museum of woman monsters' (55), a brothel, thrives on the objectification of varyingly hybrid or grotesque beings. Its heart is 'a sort of vault or crypt . . . with wormy beams overhead and nasty damp flag-stones underfoot' dubbed 'The Abyss' and used as the exhibition area for the unscrupulous woman's rare merchandize. 'The girls was all made to stand in stone niches cut out of the slimy walls, except for the Sleeping Beauty, who remained prone, since proneness was her speciality. And there were little curtains in front and, in front of the curtains, a little lamp burning. These were her [Madame Schreck's] "profane altars", as she used to call them' (61). The down-to-earth and often humorous mood typically adopted by Carter does not lighten but rather intensifies through defamiliarization the darkness of the perversions presented in the novel. Indeed, as Wisker notes, even though the 'everyday Cockney tones of the winged, iconic aerialiste Fevvers renders these traditionally gothic horrors almost domestic' (1993:167), there is something unquestionably harrowing about Carter's depiction of necrophiliac, sadistic and masochistic clients and the props they employ: 'the one I liked least,' Fevvers states, 'was the executioner's hood; there was a judge who come regular who always fancied that. Yet all he ever wanted was a weeping girl to spit at him' (Carter 1994:61). The carnivalesque flavour of Carter's fiction cannot, therefore, be regarded as a means of concealing the darkness of the desires by which sexual roles and relations are frequently imbued. As Marina Warner comments, 'humour in Carter's fiction signals her defiant hold on "heroic optimism", the mood she singled out as characteristic of fairy tales, the principle which sustained the idea of a happy ending'. Yet, 'laughter never unburdens itself from knowledge of its own pessimism' and hence 'remains intrinsically ironic' (1995:197).

The image of the 'Abyss' used to designate the underbelly of Madame Schreck's museum features again a couple of chapters later to signify, in Rosen-creutz's words, 'the female part, or absence, or atrocious hole, or dreadful chasm . . . the vortex that sucks everything dreadfully down, down where Terror rules'. The deranged Rosicrucian objectifies Fevvers by maintaining that she combines all the mythological themes he is simultaneously attracted to and terrified of – 'Flora; Azrael; Venus Pandemos!' – and claims that 'by uniting his body with that of Azrael, the Angel of Death, on the threshold of spring, he would cheat death itself' (Carter 1984:77, 79). Regrettably for the aerialiste, what he has in mind is her ceremonial immolation. A further example of the patriarch sustained by destructive fantasies is supplied by the Grand Duke. In his case, despotism is shown to rely on the support of art – a tool that has traditionally been used by Western societies as a means of fixing, freezing and framing woman and her supposedly leaky body. The Grand Duke's dehumaniz-ing urges are epitomized by the compulsion to collect, contain and ultimately annihilate the object of worship. In his world, everything is indeed hard, frozen, crystallized: his stupendous dwelling is described as 'the realm of minerals, of metals, of vitrification' and there is 'a sense of frigidity, of sterility, almost palpable, almost tangible in the hard, chill surfaces and empty spaces' (184). In the middle of the table laid for supper stands a 'life size' sculpture of Fevvers made entirely of 'ice': 'May you melt in the warmth of my house just as *she* melts', the Grand Duke lyrically and ominously intones (186). (See also **Chapter 14**.)

Like Carter, Poppy Z. Brite presents violent desecrations of the body not in order to justify sexual violence but to expose the hypocrisy of whole cultures committed to hiding the pervasiveness of both literal and metaphorical drives to rend, mutilate and dissect through exploitative power relations. (The work of Poppy Z. Brite is also discussed in **Chapters 1, 10** and **13**.) What dominant cultural paradigms expect us to perceive and commend as aesthetically and ethically rewarding is only a minute portion of the real that excludes 'the grey areas, the unclaimed zones' and labels them repulsive. As Charles Baudelaire's *Les Fleurs du Mal* and T. S. Eliot's reflections on art's penchant for elevating the sordid to the beautiful stress, developing an aptitude to live with darkness may well depend on the willingness 'to see the beauty in something that [we] would otherwise find disgusting' and even be 'disturbed' by our 'ability to see this beauty' (Brite 1998).

In its exploration of psychological darkness, the Gothic vision unremittingly proposes an interweaving of anguish and excitement, anxiety and delight, anomie and desire. Whether we follow William Patrick Day's line, according to which the Gothic transforms 'the anxiety of fear' into 'pleasure' (1985:10–11), or whether we follow Judith Halberstam's approach and see it as a translation of desire into fear triggered by libidinal anxieties (1995), what seems obvious is that narratives of darkness hinge constantly on the interplay of pleasure and pain. This links them to an apocalyptic ethos wherein baleful and hopeful visions coexist, doom and rebirth being indissolubly entangled in the concept and etymology of apocalypse, no less than in the concept of darkness. What the Gothic vision offers is not necessarily a binary opposition whereby either fear leads to pleasure or pleasure leads to fear and hence pain. This is vividly exemplified by Bret Easton Ellis's *American Psycho* (1991), where fear does not unproblematically yield either pleasure or pain. In fact, it is dissected into both its private and societal components. The exaggeration of its effects leads to the normalization of horror in the reader's perception, mainly to highlight the voraciousness of American society and the predatory instincts of capitalism at large. The lists of commodities that pepper the narrative (garments, dishes, CDs, art works) often come across, paradoxically, as more alive than any of Ellis's eminently cardboard characters. Mary Harron's cinematic adaptation of *American Psycho* (2000) emphasizes this point. It may well be the case that the ghastly episodes depicted in the novel are merely products of its protagonist's hideous fantasies. Yet this does not make them any less powerful or indeed any less concrete since, ultimately, fantasies are not at odds with reality but rather interpretations of reality in both its actual and potential manifestations. Ideating fantastic worlds may well be a way of trying to comprehend our own world.

Arguably, we go on revisiting the murky realms of aberration, excess and evil to give names and faces to the spectres that scare us most. According to the German film-maker Fred Kelemen, our attraction to diverse incarnations of physical, psychological, geographical and historical Gothicity results from a desire 'to put a spell on the demons', comparable to the attempts of cave dwellers to 'capture the demons' which they feared most acutely by painting pictures of them in animal form in the eerie depths of the earth (quoted in Mettler 1995:60–4).

— Part 2 —
Haunting

Introduction

What haunts us is something inaccessible from which we cannot extricate ourselves. It is that which cannot be found and therefore cannot be avoided. What no one can grasp is the inescapable. . . It stays with us because it has no place.

Maurice Blanchot, The Space of Literature

How can we be scared by what we know does not exist? Why should we go on seeking the sources of fear when being frightened is so obviously unpleasant? Narratives of darkness turn repeatedly to the phenomenon of haunting as a means of emphasizing the inevitability of human beings confronting the non-human that eludes explanation. The confrontation is inevitable because the inexplicable, though ostensibly non-human, is intrinsic to being human. The energies that haunt us are very much a part of our own selves; they refer to what is missing from us and hence to a fundamental aspect of our being – lack. If we find them disorienting, spooky or overtly threatening, this is because we have disavowed them in the interest of rationalist doctrines that brand anything which cannot be empirically ascertained and measured as a symptom of moral and mental degeneration. Haunting forces will not leave us alone precisely because we cannot leave them alone, in a blind and often unacknowledged quest for what we have repressed. This approach to haunting indicates that there are no obvious distinctions between the inside and the outside, since factors which we may be inclined to deem external to our selves insistently turn out to be intrinsic aspects of our psyches and our bodies. Accordingly, it is hard to establish who is being haunted and who is doing the haunting: in other words, where exactly the sense of menace originates. Uncertainty and uneasiness are therefore primary ingredients of spectrality. In *The Scarlet Letter* [1850], Nathaniel Hawthorne vividly encapsulates this idea by emphasizing the ghost's liminal status: 'Somewhere between . . . the Actual and the Imaginary . . . ghosts might enter' (1978:31). Avery Gordon further stresses the ghost's disrespect for conventional boundaries and distinctions: 'the ghost imports a charged strangeness into the place or sphere it is haunting, thus unsettling the propriety and property lines that delimit a zone of activity or knowledge' (1997:63).

The realm of haunting is not so much different from or an alternative to the real as an extension of the real into commonly unexplored territories. The more familiar and habitual the site of an apparition is, the more sudden and disquieting are its effects. Ghosts insert themselves into the texture of the quotidian in baffling ways: they walk through walls, climb out of portraits, peer through mirrors. This makes their world apparently illogical, insubstantial, oneiric. Yet, it does not make it nonsensical for even dreams speak a language based on precise and curiously logical rules, however inconsequential their images and narratives may seem. What renders ghosts more unsettling still is the fact that they cannot be univocally associated with any one of the senses. They are often related to visions, and hence to the sense of sight, but some of their scariest manifestations are frequently heard rather than seen. At times, visual images are conjured up by the haunted person out of an instinctive attempt to give shape to fear and do not pertain to the manifestation itself. It could be argued that one of the most distressing forms of haunting consists of finding oneself and one's whole sensorium in the grip of emotions that belong to an unknown Other. This can be a prelude to the paralyzing sensation that one has actually become someone else.

Despite the profound sense of vexation induced by such premonitions, tales of haunting may serve a reparative role, for 'the ghost story is, among other things, a sort of safety net. It allows us to deal with the tangibility of our own mortality from a safe distance, and allows us to explore the ideology of life after death . . . It speaks of how we deal with life' (*Deserts of the Dead*). Thus, ghost stories may ultimately help us reconfigure our very understanding of reality. That reality is never fully present may seem a banal expression of the obvious. It is nonetheless something we frequently forget or ignore. We think of ourselves as possessors of physical and psychological properties, and of such properties as the measure of our presence. Yet, as indomitable anxieties constantly force reality to shift gears, we become increasingly aware that reality is distant from us. Our own reality, both bodily and mental, is haunted by that which seems not to be there. Exploring reality means confronting its invisible aspects, seething phantoms which are either deliberately excluded from view because they are too debilitating or painful to register, or inadvertently allowed to fall into reality's interstices. Following this lead, narratives of darkness focus on the construction of identity out of lack, of presence out of an absence that will never leave it. Furthermore, the instability of identity is paralleled by the depiction of alternative worlds where all solid foundations are shaken. The shape of reality is continually sought in its invisibility, by tracing through time and space that which makes its mark by at the same time being there and not being there.

Through the discourse of haunting, the Gothic vision posits both the ghost and the persecuted subject as existentially incomplete, disabled by absences which make the equation between being and presence specious, if not downright redundant. Yet this defectiveness holds creative potentialities, for it conceives of being as something other than unadulterated presence. A lacunary subject may function imaginatively by negotiating a deal with its absences, indeed by harnessing them to a broadening of its field of mental and physical action. Being becomes a reaching out of the self into the 'no longer' and into the 'not yet': it oscillates between the plane of completion from which it has always already slipped and the plane of countless other lives still to be entered. The duplicity of being is thrown into relief by ambiguous narratives in which reality and unreality coalesce, through the production, within any one picture, of contrasting viewpoints, multiple perspectives and interlocking spaces which spurn the authority of monocularity and the tyranny of empirical evidence. Tales of haunting are ultimately pictures of a floating universe, of a transient spectacle, of virtual histories and invisible destinies. While the humanist model proclaims that the self is complete and that if it is not, it must and may be completed, the Gothic vision foregrounds the need to face up to incompleteness as a condition which may not and must not be redeemed. Phobia, horror and abjection lie with apparent fullness and fulfilment, not with the gap, for plenitude is only ever a broken promise, while the gap is the precondition of creativity. In dispersing the self into murky areas of uncertainty and doubt, dark texts emphasize that we need to experience our own deficiencies and undecidables as the *sine qua non* of any claim to identity, that our presence is only ever a mirage or hallucination predicated on our constant interaction with absence.

As the most popular and enduring incarnation of unease, resisting classification both in the province of presence and in that of absence, the figure of the ghost reinforces in exemplary fashion the notion that fear is a pervasive aspect of human life. Ghosts return to haunt the living out of a desire for revenge conducive to often extreme acts of violence and brutality that may include the victimization of the innocent. However, they are frequently also egged on by a desire for justice that does not merely point to the instinctive urge to heal a personal injury but also to wider ideological issues. This is evinced, for example, by Stephen King's *Bag of Bones* (1999), a novel to which spectrality is central not only thematically but also structurally. King's text itself is haunted throughout by Daphne du Maurier's *Rebecca* [1938]. The Southern blues singer Sara Tidwell returns to seek justice not only for herself and her child but also to expose the evils of a whole community and the chain of nefarious events initiated by fierce racial discrimination. That spectrality constitutes a communal rather than a singular phenomenon is emphasized by the fact that the harshly abused black woman is not the only ghost whose threats and warnings course through the narrative. The ghost of the protagonist's wife and the ubiquitous ghost of a crying child also feature conspicuously. Prominent amongst Sara's intended victims is the recently widowed Gothic romance writer Mike Noonan who, compelled by a recurring dream to return to his vacation cabin by Dark Score Lake in rural Maine, finds that this has become a beacon for ghoulish visitors, and that it is on this same site that decades earlier the black woman was raped and murdered. Central to the plot is the discovery that everybody related to the people who have killed Sara and her son have paid by losing a child of their own. Ominously, all the dead children's names bear a resemblance to Kito, the name of Sara's son. Among the actual and potential victims are Kia, the protagonist's unborn daughter, and Kyra, the psychic child whose rescue from the rapacious hands of the incalculably rich and no less manipulative Max Devore is central to the story. According to inveterate beliefs which we have no satisfactory reason to dispute, ghosts cannot rest until a cycle of haunting is either completed or broken. In *Bag of Bones*, the evils that have become entrenched in the very soil of the Maine community and their spectral embodiments are only partially purged when the past is reburied in the very form of Sara Tidwell's body. (*Bag of Bones* is also discussed in **Chapters 2** and **12**, and the Introduction to **Part 3**.)

The analysis of spectrality offered in the following chapters hinges on the exploration of the principal narrative structures through which dark fiction articulates the dialogue between presence and absence, with reference to an illustrative gallery of ghostly figures and to exemplary locations laden with social and psychological connotations.

— 4 —

The Rhetoric of Haunting

AUNTING IS A DISCOURSE. It encompasses a number of languages (both verbal and visual), image repertoires, performative acts and stylistic devices. These elements constitute a complex rhetoric, central to which is the principle of ambiguity: a blurring of logical distinctions, resulting in the sustained obfuscation of sense, whereby a mood of suspension and undecidability is produced. The prototypical figure associated with haunting, the ghost, typifies this rhetorical strategy, largely through its uncanny admixture of physical and incorporeal attributes. Furthermore, an atmosphere of haziness is frequently evoked through the juxtaposition of the natural and the supernatural, the ancient and the modern, the rational and the irrational. A viable point of entry into the examination of the rhetoric of haunting is supplied by the ghost stories of Algernon Blackwood and M. R. James. (See also **Chapter 2** for the link between M. R. James's fiction and Christmas.)

Blackwood is primarily concerned with conveying the all-pervasiveness of haunting forces through a vision that could well be described as spectral pantheism, as well as with emphasizing that the apprehension of those omnipresent energies, however disturbing, may be conceived of as potentially illuminating. As Paul F. Olson observes,

> In Blackwood's work, the entire world was haunted, ghosts and spirits lurked in
> every living thing, and something as simple as a snowfall or a gust of wind
> could open a doorway to another world . . . [Blackwood] liked to create stories
> about average characters who see the curtain of perception ripped away and
> catch a glimpse of the larger, life-changing, mind-altering, sometimes incom-
> prehensible truths that lay on the other side. (Olson: website)

The 'other side' is unquestionably a source of fear and yet, like fear itself, it is capable of yielding its own peculiar rewards. At times Blackwood makes nature the principal repository of haunting agents. In 'The Willows' [1907], for example, he inspires a sense of nature's awesome and spellbinding powers by representing the predicament of unwary campers threatened by a spectral grove (Blackwood 1973). At others, natural forces are intertwined with ancient and half-buried, yet indelible, traditions. This is exemplified by 'The Wendigo' [1910], a story in which Native myths come to life to haunt the present and, implicitly, its belief systems (Blackwood 1973).

The study of the genesis and evolution of fear within particular psyches is one of Blackwood's ongoing preoccupations, and this requires a certain degree of individuation in the process of character construction. M. R. James's characters, conversely, come across as relatively flat, since he is less interested in dramatizing the fear within the narrative than the fear produced by the narrative in the reader's mind. Julia Briggs draws attention to a further difference between Blackwood and James. The latter, she argues, 'did not share the concern shown by other writers (Blackwood . . . , for instance) with the significance of spirits, the state of mind in which ghosts are seen, or the condition of a universe that permits the maleficent returning dead. His stories assert a total acceptance of the supernatural that his scepticism apparently denies' (1977; quoted in Bloom 1998:101–2). One of the principal ambiguities posed by James's tales consists of his inclination to take unearthly occurrences for granted and, simultaneously, detach himself from their psychological and metaphysical import. This detachment is frequently fuelled by the writer's passion for antiquarianism and its connotations of both historical and physical remoteness. However, a further element of ambiguity can be seen to inhabit James's fiction when we turn our attention to his favourite locations. Much as his academic enthusiasm may draw him to the past, it is often by recourse to commonplace and contemporary settings that he aims at evoking the most potent feelings of dread and distress. This ensues from the writer's conviction, voiced in his Introduction to *Ghosts and Marvels* [1924], that 'a setting so modern that the ordinary reader can judge of its naturalness for himself is preferable to anything antique' (James 1998:339).

It is in his conception of the spectral figure itself that James participates most overtly in the rhetorical ethos of ambiguity. In particular, his tales exemplify the interpenetration of accepted definitions of terror and horror, terror conventionally alluding to the perception of intangible threats and horror to the confrontation of physical abomination. In James's stories, those two dimensions unrelentingly coalesce. On the one hand, he praises vagueness over explicit references to the corporeal domain as instrumental to building up and maintaining a menacing sense of the inscrutable. Undoubtedly, some of the scariest spectres are those that remain equivocal and cryptic. An imprecisely sketched ghost is especially disturbing because it refuses to be cast into a definitive shape, as typified by the creature in James's own 'Oh Whistle and I'll Come to You, My Lad' [1904], described as having a 'face of *crumpled linen*'

(James 1998:76), and by the apparition in Joyce Carol Oates's 'The Ruins of Con-tracoeur': *'A thing-without-a-face'* (1999:27). On the other hand, the pursuit of allusive vagueness consistently results in descriptions which evoke a powerful impression of physicality and even revulsion. (This concept is closely examined in **Chapter 15**.) Understating the material dimension becomes, paradoxically, a means of heightening its significance. Indeed, in 'Oh Whistle', the eyeless spirit in the bedclothes, however vaguely formed, is endowed with a disconcerting energy: it 'seemed to feel about it with its muffled arms in a groping and random fashion' (James 1998:75). James's fascination with repulsive corporeal-ity is also borne out by the recurrent utilization of varyingly satanic and vampiric insectile creatures: the flies in 'An Evening's Entertainment' [1931]; the wasp-like creature in 'Mr Humphreys and His Inheritance' [1911]; the spiders in 'The Ash-tree' [1904] and in 'Canon Alberic's Scrapbook' [1895]. The last is a paradigmatic instance of the author's ability to dramatize the unfore-seen discovery of an alien, malevolent Beyond that is apparently distinct from the everyday world, yet always ready to infringe upon it with devastating results, though often as a consequence of apparently trivial actions. The spider-like creature, with its 'pale dusky skin covering nothing but bones and tendons of appalling strength', vividly embodies the Beyond's disruptive forces by inducing 'the intensest physical fear' (James 1998:10–11), thus confirming the proposition that terror of the indefinite and horror of the corporeal are inextricably interwoven.

This admixture of the hazy and the tangible is also central to 'The Treasure of Abbot Thomas' [1904], where the menacing entity's lack of clear definition serves to intensify its horrific and disgusting attributes: 'I was conscious of a most horrible smell of mould and of a cold kind of face pressed against my own and moving slowly over it; and of several – I don't know how many – legs or arms or tentacles or something clinging to my body' (James 1998:94). What is conveyed here is a sense of repulsive intimacy hinting at an experience of sexual violation. This theme is also tangentially articulated in 'Casting the Runes' [1911], where the privacy and safety of the bed are grossly desecrated by a monstrous entity made all the more horrifying by the fact that it can be felt but not seen: 'he put his hand into the well-known nook under the pillow: only, it did not get so far. What he touched was . . . a mouth, with teeth and with hair about it' (James 1998:146). The sexual connotations of the infelici-tous encounter are reinforced by the entity's affinity with the mythical image of the *vagina dentata*. The incidents just mentioned point to undercurrents of frightful sexuality in an otherwise pretty sexless world. Women feature infre-quently in James's tales and when they do, they are only superficially described, largely because of their stereotypical association with sexuality and the writer's belief that this subject is inappropriate to the ghost story. In 'Some Remarks on Ghost Stories' [1929], he asserts:

> Reticence may be an elderly doctrine to preach, yet from the artistic point of view I am sure it is a sound one. Reticence conduces to effect, blatancy ruins it, and there is much blatancy in a lot of recent stories. They drag in sex too, which is a fatal mistake; sex is tiresome enough in the novels; in a ghost story, or as the backbone of a ghost story, I have no patience with it. (James 1998:347)

(The relationship between sex and the ghost story is also discussed in **Chapter 9** in relation to Henry James's *The Turn of the Screw*.) However, the metaphorically sexual nature of many scenes of physical disruption suggests that a world without sex may still, paradoxically, be traversed by sex-inspired horrors. James also emphasizes the pivotal role played by narrative pace in conveying a climate of haunting. In his essay 'Ghosts – Treat Them Gently' [1931], he underscores the desirability of building up a sense of threat through a deliciously slow tempo: 'Our ghost should make himself felt by gradual stirrings, diffusing an atmosphere of uneasiness before the final flash or stab of horror' (James 1998:351). In the Introduction to *Ghosts and Marvels*, it is proposed that the ideal tale should convey a 'nicely managed crescendo', whereby the sense of menace reveals itself incrementally: 'Let us, then, be introduced to the actors in a placid way; . . . and into this calm environment let the ominous thing put out its head, unobtrusively at first, and then more insistently, until it holds the stage'. A creeping feeling of discomfort is vital to the overall effect. Paradoxically, however, slowness works insofar as it is allied to opportunities for a sudden awareness of being scared. By this means, the most self-confident subjects can be catastrophically exposed to countless sources of malice and, ultimately, to their own darkness. Indeed, it is vital that the reader should be led, through a combination of 'some degree of actuality' and 'a slight haze of distance' in the representation of the characters and settings, 'to identify himself with the patient', the haunted party (James 1998:339–40).

No less central than ambiguity to the discourse of spectrality is the mechanism of repetition. In *Beyond the Pleasure Principle* (1920), Sigmund Freud relates repetition to a compulsive tendency to re-enact traumatic experiences, largely repressed, in an attempt to bind their energies and reach a state of balance or even entropy. At the same time, repetitive behaviour points to a desire to compensate for a deep-seated sense of lack. Narratives of darkness that hinge on the phenomenon of haunting comment on both facets of repetition. The recursive appearance of ghosts often articulates both the return of the repressed and the longing (having allowed the repressed to surface) to let it rest in peace. Concurrently, ghosts are, albeit subliminally, invited to enter the everyday course of life as a means of compensating for something that is painfully and inexplicably missing. Indeed, although ghosts are conventionally assumed to disrupt the natural order of things, they can also be said to complete an otherwise lacunary reality. Jacques Lacan (1982), in his study of

Shakespeare's *Hamlet* as a tragedy of desire, suggests that they fill in the gap opened by death: a fracture supposed to be especially wide in the case of violent and untimely deaths, as well as in the absence of adequate mourning rituals. Thus, in a sense, ghosts return not so much in order to unsettle the status quo as in order to mend a damaged fabric.

Although spectres are traditionally connected with the dead, and the people they haunt with the living, this conventional separation is often quizzed and rendered uncertain by narratives of darkness. For example, the narrator in Susan Hill's *The Woman in Black* [1983], though he is the victim of haunting agents, feels like a ghost himself: a gloomy 'spectre at some cheerful feast' (1998:46). Likewise Barney, the protagonist of Margaret Mahy's *The Haunting*, feels that *'he* might be the one who was not quite real' when faced with a baffling spectral vision (1999:20). The dead may turn out to have a more solid identity than their living counterparts, and the latter, in turn, may become akin to phantoms. In Daphne du Maurier's *Rebecca* [1938], the second, and ominously unnamed, Mrs de Winter often perceives herself as a ghostly entity trailing in the shadow of the dead woman she has replaced. Paradoxically, although Rebecca is the spectre that relentlessly haunts the second Mrs de Winter's world, it is the latter who perceives herself and her surroundings as ghostly. Mrs Danvers (the housekeeper) fuels the heroine's doubts about the substance of her own identity by stressing Rebecca's enduring hold on Manderley: 'You'll never get the better of her. She's still mistress here, even if she is dead. She's the real Mrs de Winter, not you. It's you that's the shadow and the ghost. It's you that's forgotten and not wanted and pushed aside' (1992:257). Spectral identities crowd upon the second Mrs de Winter and her subjection to the past reaches a climax in the episode of the masked ball. Maxim teasingly speculates about the appropriateness of his wife's dressing up as 'Alice-in-Wonderland', thus supplying her with a ghostly persona consonant with her characterization as a child. But an alternative role is also forged for the second Mrs de Winter at this juncture: the fact that she actually appears wearing a dress copied from a portrait of Caroline de Winter, identical to the one worn by Rebecca for her last fancy-dress ball at Manderley, invests her with an adult identity. However, this subject position is no less spectral than the infantile one, for it dissolves the heroine into irreconcilable opposites: a capable woman possibly ushering in a new lifestyle for both Maxim and Manderley and a second-rate replica of Rebecca, physically possessed by her phantom in vestimentary form.

It could be argued that du Maurier's novel in its entirety constitutes something of a ghost lurking beneath the assumptions of romance fiction. This reading would confirm Alison Light's suggestion that the text explicitly articulates what more conventional romances have insistently spectralized: 'I would like to see *Rebecca* as the absent subtext of much romance fiction, the crime behind the scenes of Mills and Boon . . . *Rebecca* acts out the process of repression which these other texts avoid by assuming a fully achievable, uncomplicated gendered subject whose sexual desire is not in question' (1984:10). *Rebecca* haunts romantic fiction by showing that what is customarily taken for granted by tales in that tradition should be questioned and the underlying ambiguities exposed. One of the most poignantly ambiguous issues highlighted by *Rebecca* is the tension between the plausibility of attempting a radical break with the haunting past and the recognition of an ungenerous lack of prospects. As Nicholas Rance observes, the 'destruction of Manderley' might well symbolize 'the demise of an aristocratic lifestyle . . . with the heroine embodying a more rooted if less elevated future' (1993:88). Yet, the second Mrs de Winter's childlessness symbolically militates against the vision of fresh beginnings. This theme is painfully developed by Susan Hill in her sequel to du Maurier's novel, *Mrs de Winter* [1993].

Hill defines haunting as the phenomenon capable of leaving a person 'with all one's certainties and reasoning undermined, and thrown about like toys by a malevolent gleeful child' (1999:79). Central to the protagonist's predicament is her faith in a new dawn capable of erasing Rebecca's ghost. The delusory character of this aspiration is symbolically encapsulated by the episode in which Mrs de Winter finds a photograph of her predecessor in an old magazine and is so stunned by its vitality that she cannot at first bring herself to 'rip out the page'. When she does succeed, she is overwhelmed by the sense of having performed some sacrilegious act of mutilation. Moreover, Rebecca's 'face' remains ominously unscathed (147–8). The photograph is much more than an old picture of a dead woman. First its resistance and then its resilience to the protagonist's attacks endow it with potent energies which suggest that what haunts us most indomitably is not presence or the present but rather submerged relics from a past that has never quite passed away: images, imaginings, the imaginary. In Mrs de Winter's case, these ultimately amount to a concatenation of might-have-beens, in which a critical role is played by the absent presence of the children denied her by Rebecca's unexorcizable resurgence. Repeatedly, she senses the unborn 'following' her (231), as so many 'faces peeping out from the shrubbery' (295). Like du Maurier's heroine, Hill's Mrs de Winter is no less spectral than Rebecca. Indeed, she presents herself as an assortment of phantom identities:

> the child I myself had been, and the growing girl, and then the gauche young
> woman who had met Maxim, the bride arriving at Manderley, the passionate,
> loving, bewildered wife in awe of it all . . . had led here, to this woman with the
> beginnings of grey hair . . . Me. And yet they were not, they were ghosts, and
> they had vanished. . . They were not dead, as she was dead, but they no more
> existed than the newborn baby or toddling child I had also once been. (324–5)

Both *Rebecca* and *Mrs de Winter* conjure up a pervasive sense of uncertainty by dramatizing unresolved conflicts engaging the present and the past, and by rendering the dividing line between the living and the dead nebulous. In so doing, they do not merely depict the vicissitudes of singular sensibilities for, when contextualized, they evince a commitment to wider ideological concerns pertaining to economic and sexual structures of dominance. They make the romantic genre itself ambiguous by intimating that it may serve more complex purposes than vicarious wish-fulfilment.

Articulating a complex dialogue between the past and the present, Toni Morrison's *Beloved* (1987) foregrounds the ideological dimension of spectrality with reference to the legacy of slavery and racial oppression. The novel, as Avery Gordon observes, 'problematizes the retrieval of lost or missing subjects by transforming those who do not speak into what is unspeakable' (1997:150). Morrison intimates that what is invisible is not, necessarily, *not there*: what seems absent may actually be a seething presence, the protagonist of an occluded history, the product of an ideology of blindness such as the one that renders Ralph Ellison's excluded subject an *Invisible Man* [1952]. The theme of ghostliness enables Morrison to constellate a whole galaxy of collective memories that may prove far too debilitating if recorded directly in a documentary fashion but become a means to illuminating discoveries when mediated through the rhetoric of haunting. It is important, in this respect, to appreciate Morrison's distance from the tradition of reportorial slave narratives. These have undoubtedly created scope for a narrativization of suffering that ostensibly gives the dispossessed a voice and rescues them from a destiny of anonymous obscurity. Yet, they risk pandering to distinctively American hegemonic priorities by subscribing to the glorification of the individual, by suggesting that all people are free to express themselves and thus effacing the fact that the majority of oppressed subjects has actually remained silent and ghostly. *Beloved* supplies voices for the disenfranchised but such voices are displaced and decentred and thus serve to challenge the ideology of individualism. (*Beloved* is also discussed in **Chapter 1** as an instance of Southern Gothic.)

The interplay of past and present so crucial to the themes and structures of the texts examined above also plays a major part in Peter Ackroyd's *Hawksmoor* (1985), where spectrality is inseparable from the rhythms of history and from the coalescence of disparate temporal dimensions in a cacophony of overlapping voices. In the novel, the eighteenth-century narrative and its twentieth-century counterpart unremittingly haunt each other through a plethora of correspondences and parallelisms. While the protagonists of the text's two strands continually echo one another in their psychologies and actions, Ackroyd simultaneously weaves a tapestry of images that recur throughout the novel with uncanny insistence. Two of these images feature with the disquieting regularity of a repetition compulsion: the 'shadow' (e.g.

1985:86–7, 209–10) and 'dust' (e.g. 17, 34, 69, 109, 119), as proverbially spectral vestiges of things gone and yet abiding. Not only do the two narratives haunt each other: they are also self-haunting, persecuted from within by harrowing intimations of the flimsiness of the belief systems upon which their cultures claim to thrive. The pretensions of the Enlightenment, most notably championed by the Royal Society and by Sir Christopher Wren, are punctured by the persistence of satanic allegiances, at the same time as the graphic portrayal of the horrors of Bedlam points to the eruption of the irrational and the diabolical in the very cradle of reason. As the eighteenth-century architect Nicholas Dyer, whose ethos is nourished by more ancient and far darker ideals than the ones fostered by the Age of Reason and its passion for 'Systems', points out, 'there is no system to be made of those Truths which are learnt by Faith and Terrour' (146). Likewise, the twentieth-century detective Nicholas Hawksmoor, intent on investigating a series of murders that repeatedly lead back to the spooky churches executed by Dyer, is tormented by doubts regarding the viability of rational explanations. There is little conviction in his assertions that 'There are no ghosts' and that 'We live in a rational society' (158), and this is confirmed by his recognition that if mysteries are ever resolved this is a result of accident, not of logic: 'He had come to the end by chance' (215). Moreover, while the modern Gothic tale of paranoia, pursuit and self-persecution harks back to an eighteenth-century Gothic tale of tenebrous lawlessness, both narratives evoke a pre-Gothic city of darkness, the London of the Great Plague and the Great Fire, and, beyond that, the London of ancient cults and rites. (The relationship between the urban construct and Gothic darkness is examined in detail in **Chapter 1**.)

The ambivalent logic that makes the past and the present both competing and complicitous parties also animates the individual psyche's hauntings and self-hauntings. This is evinced, for instance, by Peter Straub's *Mr X*, where it is proposed that some of the most stubborn haunting agencies are the doubles and alter egos which we perceive both as parts of ourselves and as separate entities. Straub ideates those agencies as shadows which his characters are at once alienated from and dependent upon, in the knowledge, albeit semiconscious, that the more they endeavour to escape them, the more they will yearn for them. From a young age, the protagonist Ned Dunstan is haunted by a nightmare in which his shadow acquires a life of its own. The shadow is daring and adventurous, refuses to remain anchored to Ned and to a life it considers dull, and repeatedly draws the protagonist into dark and menacing worlds. This spooky entity foreshadows Ned's flesh-and-bone alter ego, an identical twin named Robert snatched away at birth, whose existence Ned does not discover until the eve of their thirty-fifth birthday. Like the shadow, Robert is the unscrupulous counterpart of Ned's putatively self-restrained being. The protagonist simultaneously resists his brother's lure and yields to the desire to be finally united to what he feels he has been lacking all along: 'Right from the beginning, I had the sense that something crucially significant, something without which I could never be whole, was missing' (2000:10). Straub has commented on the relationship between Ned and Robert as 'a literalization of the protagonist's divided impulses, a kind of metaphor for lost wholeness. His public self, Ned, is kind, rational, well-mannered, civilized, reflective to the point of passivity; his split-off self, Robert, is angry, selfish, criminal, impulsive, childish, wild, cruel. Robert is free to act as Ned cannot dare to act'. And yet, Ned may have one advantage over Robert: 'only Ned can admit the yearning for unity both of them feel' (Straub:website). This suggests that the encultured self is inevitably more aware of loss, of what it intrinsically lacks, and hence of the attractiveness of achieving a fusion with its Other: namely, something that either has been denied or has deliberately resisted socialization, thus bypassing the ethical and legal imperatives of the adult world. In Lacanian terms, it can be argued that whereas Ned has accessed the Symbolic order, Robert has not.

In exploring Ned Dunstan's haunting by his twin brother, Straub articulates two further levels of spectrality: the haunting of Mr X, a homicidal misanthrope, by H. P. Lovecraft's otherworldly horror fiction and by the shadow-son he seeks to annihilate in order to achieve his dark objectives; and the haunting of *Mr X* itself by Lovecraft's story 'The Dunwich Horror' [1928]. Straub's narrative resonates with well-known Lovecraftian images, most notably that of the 'Old Ones': the paradigm of a deeply malevolent Beyond construed as the haunt of spectrality at its most demonic. Terrifyingly liminal creatures, the Old Ones exist 'not in the spaces we know, but between them', moving 'unseen and foul in lonely places where the Words have been spoken and the Rites howled' (Lovecraft 1997:134). The powerful feeling of presence associated with these preternatural beings gives way, in Straub, to a pervasive sense of the pockets of absence that riddle human subjectivity. What *Mr X* ultimately foregrounds, by transforming the cosmic mystery projected by Lovecraft into a tale of self-exploration, is our inexorable exposure to an Other that is simultaneously distinct from and inherent in us: the Dionysian twin without which the Apollonian self could not subsist. The topos of identical twins operating as each other's haunting shadows could almost be considered a blueprint for the narrative mapping of rhetorical ambiguity, insofar as it radically problematizes various adversarial binaries by underscoring the inevitability of interdependence. This is clearly borne out by Wally Lamb's *I Know This Much Is True* (2000), where Dominick and Thomas unremittingly haunt each other out of a recognition of being, paradoxically, opposed and complementary facets of one single personality. If Dominick, the pluckier and more successful of the two, haunts Thomas, Thomas, in turn, haunts Dominick through his childlike neediness and, above all, his incurable illness. Locked together in a violent and deceitful world where the sick are treated as criminals and the healthy are denied the power to exercise reason in the face of disciplinary systems far more irrational than the schizophrenic mind, the twins are ultimately 'interchangeable' (2000:604).

A further element of indecision is instilled into tales of haunting by the realization that the ghost is not inevitably malevolent. It is plausible, in fact, to conceive of the ghost as a dispossessed and somewhat pathetic entity: 'a leftover shred of ego, unable to believe it had been jilted by its own corruptible flesh' (Brite 1997:16). More importantly, as stressed by Lacan in his assessment of *Hamlet*, the spectre may play a reparatory role. Gordon embraces the proposition that haunting may hold positive potentialities by suggesting that 'From a certain vantage point the ghost . . . represents a future possibility, a hope' (1997:64): indeed, while symbolizing lack and loss, it implicitly points to levels of experience that could be obtained or regained. The ghost's compensatory function is often highlighted in German ghost stories. J. W. Goethe's conviction that all crimes are eventually punished encapsulates a world view, also promulgated by Hegel, according to which the universe strives towards equilibrium and the reconciliation of opposites. In this scenario, spectres too participate in the construction of a balanced order of things, regardless of their presumed unreality. Indeed, for harmony to prevail, fantasy and reality must be seen to coincide. E. T. A. Hoffmann's stories emphasize this idea by recourse to what Poe once tagged the *genius of the bizarre*. Goethe's own masterpiece, *Faust*, typifies the holistic ethos by annihilating both space and time and by giving visions and real occurrences equal solidity.

Finally, the rhetoric of haunting erodes not only the dividing line between the real and the imaginary but also the boundaries of the self. Haunting puts us in situations where we cannot be certain whether we are perceiving actual things or hallucinating. At the same time, it makes us unable to establish whether the vision is our own or if somebody else is dreaming it on our behalf. By capitalizing on the systematic dismantling of physical, psychological, spatial and temporal demarcations, the rhetoric of haunting shakes the very foundations of the edifices we like to conceive of as impregnable identities. It locates the phantom of ambiguity at the core of selfhood by positing the ultimate haunter as a lacuna within the subject. At the same time, it stresses the cultural and historical specificity of both haunting agents and the inner gaps they symbolize. Ghost stories are punctuated by daunting allusions to ideological tensions that point, elliptically, to fantasy's proclivity to infiltrate hegemonic agendas, suggesting that the latter are no less fictitious, upon close inspection, than the most preposterously tall tale of haunting.

Spectral Forms

GHOSTS ARE OFTEN REFERRED TO AS SPECTRES. Although the word 'spectre' is by no means more evocative that the word 'ghost', the phrase 'spectral forms' has been adopted, in the present context, because 'spectre' encapsulates the prismatic character of haunting in its entirety by problematizing the relationship between presence and absence, thereby indicating that any chain of associations triggered by ghostly phenomena is always open to negotiation. 'Spectre' derives from the Latin *spectare* and *specere* ('to look at') and its association with looking is confirmed by the fact that, as well as being synonymous with 'ghost', it also signifies an 'apparition' (from the Latin *apparere*, 'to come forth') or a 'phantom' (from the Greek *phos*, 'light'). Other words more or less overtly associated with sight share the same root: 'spectacle' (literally, 'a sight'); 'expectation' (understood as 'looking forward' to something); 'spectrum' (the range of colours or sound vibrations identifiable through diffraction and, by extension, the variety of available views on a given issue). The etymology of 'spectre', therefore, relates it to the realm of vision. Yet, as intimated by the realization that ghosts do not always manifest themselves as optical illusions, it also proposes an extension of the range of entities and situations encompassed by our visual experience: the spectrum of ghostliness includes both the visible and the invisible, the seen and the unseen.

A product of folklore, myth and fantasy, the ghost also embodies cultural anxieties. In much early Gothic fiction, spectres are not merely larval forms creeping back from the desolate world of the dead but also, more poignantly, effects of intrigues and betrayals grounded in the unsavoury realities of legal sleaze and religious hypocrisy. (See **Chapter 1** for a detailed evaluation of this theme.) Moreover, the forms which ghosts assume are closely connected to the sociohistorical circumstances in which they are born. The multi-facetedness of the discourse of haunting is attested to by the semantic and symbolic connotations of the word 'spirit', another term frequently employed as interchangeable with 'ghost'. If in the domain of popular culture in its diverse incarnations –

from Victorian Yuletide hampers replete with spook-infested tales to Hollywood's rendition of haunted settings – spirits are fundamentally commercialized icons, the word 'spirit' is nonetheless rife with mythological, theological and metaphysical implications. Indeed, it is often coterminous with 'soul', with a creature's intangible and, in many creeds, immortal essence. The virtual interchangeability of 'spirit' and 'ghost' is confirmed by the fact that words etymologically related to ghost, such as the Old English *ghast* and the German *Geist*, mean 'spirit' in both the ghoulish and the religious connotations. Taken out of their most overtly fictitious or commercial adaptations, spirits embody ideals and principles that form the bedrock of disparate belief systems. Far from standing as incontrovertibly malevolent forces to be exorcized, spirits consistently operate as the guarantors of societal continuity. While it is not compatible with the scope of this book to document the ascendancy of spirits as either explicitly or latently organizing agents, it is possible to argue that their portentous recurrence is testified by worldwide cults.

The 'Holy Ghost', or 'Holy Spirit', occupies a privileged position in the Christian Trinity and indeed requires two taps, one on each shoulder, in the act of crossing oneself, whereas the 'Father' and the 'Son' only require one. Shamanism, a phenomenon endemic in tribal cultures throughout the world (from South and North America to Siberia, from Africa to Australia, from Europe to the Far East), makes the spirit world central to its system of values. Aided by ritual practices such as rhythmic chanting, dancing and drum-beating, and by the consumption of hallucinogenic substances, shamans are able to transcend their material bodies and let their spirits fly to otherworldly destinations, where they obtain the knowledge necessary to heal the sick or assist them in their final hours if they are deemed ready for death. The Native American medicine man and the African witch doctor are well-known variations on this theme. The shaman's universe is a fluid spectrum linking the human sphere and the spiritual domain through a creative respect for the unknown. Spirits are likewise pivotal to voodoo (from *vodu*, the term designating 'spirit' in French West Africa), a cross-breed religion formed by the intermeshing of the native beliefs of Africans conveyed to the Caribbean by the slave trade, and Catholicism. The function of voodoo priestesses (*mambos*), priests (*houngans*) and their apprentices (*hounsis*) lies primarily with the imperative to summon the *loas*, superior spirits who have the power to secure peace or initiate conflict appropriate to the situation in hand, thereby balancing the effects of good and evil, love and hate.

In Celtic mythology, spirits play no less prominent a role. The Irish tradition, in particular, is pervaded by a potent sense of the omnipresence of non-human, semi-human or post-human entities who, in their proclivity to threaten and scare, also promise highly palatable gifts for their human counterparts. Their intrusiveness is daunting, but is not an irrevocable curse for those who are prepared to acknowledge their ubiquity and even revere it. These spirits' most salient features are their hybrid and liminal character, and their juxtaposition of apparently conflicting properties. *Taidshe* (ghosts), who inhabit a threshold realm between life and death, often feature side by side with the *Little People*, or *Tuatha De Danaan*, the descendants of Earth gods and goddesses once prodigally worshipped through lavish offerings and rituals, and gradually reduced to gnome-like creatures lurking in the woods, whose powers are only a pale trace of their bygone glory. Those who catch a glimpse of the Little People, particularly on May Eve, on Midsummer Night or at Hallowe'en (see also **Chapter 2**), may have their wishes fulfilled but should savour their pleasures cautiously, for the downgraded progeny of ancient deities has an odd sense of humour that often verges on the macabre. In one of their spookiest incarnations, the Little People are the demons that snatch humans away into the unfathomable Beyond of Faeryland, steal babies from their cradles and replace them with mischievous changelings. No less mystifying are the *deenee shee* (fairies), traditionally described as fallen angels too deeply marred by evil to be saved, yet not degenerate enough to deserve eternal damnation. Ambiguity is also central to the *Murrughach* (from *muir*, 'sea' and *oigh*, 'girl'; hence, 'mermaids'), figures that combine exceptional beauty (only marginally impaired by their webbed feet) and a penchant for handling their male victims with proverbial malice. The young roam the seas in their search, blind to all danger, while the old are dragged to the abyss, where their bones turn into coral. Siren and fairy at once, the *Banshee* (from *ban*, 'woman' and *shee*, 'fairy') leaves her mark by haunting the most ancient and illustrious families, and by making her heart-rending song heard whenever a premature death is imminent. (Related mthological figures are examined in detail in **Chapter 14**.) Other recurring spirits endowed with spectral attributes are the *Leprechauns* (incarnations of erotic desire and laziness), and the *Pooka*, the imposing stallion endowed with the power of speech. Various stories by Joseph Sheridan Le Fanu, Fitz James O'Brien and Bram Stoker, as well as Anne Rice's *Witches' Chronicles*, often hark back to this tradition.

The inevitability of our encounters with supernatural occurrences and entities is not simply a corollary of our persecution by haunting forces. We actually seek such experiences once we have sensed, consciously or unconsciously, that the seeds of darkness are sowed by human beings no less than by preternatural energies. This is evinced, for example, by early American history and its shaping by the dark visions of the Puritan settlers, especially the image of Hell as a dimension capable of infiltrating the sphere of the living and of undermining both the stability of the real and the very foundations of its divinely ordained architecture. (The Puritan vision is also discussed in **Chapter 2**, in relation to Charles Brockden Brown, and in **Chapter 3** in relation to Nathaniel Hawthorne.) Furthermore, a deep fascination with related otherworldly experiences is indubitably a major feature of much American writing from Washington Irving and Nathaniel Hawthorne to Edgar Allan Poe, Henry James, Ambrose Bierce and Mary Freeman. It is perhaps not surprising, given this background, that Spiritualism, as a cult that promises access to the Absolute Beyond by means of direct communication with the dead or with the angelic domain, should have originated in the United States. The origins of Spiritualism are often connected with the weird events surrounding the Fox family, and a brief exposition of the case may cast some light on the inception of that intriguing phenomenon.

John D. Fox, his wife and their young daughters Kate and Margaret moved into a reputedly haunted cottage situated in Hydesville (New York State) in 1847. Not unaccustomed to the supernatural, thanks to the visionary faculties of a great-grandmother and an aunt, the family were not intimidated by the building's sinister reputation. After three months of relative peace, the cottage started unleashing its occult energies in the guise of nocturnal noises including rhythmic knocking, whispers and wailing. Gradually, the family realized that whatever the nature of the force inhabiting the house's interstices, it was clearly attempting to engage them in some kind of dialogue. Willing to communicate with that mysterious power, the Foxes soon discovered that taps on the walls produced by human hands would be answered by corresponding taps and knocks. The spirit behind these messages was eventually identified as a door-to-door salesman who had been murdered in the cottage 31 years earlier and then buried in the cellar. Flocks of curious visitors began to descend upon the haunted dwelling and supernatural occurrences escalated to riotous proportions: guitars would play themselves, furniture would shift about the house and ornaments would float in mid-air. When the Foxes' son David visited the parental home, he became the recipient of sybilline messages from the Beyond announcing the dawn of a new era in the relationship between the dead and the living. By this time, few doubted that the cottage was a gateway to the Otherworld, and on 4 November 1849 the first official Spiritualist gathering was held within its walls. The new cult spread rapidly and gained for Kate Fox, in particular, considerable fame. As a result, she moved to England, where several eminent personalities converted almost instantly to Spiritualism: Sir Arthur Conan Doyle virtually made it his *raison d'être*. Whatever empirical value one may wish to ascribe to the events surrounding the Foxes and their home, it is hardly deniable that they constitute the first instance recorded in modern times of an exchange between this world and the Beyond.

Ambrose Bierce develops the motif of the tapping code in 'Beyond the Wall' (1909–12). Its protagonist, Dampier, is restrained from openly seeking the favours of the woman he cherishes, a charming neighbour, by the undesirable combination of an aristocratic background and a limited income, and by his ingrained prejudices (she is a lower-class orphan). He endeavours to avoid meeting her 'by a mighty effort of will' but eventually yields to the impulse to reach her by other means: one fateful night, he raps on the wall that separates his bedroom from hers. His 'signal' having been answered, the unusual conversation continues 'for many evenings afterwards'. Unexpectedly, the woman stops responding and when she resumes her part in the dialogue, it is only through 'a faint tapping . . . the mere ghost of the familiar signal'. The protagonist soon after finds out that his beloved has died after a protracted illness, and realizes that the only companion he is left with is his vacuous pride. Yet, he is not utterly alone: the woman's messages follow him, and indeed ten years later 'a gentle tapping' can still be heard in the gloomy tower to which Dampier has retired (Bierce 1964:26, 29, 30).

Many people would probably be disinclined to confront disembodied voices and floating shapes, let alone share a dwelling with them. There are, however, some potentially amusing exceptions, not only in fiction but also in real life. In *The History of Supernatural*, Karen Farrington cites the example of the Canadian professor Trevor Kirkham and his wife Judy, who turned to the law when they discovered that the mansion they had purchased was not haunted as originally promised:

> They had bought Cringle Hall at Goosnargh in Lancashire in the belief that it housed a clutch of ghosts, including that of Catholic martyr John Wall. When the ghosts – and ghost-hunters – did not turn up they regretted their investment and subsequently claimed the property had been misrepresented to them. (2000:75)

The Kirkhams' case patently draws attention to the commercial side of spectrality. Whether or not real estate is involved, ghosts can mean big business. This is demonstrated by the ongoing proliferation of spooky films that simultaneously pander to the audience's desire for jolts (rendered tolerable by the safety of the environment in which they are received) and symbolically tame the unknown through the homogenization of the natural and the supernatural.

Spectres are often manifestations of dead people who, having been viciously wronged in their lifetime, seek to wreak vengeance upon their erstwhile oppressors. In some of the most tantalizing ghost stories, the spectre is hell-bent on drawing its enemy to death and, ideally, perdition. In Ambrose Bierce's 'The Ways of Ghosts: PRESENT AT A HANGING' [1909–12], for example, a preternatural creature returns seven years after his assassination to compel his murderer to hang himself on the very spot where his bones were buried. In 'The Ways of Ghosts: AN ARREST' [1909–12], a criminal on the run is noiselessly and effortlessly led back to prison and to certain execution by the spirit of the jailer he has killed in order to escape. No less intriguing are those narratives in which otherworldly entities are not merely intent on precipitating the demise of their living adversaries but also on causing them to acquire spectral forms of their own. In these cases, the enemy's punishment lies primarily in his or her injunction to taste the anguish inherent in the ghostly victim's fate of tormented wandering. A case in point is Mary Freeman's 'Shadows on the Wall' [1920]. In this story, Edward returns to haunt his brother Henry (who is suspected by his sisters of having caused the former's untimely death) in the guise of a shadow that remains intact and unchanging despite the felonious brother's frantic re-arranging of the household furniture. At the story's climax, the sisters face not one but two spectral shadows projected on the wall and, seconds later, are informed that Henry has passed away. Edward has obviously succeeded in leading his malevolent sibling not only to death but also to an accursed state germane to his own. What is most disturbing about Freeman's tale is the spectre's uncanny ability to evince a physical form that is both immaterial and stubbornly present. (See also **Chapter 4** for a discussion of the use of this strategy in supernatural fiction.) An analogous effect is conveyed by Mary E. Braddon's 'The Cold Embrace' [1867]. Haunted by the ghost of his betrothed, who was driven to suicide by his callous indifference, the protagonist repeatedly feels trapped in the grip of 'cold arms clasped round his neck'. Struggling to rationalize the blood-chilling occurrence, he meets an impasse caused by the spirit's ambivalent status: 'It is not ghostly, this embrace, for it is palpable to the touch – it cannot be real, for it is invisible' (quoted in Dalby 1992:48). It is the spectral presence's simultaneous participation in the spheres of the corporeal and the incorporeal that makes its interventions so distracting. Likewise, the character of Cecilia Montresor in Rhoda Broughton's 'The Truth, the Whole Truth, and Nothing But the Truth' [1873] declares that nothing is capable of inducing a more 'unutterable fear' than 'the "bodiless dead"': an entity rendered overwhelming by its knack of imparting the illusion of presence to the intangible (quoted in Dalby 1992:84).

Ghost stories are a vehicle through which writers and readers may confront the destructive undercurrents of the pride, corruption and jealousy that treacherously course beneath the apparently respectable surface of family life. Elizabeth Gaskell's 'The Old Nurse's Story' [1852] exemplifies this idea. The innocent orphan Miss Rosamond is the victim of a haunting that reanimates ancient sexual rivalries and ruthless patriarchal punishments. The spirit to whom she feels fatally attracted is that of a 'Phantom Child' (quoted in Dalby 1992:15) who knocks wildly against the window panes of Rosamond's ancestral home and eventually beckons her into the lethally icy night. The potentially murderous spectral girl is, however, no less innocent than Rosamond herself: a pawn in a vicious game played by departed adults to take revenge on their persecutors and poison the present with the venom of their thwarted desires. Indeed, behind the Phantom Child lies a family history of scornful pride and hatred revolving around the battle between her mother Maude and her aunt

Grace over the common object of their passion, and culminating with the expulsion from the mansion of the little girl and her mother by a merciless patriarch devoured by an all-consuming sense of self-righteousness. Spectral forms such as Gaskell's Phantom Child tend to elicit sympathetic responses from the reader willing to conceive of the ghost as more than a sinister violator of the familial and social fabric, and to acknowledge its own dispossessed and alienated status. One of the most moving examples of a supernatural being capable of eliciting compassion in spite of its malevolence is supplied by James Fitz O'Brien's 'What Was It?' [1859]. Sympathy for the protagonist, savagely assaulted by a monstrously tangible yet utterly invisible spirit, gradually gives way to distress about the fate of the thing itself, as it lies starving on a bed that merely records its existence by means of the sheets rippling under the indiscernible body and of the rope used to keep it under control.

Frequently ghosts are capable of engaging sympathetic effects insofar as their return is not motivated exclusively by their thirst for revenge but also by their determination to right a wrong. This topos, already central to Greek tragedy and subsequently reworked by Elizabethan and Jacobean Revenge Tragedy, is still recurrent in fictional and filmic elaborations of the discourse of haunting. In the film *What Lies Beneath* (Robert Zemeckis, 2000), for instance, the ghost of the young woman, Madison, with whom the prestigious scientist Norman Spencer has had an affair and then murdered, resurfaces to haunt both the killer and his wife, Claire, and initially appears to take the deceived wife as its principal target. Once Claire, having embarked on a quest for the spirit's identity and discovered Norman's culpability, becomes her husband's next likely victim, it is intimated that Madison is no less concerned with protecting Claire than with taking her revenge. The murdered woman is not overtly summoned by the séance that Claire stages in the bathroom where the spirit tends to manifest itself most spectacularly. However, it becomes increasingly clear that each of the spectre's threats is also a warning, both re-enacting and foreshadowing the brutal dispatch of a female victim to a watery grave.

The evocation of compassionate responses is often of paramount significance in narratives featuring spectral forms that are not so much reanimations of the dead as living beings who have been constructed and consequently come to be perceived as ghostly. One of the most memorable apparitions of a living character rendered eerie by her actions and surroundings is supplied by Wilkie Collins's *The Woman in White* [1860], in the scene where Walter Hartwright encounters 'the figure of a solitary woman, dressed from head to foot in white garments' (1985:47) in the moonlight, at the crossroads where the road from Hampstead Heath intersects the Finchley Road. What makes Anne Catherick, the woman of the title, spectral is fundamentally her victimization by a patriarchal system intent on stripping its female subjects not only of their basic human rights but also of their identities, by relying on the legitimizing authority of the law: Collins's plot is indeed structured around legal issues involving wills, inheritance laws and marriage laws. Anne's white garments further emphasize her passivity, since white often, in nineteenth-century fiction, connotes purity, virginity, and the angelic self-restraint beloved of many a Victorian. Despite her centrality to the narrative, Anne remains a pathetically ephemeral figure right to the end. In Walter's words: 'So the ghostly figure which has haunted these pages, as it haunted my life, goes down into the impenetrable gloom. Like a shadow she first came to me in the loneliness of the night. Like a shadow she passes away in the loneliness of the dead' (576).

The image of the pathetic ghost features frequently in children's literature. Hairy the Horrible Hound in 'Hoots 'n' Owls', for example, howls relentlessly because he is lonely: 'He wanted someone to talk to, someone to play with. But because he was a ghost hound no one would come near, let alone throw him a stick to chase' (Repchuk *et al.* 1999). Comparably, the ghost of Moaning Myrtle in *Harry Potter and the Goblet of Fire*, feels deeply hurt whenever she is reminded that she is dead. Asked by Harry how he could possibly breathe under water, she explodes: 'Tactless! . . . Talking about breathing in front of *me*! . . . When I can't . . . When I haven't . . . not for ages . . .' (Rowling 2000:404). In *Harry Potter and the Chamber of Secrets*, the Hogwarts spectre Nearly Headless Nick, for his part, is upset by not being allowed to join the 'Headless Hunt' due to the fact that despite 'getting hit forty-five times in the neck with a blunt axe', his head is still minimally attached to his body (Rowling 1998:95). That headlessness, quite apart from its symbolic associations with castration, can lend itself to comic treatment is also demonstrated, incidentally, by Washington Irving's *The Legend of Sleepy Hollow* [1819–20]. Ichabod Crane is so scared by the nocturnal recounting of ghost stories that he is quite taken in when his rival Brom Bones confronts him with the sight of a pumpkin that looks like a severed head. The facetious mood of Irving's narrative is taken to melodramatic extremes in Tim Burton's film *Sleepy Hollow* (1999).

Paradoxically, feelings of pity are also invited by several fairy-tale characters who, though not literally spectral, are metaphorically made so (not unlike Collins's woman in white) by their vulnerable status. Varyingly enslaved to a routine of drudgery, marginalized, scorned, ostracized and often ruthlessly persecuted by patriarchy's inflexible laws, popular heroines such as Cinderella, Snow White, Sleeping Beauty and Donkeyskin, to cite a few well-known stories, could be considered paradigmatic examples of a human being's spectralization by inhumane cultural formations. Not only are those heroines pacified to the point of invisibility by their tormentors, they are also portrayed as self-spectralizing, as haunted by the imperative of self-denial. Hans Christian Andersen's *The Little Mermaid* [1837] is possibly one of the most harrowing dramatizations of self-abnegation. Turned into a ghostly vestige of her original self by dire mutilations (she is only allowed to join the prince and his milieu once her tongue has been cut out and her tail shaped into sword-like limbs), she continues serving her ungrateful beloved until, in order to save his life, she feels compelled to forfeit her own, thereby becoming an utterly unearthly creature.

Of course, not all fairy tales featuring disenfranchised heroines offer such gloomy resolutions. In fact, their most disturbing implications are generally sweetened and mellowed by the presence of a happy ending and even, at times, by the infusion of a modicum of humour. Restorative denouements, especially when endowed with moral messages, are instrumental to the socializing and enculturing programmes pursued by much fantasy literature aimed at young audiences. (This idea is discussed further throughout **Part 4.**) The representation of spectral forms, whether literal or metaphorical, as deserving of the reader's compassion can also be seen to proceed from the desire to set exemplary standards of conduct by encouraging children to grow out of amoral, or even aggressive, dispositions and hence develop a sense of respect for the weak and the unhappy. Yet, compassionate responses are invited to the extent that these may be justified not only by the persecuted character's intrinsic virtuousness but also by the eventual achievement of enviable rewards. Children's tales that hinge on pitiable victims of merciless systems do not transcend the strictures of the adult world but rather articulate them in symbolic forms that enable some harsh truths to appear in a subtly mediated fashion. Spooky narratives for children, in particular, deal with the same elemental themes that animate ghost stories for adults. When they suggest that certain ghosts are worthy of our sympathy, they do so with reference to a cluster of frustrating emotions presumed to afflict otherworldly creatures no less than humans: solitude, the fear of exclusion, the tormenting awareness of the infinity of death-in-life or life-in-death. Simultaneously, they implicitly draw attention to the demands and prohibitions inherent in structures of power and knowledge that will only convict the evil and elevate the good as long as the good are willing to rejoice in culturally determined notions of pleasure and success. The very genesis of scary tales for the young is often explicitly associated with an attraction to fear that is generally recognized as central to the adult reader's ongoing fascination with the supernatural, its terrors and its horrors. This idea is succinctly encapsulated in a remark made by the narrator of the children's ghost story 'Smoky Smells Success': 'After all, everyone likes being a little bit scared now and then, don't you? (Repchuk *et al.* 1999).

Finally, if spectres lend themselves to sympathetic portraiture, this is largely because, being evidently not alive and only inconclusively dead, they symbolize one of the most intractable aspects of embodied existence – our status as biomachines whose functioning depends on the continuous coexistence of birth and death, growth and decay. On the psychological plane, this physical reality is replicated by comparable rhythms of production and destruction, as patently demonstrated by the mind's proclivity to oscillate between states of hope and states of despair. It is in the apprehension of the pervasiveness of fear that the psyche echoes most forcibly the ghost's ambivalence, fear that both numbs the mind through its deathly threats and revives it through a stimulus to survive. Fearing ghosts/spectres/spirits amounts to fearing the gaps in the fabric of being that allude to the prospect of eventual annihilation. The dread inspired by an indefinite something, simultaneously seen and unseen, that may well be akin to nothing, is akin to the abiding fear of death. However, insofar as the spectral nothing is located, by a plethora of diverse cults, in a realm beyond-the-human, the human urge to commune with spirits cannot be regarded univocally as a cause of paralysing anxiety, for it actually underlies the auspicious possibility of participating in an endless becoming, an ongoing cycle of birth and death.

— 6 —

𝕳𝖆𝖚𝖓𝖙𝖎𝖓𝖌 𝕾𝖊𝖙𝖙𝖎𝖓𝖌𝖘

THE PRISMATIC QUALITY that distinguishes both spectral forms and the reactions they elicit in their victims also characterizes many scenes of haunting. Aptly corroborating one of my principal propositions – the notion that terror and horror are interacting components of the phenomenon of fear – the material circumstances in which human beings confront the spectral Other have the power to produce simultaneously terrifying and horrifying effects. On the one hand, they are capable of depriving both natural and architectural objects of their solidity, thus turning them into distressingly indefinite sources of fear. On the other, they have a proclivity to accord tangible reality to otherwise amorphous intimations of the mysterious. They therefore evoke a distinctively Gothic atmosphere of hesitation and anxiety in which both ethical and aesthetic standards are suspended or even irreverently mocked. However, partaking of the very ethos of ambiguity that shapes the rhetoric of spectrality as a whole, haunting settings are both intimidating and inviting for, as they threaten to trap or harm their inhabitants, they are also venues wherein the Beyond's tantalizing powers may be apprehended and negotiated. Like fear itself, they sharpen consciousness in the same movement as they appear to paralyse it. (This chapter is closely related to **Chapters 1** and **10**.)

The contention that Gothicity constitutes the major representational field where the dynamics of fear are explored is confirmed by the historical association of that discourse with cultural darkness. Although the haunter of many dark spaces is proverbially the ghost, the Gothic vision is also haunted by the derogatory connotations carried by 'Gothic' as a stylistic term. Among the various spectre-infested locations portrayed by dark fiction, Gothic architecture as an aesthetic concept is pervaded by disquieting undertones due to its conventional connection with barbarity. The buildings classed as 'Gothic' are the ones erected in the Dark Ages over the wrecks of classical civilizations. As an architectural term, 'Gothic' entered the Western lexicon in the eighteenth century, at the time when the concept of 'home' was beginning to reflect the values of the rising bourgeoisie. It came to signify everything which a middle-class residence should disdain: discomfort, coldness, extravagance, unclear boundaries between the inside and the outside, and, above all, sprawling structures suggestive of lack of control over one's space. In using outlandish castles and maze-like mansions, narratives of darkness challenge the bourgeois ideal of the sheltering home. Buildings, then, become ways of commenting on class politics, gender politics and related structures of power and knowledge. They often depict, more or less elliptically, the spaces disavowed by entire cultures. A haunted house is the site/sight upon which collective anxieties converge. Henry James's *The Turn of the Screw* [1898], for example, makes a haunted house the symbol of a whole society stifled by a repressive ethos of decorum. Whether or not psychoanalytical interpretations of the tale hinging on the notion of the Governess's sexual repression and attendant neurotic disposition are tenable, the image of suffocation undoubtedly dominates the narrative, both figuratively and literally. (*The Turn of the Screw* is discussed in detail in **Chapter 7**.) In a number of late-twentieth-century texts, the heir of Gothic castles and mansions is the bourgeois house itself, the location in which disorder is most likely to erupt with devastating repercussions on its owners' certainties and values. Echoing corridors, dark towers, misty graveyards, crumbling abbeys and labyrinthian woods are no longer indispensable stage sets. Suburban districts and houses, as demonstrated, for example, by John Carpenter's *Halloween* (1978) and Wes Craven's *A Nightmare on Elm Street* (1984), can prove just as daunting.

Anne Rivers Siddons's *The House Next Door* [1978] offers a paradigmatic example of the disruption of an orderly district by malicious haunting forces: relationships are dramatically shattered, conventional defences crumble and the armour provided by economic and sexual hierarchies becomes utterly irrelevant. The most radical transformation is evinced by the characters of Colquitt and Walter Kennedy, whose lives and attitudes are drastically modified by their proximity to a haunted house and who end up, as a result, 'ostracized by their neighbours, hated by city realtors, and ready to burn the house next door to the ground' (King 1993:303): quite a reversal for a wealthy and orderly couple in suburban Atlanta. What makes the Kennedys' deterioration from model citizens to deranged pariahs especially disturbing is their gradual engulfment by the neighbouring dwelling. At first, all that lies next to their home is a wooded lot. The situation begins to acquire harrowing connotations as soon as the ambitious young architect Kim Dougherty decides to build a house on the lot. Even before the actual construction starts, Colquitt hears an owl hooting in the night-shrouded location and instinctively ties a knot in her bedsheet as though guided by an unconscious urge to exorcize the ill omen. From now on, inauspicious events escalate. The new house's first owners, the Harralsons, lose everything to the place, including a potential baby and a dog. The Sheenans, the next couple to own the house, fare no better and Anita, in particular, is persecuted by horrendous filmic images unrelentingly replaying her son's death in Vietnam. The final and by no means less portentous occurrences befall the next family, the Greenes. The haunting ultimately amounts to a desecration of bourgeois ideology itself and exposes its representatives as 'vain, class-conscious, money-conscious, sexually priggish' (King 1993:313): that is to say, narcissistic cultivators of totally flimsy, albeit stylish, facades.

In mirroring cultural preoccupations, haunted houses also symbolize psychological vicissitudes. As Peter Brooks has commented, the layered map of many Gothic buildings bears affinities to the Freudian topology of the psyche: 'The Gothic castle, with its pinnacles and dungeons, crenelations, moats, drawbridges, spiralling staircases and concealed doors, realizes an architectural approximation of the Freudian model of the mind, particularly the traps laid for the conscious by the unconscious and the repressed' (1976:19). Anne Williams elaborates the concept of 'the psyche as house' with an emphasis on the dynamics of infraction brought into play by architectural enclosures and demarcations:

> Building walls and declaring boundaries . . . creates both the possibility – and the desire – to transgress any or all of them . . . A house makes secrets in merely being itself, for its function is to enclose spaces. And the larger, older, and more complex the structure becomes, the more likely it is to have secret or forgotten rooms. (1995:44)

Horace Walpole's *The Castle of Otranto* [1764] had already intimated that the mind's inner world and the outer reality of buildings and architecture are interconnected. Walpole's formula has found several applications in modern and contemporary fiction. Frequently what is stressed is the impossibility of drawing a neat distinction between internal and external dimensions, the haunted self and its surroundings. Edgar Allan Poe's 'The Fall of the House of Usher' [1839] can be said to have generated a matrix for the exploration and portrayal of haunting situations as locations inseparable from their inhabitants' mental states. The House of Usher itself and Roderick Usher's mind are reflections of each other, to the point that when the one collapses so does the other: 'my brain reeled as I saw the mighty walls rushing asunder – there was a long tumultuous shouting sound like the voice of a thousand waters' (1986:157).

Poe's settings almost invariably mirror and replicate his characters' haunted psyches. His protagonists insistently seek an aesthetic sphere of refined sensibility and opportunities for a mystical transcendence of everyday conventions. While their quest promises illuminating insights, it also, somewhat inexorably, paves the way to madness. Indeed, emotional disturbance seems the inevitable culmination of the withdrawal from the quotidian preoccupations which the aesthetic pilgrimage requires. Thus, Roderick Usher, having cultivated his passion for a superior realm to obsessive extremes, is left staring at the overwhelming reality of 'the grim phantasm, FEAR' (144). The alternately grotesque and claustrophobic attributes evinced by his palace echo not only the frenzied disreality of the protagonist's mind but also the deterioration of a whole culture committed to the ferocious repression of the search for ideal beauty. The retreat from society finally yields not gratification but 'a morbid acuteness of the senses' (143) relentlessly haunted by the ineluctability of death. This is vividly dramatized by 'The Masque of the Red Death' [1842], where a thousand knights and ladies under the leadership of the 'dauntless and sagacious' Prince Prospero retire to 'the deep seclusion of one of his castellated abbeys' (Poe 1986:254) in order to escape the plague and devote themselves to the pursuit of beauty of the most voluptuously magnificent and indeed 'bizarre' (255) kind. Yet the party cannot ultimately escape destruction, as the Red Death, having insinuated itself into the building with the stealthiness of 'a thief in the night', vanquishes the revellers one by one and asserts its 'illimitable dominion over all' (260).

The trope of withdrawal that characterizes the doomed life choices of many of Poe's characters also informs the ideal location portrayed in 'The Philosophy of Furniture' [1840], an essay that hints at important correspondences between the psyche and its environment. The shape of the room described by Poe is simple, the furniture sparse and further ornamentation carefully selected. The abundance of minute detail encouraged by much nineteenth-century interior design is openly disdained in favour of 'a small and not ostentatious chamber with whose decorations no fault can be found' (Poe 1986:418). As a metaphor for the psyche, the room suggests that the absence of clutter is the prerequisite for the ability to be stimulated by one's surroundings, since minutiae tend to numb the senses and impair the creative impulse. Of course, stimulation may well occur in the form of disturbing apprehensions. After all, 'the "ideal" chamber bears close comparison,' as David Galloway observes in his Notes to *The Fall of the House of Usher and Other Writings*, 'with descriptions of the haunted chambers in which so many of Poe's characters find themselves' (537). Indeed, while the style commended by Poe is supposed to induce a sense of 'Repose' (419), the overall mood which the room should inspire is one of 'tranquil but magical radiance' (420), which suggests that intimations of the mysterious should also be kept alive. This is confirmed by the fact that in spite of the chamber's uncluttered beauty, elements of opulence are introduced, especially in the description of the windows: these 'have deep recesses' and panes of 'crimson-tinted glass', and 'are curtained within the recess, by a thick silver tissue' and outside the recess by 'curtains of an exceedingly rich crimson silk, fringed with a deep net-work of gold' (418). Special significance is thus attached to secluded spaces, as if to suggest that the most eminent of the mind's eyes are remote, private and very possibly hidden portions of the psyche. The tinted glass image is pivotal – it intimates that the most sensitive windows of the soul are those that do not presume to have immediate/unmediated access to the real and that do not trust empirical evidence, since perception inevitably occurs through filters and screens that tantalizingly alter images and objects. What is ultimately haunting about the setting itemized by Poe as ideally conducive to relaxed and imaginative speculation is its ability to evoke, despite its rational organization, its luminous openness and its simplicity, a troubling sense of the unknown. This is most acutely apprehended when the chamber is ideated as a metaphor for the mind and particularly the contemplative psyche, as a space in which rationality and apparently lucid and uncomplicated processes are inexorably interfered with by distorting factors. (Poe is also discussed in **Chapter 7** with reference to the relationship between the psyche and narrative.)

Symbolic analogies between psyches and buildings as contexts for unresolved hauntings are sometimes reinforced by the meandering and unchartable character of both. William Peter Blatty's 'Elsewhere', for example, suggests that spatial and psychological confusion are intimately intertwined, both resulting from a disquieting sense of directionlessness. The character of Dare, 'in moving from hall to connecting hall', soon finds himself 'wandering in a maze and completely unable to retrace his steps' (1999:162). *Elsewhere*, the haunted house, contains mysterious rooms that are there one moment and invisible or inaccessible the next, and unpredictable spaces that both belong and do not belong to its main body. Its metamorphic architecture closely mirrors the rambling nature of the thoughts and emotions which it is capable of inducing in its inhabitants. Moreover, several dark texts show that it is often impossible to ascertain conclusively whether the menacing agent is situated in a specific portion of the mental and physical contexts of a haunting or is, in fact, floating in an unspecified somewhere else.

Rick Hautala's 'Knocking' elaborates this idea by building up an agonizing atmosphere of inevitability, as the haunted protagonist gradually loses the ability to discern whether he is refusing admission to his haunters or whether he is being refused access to an unhaunted domain. The story makes it arduous for both its protagonist and its reader to establish what lies either within or without the setting's boundaries. Martin Gordon locks himself up in his house as the 'millennial celebrations' rage outside (1999:301) and his sole preoccupations, at first, consist of strengthening the barricades meant to protect him from the forbidding outside and of rationing the food he has squirrelled away in preparation for his self-imposed confinement. Unexpectedly, his life comes to be dominated by 'the sound of someone knocking . . . knocking on the front door', a noise made particularly ominous by the impenetrable darkness in which it is heard (304). Martin soon begins to suspect that the person 'out there' might be his dead mother: 'He couldn't help but remember how during those last horrible years, when she was ill and bedridden, she would bang on the wall to get his attention, pulling him away from his time alone with his trains. He tried not to think of it, but the sounds were practically identical' (305). *The Haunting of Hill House*, discussed later in this chapter, uses an analogous image in comparing some of the disturbing sounds perceived by its heroine with those produced by her ailing mother to attract her notice. As he works himself up into a paroxysm of fear and resentment, Hautala's protagonist next speculates that the knocking may come from 'his father, come home after all these years' (306), having disappeared 'when Martin was only one year old . . . gone to the store for cigarettes and never come back' (303).

That Martin is being haunted by his own history of deprivation, anger and guilt is confirmed by the story's climactic moments: echoing the psychoanalytical notion that the fearful child often tends to fuse the two parents into a single menacing force, Hautala's character ends up wondering: 'Could it be both of them out there on the stoop?' (307). Martin inescapably plunges from a position of relative control and confidence about his ability to protect the privacy and safety of his fortified sanctuary from the menacing outside to a situation in which his indoor territory becomes the principal source of dread. Willing to confront 'whomever was out there on his doorstep' (308), he finds that the door resists his mightiest efforts to undo the lock. Martin is now a prisoner in his own shelter, a victim not so much of external forces as of the nagging fear bred by his own inner self. This reaches its zenith as the knocking, initially associated with an external threat, pervades the house and begins to pulse unrelentingly throughout its entire fabric: 'from every door . . . from the hall closet, the basement, the kitchen pantry, came knocking' (310). Significantly, the terrifying change takes place shortly after the haunted character has found himself unwittingly whispering the word 'Mother' (309): an ominous echo of the rumour, encouraged by the inquest following Martin's mother's death, that he had 'smothered her with her pillow' (305).

The role played by parental spectres in haunting situations is also highlighted by Shirley Jackson's *The Haunting of Hill House* [1959]. Whether Eleanor Vance is possessed by the spooky house and impelled by it to relive sordid events to do with its past or whether she is projecting her own emotional instability onto her surroundings is never explained. Alternative treatments of this theme are offered by Robert Wise's *The Haunting* (1963) and by Jan De Bont's remake of that film in 1999. Wise's film offers a psychodrama in which the house's disruptive messages interweave with sexual, and specifically lesbian, desires longing to express themselves. De Bont's film, arguably less scary, prioritizes the association between self and environment by recourse to a quintessentially Gothic theatricality of stunning special effects. Eleanor's predicament exemplifies the state, theorized by Julia Kristeva in *Powers of*

Horror (1982), of the child who experiences severe difficulties in becoming an autonomous subject due to its inability to conceive of itself as an entity separate from others. (See also **Chapter 15.**) In the following paragraphs, Kristeva's positions on this subject are briefly outlined and related to the experiences articulated by Jackson's novel.

To begin with, argues Kristeva, our bodies seem to merge with everybody and everything else around them. Indeed, they can hardly be conceived of as bodies, if what is meant by 'body' is an object with clearly identifiable contours. As we emerge as adult subjects, we form an idea of our distinctions and, simultaneously, of our physical boundaries. The first crucial moment of separation which the child must negotiate consists of its self-severance from the mother, since the close connection between the infant and the maternal body that characterizes the preliminary stages of psychosexual development, while providing a pleasurable sense of plenitude, also symbolizes the threat of engulfment, the swamping of the self by an overwhelming (m)other. The failure to perceive oneself as distinct and bounded becomes coterminous with one's entanglement in a pre-adult world (Kristeva 1982). In *The Reproduction of Mothering* (1978), Nancy Chodorow develops a related argument by proposing that prior to the formation of an individual identity, the child is concurrently seduced and horrified by its unruptured closeness to the mother. Although the sensation of being seamlessly united to another body is in many ways blissful, it is also a troubling marker of one's dependence, lack of autonomy and entrapment in a potentially stifling embrace. Albeit painful, self-definition is the *sine qua non* of one's ability to function independently in the socialized sphere.

The process of separation and the concomitant process of identity formation are inextricably linked to the acquisition of language: the system of signs, symbols, codes, conventions, laws and rituals sanctioned by a culture as the means through which intersubjective communication is effected. The double body formed by the virtual fusion of the infant and the mother in the early phases of human life must be dissolved upon entry into the adult domain because it is incompatible with the structures and operations of language. Whereas that body vividly suggests a lack of distinctions between one person and another and, by extension, between one category and another, language pivots precisely on an ethos of separation, on groupings, classes and compartments. The moves through which humans learn to access the symbolic order of language are no less a source of distress than the strategies through which self-definition is achieved. This is because language is inexorably predicated upon the principle of loss: when we acquire language, we have no choice but to adapt our private desires and fantasies to the collective networks of symbols that conform to our culture's value systems. These are largely ineffectual, for they can never fully express individual longings deemed incompatible with communal expectations and demands. Indeed, the more we yearn to make language mean what we wish to say, the more we stumble into a painful awareness of its inadequacy, of its proclivity to spawn limitless webs of signifiers which struggle to reach a signified and invariably fail. Nevertheless, in the absence of language and its symbols, however limited and limiting these may be, we would have no means of communicating with others and would therefore be most likely to experience baneful feelings of alienation and withdrawal. These potentially destructive emotions play a central role in the condition of melancholia: a depressive state associated with an inability or unwillingness to conform to the rules of symbolic language and with a general devaluation of social bonds. According to Kristeva, melancholia is frequently the corollary of a subject's failure to conceive of itself as a separate entity, and a related determination to hold onto its primordial desire – the desire for wholeness typified by its union with the mother. Melancholia is fundamentally an inability to come to terms with the inevitability of loss that renders it impossible to enter the stage of mourning, where the subject accepts that the lost object of desire is irretrievable but at least draws some solace from the notion that it may be recalled through signs, that its loss may be symbolically recorded and hence endured.

Eleanor Vance's ordeal at Hill House exemplifies the condition of a subject that has not managed to differentiate itself properly and hence feels threatened by the laws and expectations of the symbolic order. This is primarily conveyed by the symbiotic nature of the relationship which the character develops with Hill House as a substitute mother or substitute womb. In its ferocious persecution of Eleanor, the house constitutes a stark replica of the departed parent and of her callously selfish behaviour. Like the child described by both Kristeva and Chodorow, Jackson's heroine feels simultaneously attracted to the maternal body in its literal and figurative configurations, as the potential provider of a pleasing sense of plenitude, and threatened by its overpowering embrace. Incapable of severing herself from this ambiguous entity, she falls into a state comparable to melancholia, evinced by her social incompetence and indeed by her inability to relate to others. Eleanor's experiences seem to confirm that once the formation of an adequately socialized self has been thwarted (primarily by familial pressures) intersubjective relations become unviable and the psyche is trapped in the vicious circle of compulsive fantasies it cannot share with anybody else. Indeed, the character is repeatedly portrayed as narcissistically obsessed with herself. The pathological degree of Eleanor's self-absorption is highlighted by her attempt to establish a connection with Theo. This could have feasibly provided an alternative to the suffocating mother–daughter relationship, but it is abortive and culminates, as Judie Newman observes, in 'the replication rather than the repudiation of the symbiotic bond' (1998:163).

Hill House does not merely simulate the heroine's mother – it is also

Eleanor's own monstrous double. Thus, the injunction to 'COME HOME', written in a nasty red substance in the hall, resonates not only with the voice of the dead parent but also, as Stephen King points out, with 'the voice of [Eleanor's] own central self, crying out against this new independence' (1993:328): an independence ushered in by the mother's death which the daughter is incapable of rejoicing in as a result of her self-anchoring to the pre-adult, pre-symbolic world. Moreover, it is sadly ironic that the peremptory command to merge again with the maternal *chora* should be couched in symbolic language, and specifically in writing as the most encultured form of language. The blood-like medium in which the order is written harks back to an intensely corporeal dimension. Its verbal inscription serves to warn Eleanor in a glaringly ungenerous fashion that she cannot exist outside language, that the spectres spawned by her personal history will not rest until she is prepared to acknowledge the phantoms that infest the collective articulation of meaning. This requires a recognition of the coexistence and alternation of presence and absence across the linguistic field in its entirety. It means accepting that words mean by virtue of what they *do not say* no less than by virtue of what they *do say*, that a word which is present in an utterance is always traversed by absence, by the traces of other words which could have been used instead and by the ghosts of words which we consciously or unconsciously associate with it.

In dramatizing the connection between a haunting scene and an overbearing female figure, *The Haunting of Hill House* echoes an ancient topos that can be traced back to the fairy tale tradition. (Refer to **Part 4**, 'Child and Adult', for a discussion of the role played by fairy tales in the socializing process.) In many well-known fairy tales, young heroes and heroines are imprisoned in hostile circumstances dominated by abusive female figures, such as mothers, stepmothers and mothers-in-law, whose nefarious schemes are, as Marina Warner stresses, 'rooted in the social, legal and economic history of marriage and the family' and reverberate with 'the tensions, the insecurity, jealousy and rage' (1995:238) that persistently cloud cross-generational relationships. Charles Perrault's versions of 'The Sleeping Beauty', 'The Fairy' and 'Hop-o'-My-Thumb', the Grimm Brothers' 'Hansel and Gretel', 'Briar Rose' and 'Snowdrop', as well as various adaptations of 'Cinderella', bear witness to the collusion of haunting spaces and female tormentors. In 'Cinderella', it is the absent mother who often operates as a powerful force. Several tales hinging on the Cinderella topos situate a young heroine in a setting unsympathetic to her inherent virtue and peopled by characters adept at vilifying her. Such an environment is made markedly sinister not so much by its architecture and inhabitants as by the heroine's sense that what encumbers her most pressingly is the curse of motherlessness under which she profitlessly labours. While Cinderella's relegation to a dwelling's least desirable regions and her subjugation to the despotic demands of a wicked stepmother (and of her ugly daughters) play an important role, what haunts the forsaken heroine is not a physical but a symbolic location – the body of the mother from whom she has been prematurely separated. The fairy godmother may be said to represent a consolatory substitute. Nonetheless, her magical powers associate her with the supernatural and hence confirm the spectral status of the maternal figure that Cinderella direly misses. The Good Fairy is essentially a helper, not the provider of future happiness: what is supposed to rescue the heroine from her ignoble state is, eventually, marriage to a handsome young prince. The mother figure, whether real or imagined, remains an absent presence and a present absence, a haunting force of primordial calibre.

In the closing segment of Chapter 5 (Spectral Forms), I propose that fairy tales frequently posit the living, rather than the dead, as ghostly entities: subjects lethally spectralized by their psychological and material deprivation. What I suggest here is that fairy tales, as points of crystallization for cultural hostilities and phobias, regularly exhibit a tendency to present the familiar and the familial as haunting settings par excellence. By emphasizing the ongoing incursion of family connections (both biological and constructed) by spectral energies and by concurrently presenting the domestic sphere as pervaded by injustice and oppression, those stories defy the aphorisms that associate home with the heart, with loving and with security. In fact, they accomplish precisely what Stephen King describes as one of the defining traits of 'horror fiction': they place 'a cold touch in the midst of the familiar' (1993:299). They thus participate in the often involuted dynamics through which fear becomes an awakening agent, a function of consciousness via defamiliarization, and eventually a means of grappling with the conundrum of the self as an ephemeral effect of socialization.

— Part 3 —
Narrative and the Self

Introduction

I saw I saw him [Peter Quint] as I see the letters I form on this page.

Henry James, *The Turn of the Screw*

Texts more or less explicitly related to a Gothic matrix can be grouped into various genres and subgenres that acquire significance according to a culture's contingent values and expectations. In their sheer multiplicity, dark narratives mirror the operations of fear. Just as fear, in its pervasiveness, has a tendency to adopt a considerable variety of forms that alter according to specific historical scenarios, so its fictional manifestations change over time and space. Synchronically, the fictions embody particular understandings of fear likely to be recognized and shared by the members of a distinctive social formation and simultaneously indicate, diachronically, modifications undergone by the representation of that phenomenon in the course of time. On both the synchronic and the diachronic planes, it appears that the themes articulated by many narratives of darkness and the creative processes through which they are conveyed are consistently interrelated. There are crucial analogies between plot, character and imagery, on the one hand, and the act of writing them, on the other. Content and form are mutually sustaining. Accordingly, the fictional product can only be adequately grasped in terms of the process of its construction.

Since the Gothic vision is primarily concerned with evoking a sense of uncertainty and indeterminateness, the structures it recursively utilizes tend to be unclosed. The open-endedness of dark experiences is mirrored by the inconclusiveness of the textual weave. As Jerome Monahan stresses, 'loose ends' are a principal component of chillers and thrillers: 'the horror may be over but the survivors should be shaken to the core, incapable of explaining the mysteries that have overtaken them. Something menacing should still seem to lurk in the shadows' (1999:8). Narratives of darkness epitomize Kathryn Hume's concept of 'a literature of quest, a literature . . . in search of its proper form rather than already possessed of that form' (1984:43). This is not to say that the texts themselves lack form, for some of the most avidly read dark texts are true monuments to the principle of structural competence. Rather, the notion of quest intimates that the story should be seen to find its feet as it unfolds. Through this strategy, the tale's atmosphere of suspense and doubt can be effectively maximized. The unknown must be felt to project itself towards an unspecified future, each page the reader turns opening up a potentially novel and unexpected territory.

Although, as Robert Branham, among others, points out, 'language is a conventional system for the expression and understanding of conventional experiences', narratives of darkness are capable of challenging these normative mechanisms. If Branham's comments on fantasy fiction are extended to the broader discourse of Gothicity, it could then be argued that those narratives offer an 'unabashed presentation of imaginary and impossible worlds, phenomena, and cultures' (1983:66), thereby exceeding the boundaries of the symbolic order and reaching towards the ineffable. Linguistic inscription cannot ultimately be transcended insofar as there is no reliable evidence for the existence of a realm beyond language and, even if there were, such a realm would inevitably resist articulation. Hence, it would be preposterous to suggest that a text, dark or otherwise, may preempt, escape or rise above the constraints implicit in any system of signs. It is nonetheless fruitful to focus on a text's proclivity to express aspects of our lives that dominant discourses tend to silence by manipulating the symbolic to voice not merely conventional experiences but also desires, fantasies and nightmares insistently relegated to the murky province of the unspeakable.

One of the most disquieting facets of dark fiction is precisely its tendency to emphasize the phantasmatic nature of any apparent resolution, thereby intimating that it is not merely the narratives but also the selves that participate in their production and consumption that are deprived of certainties and anchors. At the same time, however, in stressing that fear is neither an isolated occurrence nor an exclusively personal experience but actually a ubiquitous and widely shared reality, tales of darkness provide something of a connective tissue. Indeed, they bond singular selves to a communal body by showing how, in the creative process, the individual consciousness unrelentingly taps into a reservoir of archetypal symbols redolent of Jung's concept of the collective unconscious. The omnipresence of fear is thus replicated by the enduring hold of dark themes, icons and emblems as vehicles through which the fearful may be situated and grasped.

The idea that there is an intimate connection between dark fiction's recurring themes and the narrative strategies through which those themes are articulated, and the related notion that both tend to emphasize the open-endedness of the Gothic vision, is emblematically borne out by Stephen King's *Bag of Bones*. (See also **Chapters 2** and **12** and the Introduction to **Part 2**.)

The novel's protagonist, the bestselling but temporarily blocked author Mike Noonan, describes the creative process in such a way that it bears a close affinity to the story's central themes: the haunting of the present by a submerged past; the stubborn resurgence of repressed crimes and of their victims in the face of the mightiest efforts to bury them for good; the sense of blockage experienced by those who wish to understand the past when confronted with forces that are simultaneously, and confusingly, enlightening and paralysing. Noonan's creative block echoes the abortive search for the truth about the Maine lakeside retreat, initiated by his dead wife and subsequently pursued by the writer himself. His recurring nightmare revolving around the summer home alludes to the frustrated longing to unearth occluded events to do with the house's history. This mirrors the author's desire to come to terms with hidden dimensions of his imagination: 'there's something creepy about any repeating dream, I think, about knowing your subconscious is digging obsessively at some object that won't be dislodged' (1999b:50). Moreover, *Bag of Bones* corroborates the proposition that a Gothic mood of hesitation can effectively be conveyed by creating the impression that riddles are tackled as the narrative develops, with no clear indication of either their provenance or likely solution. Indeed, the novel implies that answers to the most intractable enigmas are stumbled upon more often than they are arrived at by following reason and logic. (This idea is also discussed in relation to Peter Ackroyd's *Hawksmoor* in **Chapter 4**.) Again, an analogy is proffered between narrative themes and the writing process: just as the conclusions reached by King's text are no less a product of chance than of the will, so the creative impulse is ascribed to only dimly comprehensible forces that operate assiduously beyond the scope of consciousness. 'Getting close to writing a book,' Noonan observes, is tantamount to entering a liminal region:

> It's like some guys with a big truck have pulled up in your driveway and are moving things into your basement . . . You can't see what these things are because they're all wrapped up in padded quilts, but you don't need to see them. It's furniture, everything you need to make your house a home, make it just right, just the way you wanted it. (75)

What *Bag of Bones* exemplifies is the mutual replication of themes pertaining to the darkness of not knowing and indeed of not knowing how to know, and of narrative production as a process guided by uncontrollable energies.

In the visual field, a paradigmatic example of the collusion of content and form can be found in one of Edvard Munch's most famous paintings, *The Scream* (1893). This work vividly illustrates the principal points outlined earlier as salient traits of the Gothic vision: it stresses the interrelation of thematic and stylistic priorities; it draws attention to the process of production of the work; it suggests that the work's overall structure is not a given but something to be discovered while constructing it; it underscores the open-endedness of any psychological drama that pivots on the phenomenon of fear. Munch stressed the interdependence of content and form by relating both the painting's themes and its composition to personal impressions capable of affecting deeply his entire sensorium:

> I was going down the street behind two friends. The sun went down behind a hill overlooking the city and the fjord – I felt a trace of sadness – The sky suddenly turned blood red. I stopped walking, leaned against the railing, dead tired – My two friends looked at me and kept on walking – I watched the flaming clouds over the fjord and the city – My friends kept on – I stood there shaking with fear – and I felt a great unending scream penetrate unending nature.

A further note attached to the picture reads: 'I felt a loud scream – and I really heard a loud scream . . . The vibrations in the air did not only affect my eye but my ear as well – because I really heard a scream. Then I painted *The Scream*' (Schneede 1988:50).

Munch's experience demonstrates that a profoundly troubling stimulus is capable of modifying drastically all of one's sense impressions: whatever is causing the figure in the foreground to scream uncontrollably has the power to distort the entire scenery. All the stylistic, structural and chromatic devices employed by Munch converge to evoke consuming anguish and a tortured sensibility. Concurrently, the painting's content, with its emphasis on frenzy and torment, could be said to summon representational strategies capable of expressing most vigorously Munch's vexing fear. In this psychogram of existential defencelessness, a potent sense of persecution is conveyed by the straight lines racing towards the shouting creature. The curved and wave-like lines used in the depiction of the sky and the sea are no less foreboding – they connote confusion, estrangement and engulfment. The colours offer no relief. Any possible harmony is disrupted by the violent juxtaposition of light and shadow, and of warm and cold hues laden with symbolic connotations. Every vibration of colour, from the blood-red clouds in the churned-up sky to the blue, brown and green waves with their disconcerting whiplash effect, translates into a corresponding sensation of ecstatically painful intensity. The ostensibly bizarre handling of chromatic schemes and patterns of lines emphatically defies realistic and naturalistic agendas by drawing attention to the act of painting itself, to the process through which external scenes and inner emotions come jointly to life. The idea that form is something to be discovered in the act of constructing a work is vividly conveyed by the notion that paint and brushstrokes are not merely tools for the representation of outer reality: they speak for themselves and also speak, more importantly, about their efforts to give voice to the most inchoate of anxieties. Fear may only find a shape as it is being represented, not through the artist's adherence to a pre-established blueprint.

What is most distressing about the picture is its inconclusiveness: we will never find out what has triggered the scream or what it signifies, nor do we know whether something ghastly has already happened or is on the brink of happening. This sense of indeterminateness evokes an atmosphere of terror; it also partakes of the spirit of horror by virtue of the landscape's intense physicality. *The Scream*'s human protagonist reflects Munch's obsessive concern with the isolation of the individual, especially the creative personality, in a callous and materialistic world – cut off and hounded down, at once rushing away from an undefined menace and towards an equally undefined destination that may prove no less threatening. There is even a suggestion that the shouting death's head and its flimsy body may go on running for ever towards the edge of a treacherous chasm. Nevertheless, the fearful and persecuted figure appears to be more alive than the apparently self-possessed figures in the background: ghostly burghers with featureless faces that are no less mask-like than the face of the hollow-cheeked and saucer-eyed howler. Munch implies that fear could be considered an enlivening, albeit tormenting, energy – a force possessed of a vigour which the qualities of propriety and self-restraint fostered by the pillars of society could never presume to emulate.

The thesis here proposed is threefold. First, it is suggested that the inconclusiveness typically evinced by Gothic fiction is largely a result of the latter's inclination to combine diverse linguistic registers without any one of them gaining incontrovertible dominance. The verbal and the visual, in particular, relentlessly and often bafflingly merge in mutual suffusion. Second, it is argued that formal and psychological open-endedness is a concomitant of the relative indefiniteness of both the concept of narrative and the concept of self. It would be quite inappropriate, for instance, to view the self as a living being responsible for the construction of stories and wholly in control of their developments and outcomes, and the narrative as the inanimate product of that person's efforts. In fact, narratives are also selves, bodies endowed with distinctive identities and sensibilities. Furthermore, the text is not passive. In being written, it simultaneously writes the creative subject by giving form to the author's imaginings, yearnings and fears. Finally, the interplay of dark themes and narratorial techniques inexorably leads to unresolved endings because its parameters are difficult to define. Personal and collective experiences, in particular, play varyingly prominent roles and texts accordingly veer towards one of two extremes, autobiography and historiography, with countless variations between the two. Neither extreme is conclusively triumphant. As a result, there is no single moral or aesthetic agenda by which the textual tapestry can be contained.

Words and Visions

DARK FICTION'S PROVERBIAL lack of resolution is often effectively conveyed by its kaleidoscopic interweaving of verbal and visual effects. This strategy does not merely amount to a narrator's ability to conjure up vivid images through a profusion of descriptive details. At its most compelling it aims at producing a blend of description, narration and reflection whereby settings, characters, plot complications and thematic concerns coalesce as interrelated facets of a multi-layered picture. It is a means of painting through words which in modern literary history has gained momentum at the behest of poets such as the Imagists and T. S. Eliot, but it can also be traced back to early Gothic fiction and particularly the writings of Ann Radcliffe. According to George P. Landow, Radcliffe could be credited with inventing 'the technique of proto-cinematic – or narrative – description called word-painting' (Flaxman:website). This, argues Rhoda L. Flaxman, consists primarily of 'passages of visually oriented descriptions whose techniques emulate pictorial methods'. Such practices are not simply intended to produce 'a static catalogue of visual data' for, by 'implying progress from one element to the next in a "narrative of landscape"', they offer a 'dramatization of the visual' and thereby make visions and words interdependent (Flaxman:website).

Replicating fear's protean plasticity, dark fiction articulates disquieting experiences by recourse to a plurality of codes, registers and procedures, a vitally important technique consisting of the employment of words and visions as alternately complementary and conflicting dimensions. Both verbal and visual images are capable of clarifying and obfuscating matters at the same time. They may operate in tandem by performing jointly either of those operations and, equally well, they may function oppositionally by pursuing contrary aims. The instability that characterizes the relationship between the verbal and the visual also echoes the unresolved tension animating the dynamics of terror and horror – the oscillation between the impalpable and the physical. Both linguistic codes are implicated in the discourse of horror by virtue of their corporeal qualities. Indeed, words possess tactile attributes on the basis of which they may be perceived as solid presences: marks on a page or patterns of sound that are both produced and consumed by material bodies. Visions, for their part, may be felt as materially present insofar as the images on which they pivot, illusory as they may be, have a powerful hold on the perceiver's entire sensorium. However, both visions and words partake of terror's proverbial intangibility. Visions are elusive apparitions whose connection with the empirical world is ultimately impossible to ascertain: the process of reality-testing intended to establish whether the mind's contents correspond to the outside is by no means unproblematic, for the mind is perfectly, if perversely, capable of taking a subjective imaginary perception as a presentation of reality. Words, in turn, are ghostly substitutes for the real: abstract signs. They have a physical presence, yet the objects to which they refer are inevitably absent from the page and the voice. Words, like phantasms, are presences unremittingly traversed by absences, paradoxically disembodied bodies.

Henry James's *The Turn of the Screw* [1898] is possibly the best-known example of a narrative of darkness concerned with the relationship between narrative and the self as predicated upon an interplay of visions and words. This text intimates that forming and seeing letters, that is, the acts of writing and reading, could be compared to the experience of dealing with ghosts. *The Turn of the Screw* establishes a powerful and unsettling connection between the verbal signs that constitute a narrative and the visual experiences of the narrating self. In so doing, it speculates about the nature of power: the power one may or may not gain over language, story-telling, knowledge and, ultimately, oneself. Above all, it suggests that words and visions constantly slide, flit and glide. Trying to arrest them through the exercise of power only leads to a loss of control and sanity. The governess teeters on the edge of lunacy because she struggles to quantify and contain an intractable enigmatic situation. Early readings of the story evince an obsession with the attainment of conclusive answers analogous to the frustrated heroine's own quest. Edmund Wilson (1934:385–406), for instance, explains the text by portraying the Governess as a neurotic subject haunted by her repressed sexual urges, whose dark yearnings take the form of spectral hallucinations. The children, he believes, are totally innocent. Although this reading is hard to substantiate with exclusive reference to James's work, it is not altogether preposterous if assessed in relation to the story's cultural context. Indeed, as Millicent Bell observes,

> The suggestion that James's governess is delusionary or neurotically obsessed has a basis in the historic fact that many governesses found their lives unbearable and broke down. It was said that in the 1840s more female inmates of institutions for the insane came from the ranks of governesses than from any other occupation. (Bell:website)

Robert Heilman (1947:433–45) radically questions Wilson's interpretation by maintaining that the ghosts are real and have actually corrupted Miles and Flora.

The approaches of both Wilson and Heilman are characterized by a monolithic single-mindedness, a compulsive concern with establishing the proper meaning of the tale, that is patently at odds with James's own project and, specifically, his desire to inspire an atmosphere of uncertainty and inconclusiveness by means of adumbration. In his Preface to *The Turn of the Screw*, James posits as his central preoccupation 'the question of how best to convey the sense of the depths of the sinister without which my fable would so woefully limp' (1992:liii). He explicitly objects to the type of dark narrative that strives to deprive supernatural occurrences of their inexplicable components by attributing them to the individual psyche's vicissitudes, for this strategy serves to wash it 'clean of all queerness as by exposure to a flowing laboratory tap' (xlvii). According to T. J. Lustig, the limitations inherent in the readings proposed by both Wilson and Heilman are borne out by the fact that James himself 'neither provides nor claims to possess the supreme key to meaning. A ghost behind the ghosts, he establishes his mastery by disappearing from the scene, leaving in his wake eddies of unfixable significance' (1992:xiv).

Moreover, James draws attention to the nebulous nature of the materials from which he has drawn inspiration. In an Appendix to *The Turn of the Screw*, he states that he first received the story in its embryonic form from the Archbishop of Canterbury and that the latter's narrative was inevitably 'vague' due to the hazy style of his own source: 'a lady who had no art of relation' (1992:244). Therefore, the Archbishop 'himself could give us but this shadow of a shadow'. What would have indubitably baffled and frustrated a listener longing for neat answers gives James a reason to rejoice since, in his aesthetic, vagueness has 'the immense merit of allowing the imagination absolute freedom of hand' (xlviii). The fragments of real life organized by the fiction writer into a story are not robbed of authenticity by their imaginative orchestration. Rather, they attain to a different and very possibly more complex level of reality. As Pope Brock observes, commenting upon his own reconstruction of a true story as a written narrative, when the record at one's disposal is 'fragmentary' or indeed 'missing altogether', it is the creative self's responsibility to ideate viable links amongst the existing data: 'Ultimately the facts formed a line of buoys in a sea of my own imagination' (2000:vii).

There is an important parallel between writing and the ability to conjure up visions. Margaret Mahy's *The Haunting* corroborates this point: Tabitha the would-be bestselling novelist and Troy the magician, both children, equally play with 'dreams of spinning the world' (1999:135). As Stephanie Nettell points out in her 'Afterword' to the tale, 'novelists . . . have much in common with magicians' (141). The words that eventually materialize on the page may be the result of subliminal operations: writers may have visions without quite knowing that this is the case until the visions have taken shape as narratives.

The case of *The Turn of the Screw* makes it abundantly clear that critics solely concerned with ascertaining a text's meaning repeat James's Governess's error by trying to impose order upon the inexplicable and becoming lost in what Shoshana Felman describes as the narrative's 'labyrinth of meaning' (1982:190). Psychoanalysis, in particular, 'in its efforts to master literature . . . can thus but blind itself' (199). Allan Lloyd Smith agrees that 'critics have been led into hallucinatory readings, on occasion even inventing their own ghosts', thereby allowing the words which the narrative supplies, the said and more importantly the unsaid, to engender 'peculiar tricks of vision' (1993:47). More productive interpretations may ensue from an approach that focuses on the broader social and historical implications of James's story. Such an approach is rendered especially relevant, argues Jane Nardin, by the realization that 'the ghosts are the logical offspring of the Governess's attempt to understand a complex human situation in terms of a cultural tradition incapable of yielding real insight' (1978:135). Nicholas Abraham likewise emphasizes the tale's cultural dimension with reference to the concept of transgenerational haunting. He states that 'What haunts are not the dead, but the gaps left within us by the secrets of others'. Such secrets coalesce into the figure of the phantom: 'a formation of the unconscious that has never been conscious', and is therefore not so much produced by 'dynamic repression' as by its transposition 'from the parents' unconscious into the child's'. The secrets alluded to by Abraham are not exclusively familial for they also encompass situations and affects that entire cultures deem unutterable and which, as a result, end up surreptitiously influencing people's development to the point that they may become incapable of approaching their lives as their own (1987:287–92). An especially potent extra-familial secret is the spirit of perversity which, in Edgar Allan Poe's philosophy, is not merely the energy animating the creative writer's dark imagination but actually 'a fundamental force which permeates human existence', rendered particularly overbearing by the fact that 'humanity seems so unaware of its presence' (Grantz:website).

Miles and Flora could well be considered products of transgenerational haunting, of their subjection to secrets which they cannot consciously grasp and which cause them to behave peculiarly. (Related issues are addressed in **Chapter 11.**) The children's behaviour, though disturbing by virtue of its elliptical hints at the possibility of sexual abuse, is not the only or indeed principal problem posed by the tale. Indeed, what is even more disquieting is the Governess's determination to construct incontrovertible meanings by filling in the lacunae produced by both familial and extra-familial secrets, here epitomized by the paradoxically absent presence of Peter Quint and Miss Jessel. Moreover, the Governess's visions are indissociable from her words: the words actually uttered so as to make sense of a distressingly alien state of affairs and, more pressingly, the words that remain unsaid, unspeakable. Reflecting on Miles's background, she anxiously admits: 'I could reconstitute nothing at all' (James 1992:141). Unutterable sounds echo as many occluded images, scenes relegated to the province of invisibility by their tabooed status. Indeed, what may well lie at the root of the ordeal dramatized by James is a secret stemming from a pervasively haunting legacy. Part of this heritage, argues Millicent Bell, is 'the real predicament of the gentleman's daughter of slender means, who is hired to care for another gentleman's children. She must accept the lonely, de-classed status of the woman who takes over the tasks of more fortunate women, supplying care and education for the children of a family no more "polite" (in the social sense) than her own . . . she belonged to no class and suffered from what sociologists call "status incongruity"' (Bell:website).

The epitome of this societal hybrid is, arguably, the eponymous heroine of Charlotte Brontë's *Jane Eyre* [1847], another Victorian female famously haunted by the sinister alliance of ominous words and visions. The iconography of Jane's dreams and paintings testifies to her inscription in a complex network of signs. Moreover, Thornfield Hall reaches out to Jane through powerful words of intimidation and daring, a vibrant cluster of characters engraved on the visible surface of its very architecture. The challenging signs irreverently alert the heroine to a secreted history of guilt and disgrace that is mirrored by the mansion's deceptive nature: 'the gilding is slime and the silk draperies cobwebs . . . the marble is sordid slate, and the polished woods mere refuse chips and scaly bark' (Brontë 1981:244). However, whereas Brontë's heroine eventually gains access to the upper ranks, James's Governess remains a tabooed woman.

It is paradoxical, given her inherent weakness, that the Governess herself should be in a position to cast a shadow of doubt upon her own decoding enter-prise, by equating letters and spectres: 'So I saw him [Peter Quint],' she states, 'as I see the letters I form on this page' (James 1992:137). In so doing, she implicitly draws attention to the interplay of content and form: her inter-pretive efforts resonate with the strategies characteristic of the realist text, its normative readings, reparative conclusions, repression of textual aporias and reliance on the undisputed mastery of an omniscient author. The versions of the real asserted by this kind of text are ultimately as oppressive as the Governess's literally suffocating action. *The Turn of the Screw*, conversely, typifies the modernist ethos by positing the related processes of writing and reading as unlimited. The narrator stresses that meanings are in constant flight: 'the story won't tell . . . not in any literal, vulgar way' (118). At the same time he admits, in response to the question 'What is your title?': 'I haven't one' (122). The only available form of mastery, finally, consists of the acceptance of one's inability to know and control reality, of self-dispossession, as epitomized by the absent figure of the Master and, as we have seen, by

James's own withdrawal from the text. (*The Turn of the Screw* is also examined in **Chapters 4** and **6**.)

Edgar Allan Poe also equates power to self-dispossession. The detective Dupin is successful insofar as he is able to divest himself of his own identity and to identify with his criminal counterparts. In 'The Purloined Letter' (1845), in particular, he succeeds where the Police fail because he is able to imagine himself in the situation of the criminal, namely, to erase his own personality and adopt a narrative self or persona. Like *The Turn of the Screw*, 'The Purloined Letter' emphasizes that we can only grasp words and their potential messages when we are not trying to dominate them. Meanings, like our very identities, are fleeting effects of performative and narrative acts. Neil Gaiman even suggests that we can only read properly when we are dreaming. At one point, the protagonist of *The Sandman: The Dream Hunters* realizes: 'And it was then, if he had had any doubt before, that he knew for certain that he was dreaming. For he could read the characters on the paper he carried. They were simple characters, so simple he thought it a wonder he had not been able to read them before' (1999:8). The idea of simplicity also features prominently in Poe: much of the time, he maintains, meaning eludes us because we seek it in complex and hidden regions of reality while, in fact, it is merely a ripple on the surface of language. There is no truth except as inscribed in the systems of verbal and visual signs that constitute the symbolic order: namely, a construct predicated upon the continual deferral of sense and destination. Truth is an effect of our ability, or inability, to extend the boundaries of the perceivable: 'I suppose . . . there is nothing much to see', opines the narrator in Susan Hill's *The Woman in Black* [1983]. His fellow traveller points out that 'it all depends what you mean by "nothing"' (1998:38). Indeed, there is an important difference between seeing *nothing* and *seeing* nothing: that is, between the unwillingness or willingness to perceive and accept the invisibility that riddles inner and outer landscapes alike.

Poe's representation of the operations of language as a process of endless diversion and digression has only become an object of critical interest relatively recently, thanks to Jacques Lacan's ground-breaking reading of 'The Purloined Letter'. On the whole, Poe's work has encountered an exegetic fate not dissimilar from that of *The Turn of the Screw*: a domestication of its most troubling aspects through the application of psychoanalytic concepts. It is not until Lacan that the analysis has moved beyond the narrow confines of the biographical approach into an investigation of the structural characteristics of Poe's writings and, relatedly, of the reading performance it calls for. Joseph Wood Krutch (1926) was quite happy with diagnosing Poe's presumably pathological condition and interpreting his literary talent as a means of compensating for his private sense of loss and inadequacy. Marie Bonaparte (1949), while making allowances for the more universal implications of Poe's texts, was still primarily concerned with the pathological drives underlying the tales. The minute scrutiny to which she subjected Poe's corpus was governed by the determination to relate the events and figures in the writer's life to textual materials and hence explain the writing in terms of narcissism, necrophilia and anxiety dreams. The methods of inquiry exhibited by these critics reveal a desire to relate the text's conflicts to the single discourse of psychobiography.

What Lacan's reading of Poe suggests, conversely, is a methodology that does not attempt to resolve the text's aporias and contradictions so as to extract from it a univocal meaning but rather recognizes those problematic dimensions as pivotal to its aesthetic and psychological appeal. The emphasis shifts from the investigation of content to the study of form and structure, from an analysis of the signified to an analysis of the signifier. What Lacan is concerned with is the story's superficial movement as a double metaphor for the process of constant displacement of meaning, authority and knowledge and for the discontinuity of human consciousness. The subordination of content to form and structure which distinguishes the Lacanian approach is corroborated by the tale itself insofar as certain key factors pertaining to the origins and function of the purloined letter are never disclosed. What becomes paramount, as a corollary, is the extent to which the psyche is governed not so much by what it knows or might know but by fatuous hints at something that inexorably remains both unknown and unknowable: 'the signifier,' argues Lacan, 'is not functional . . . We might even admit that the letter has an entirely different (if no more urgent) meaning for the Queen than the one understood by the Minister. The sequence of events would not be noticeably affected, not even if it were strictly incomprehensible to an uninformed reader . . . We shall find illumination in what at first seems to obscure matters: the fact that the tale leaves us in virtually total ignorance of the sender, no less than of the contents, of the letter' (1972:56–7). The reader's task, then, would consist of recognizing not meaning but its absence or negation.

Moreover, as Lacan's reading of 'The Purloined Letter' intimates, in both of the tale's key scenes, the tension between the verbal and the visual plays a prominent role. In the first, where the Minister steals from the Queen the letter of the title, the spoken word is evidently not a viable option: it is not in the thief's interest to advertise his felonious act verbally. As for the Queen, she must hold her tongue for, were she to incriminate the Minister, she would inevitably draw her husband's attention to the missive while it is her main aim to conceal its existence. Words being thus sequestered from the spectacle, the resulting balance of power rests on sight. The King sees nothing: he is utterly oblivious to both the letter and its theft. The Queen sees that her property is being abducted but is helpless to act. The Minister holds control over the situation by perceiving that the King does not see and that the Queen's sight cannot benefit her. The second principal incident in the tale mirrors the one just outlined. Dupin steals the letter from the Minister, having spotted it in a far from obscure area of the latter's office, and thus outwits the Police, who have vainly searched for it in the remotest nooks and crannies. Dupin's power of vision in the second scene replicates the Minister's in the first, while the Minister finds himself in the seeing but powerless position previously occupied by the Queen and the inane Prefect's performance repeats that of the insensitive King.

What 'The Purloined Letter' implies is that human beings are capable of perceiving things only as long as these occupy predictable locations: as long as they are where they are expected to be. Thus, anticipating the stolen epistle to have been concealed in some cryptic recess, the Police are unable to see it in its conspicuous situation, a letter-rack on a mantelpiece. The letter, as John Lechte observes, 'is hidden only because it is in a place too unexpectedly obvious for those who do not have eyes to see' (1990:40). Human beings' responses to fear exhibit comparable traits. Culturally trained to keep frightening occurrences and emotions at bay by regarding them as sporadic disruptions of an otherwise smooth fabric, we are often incapacitated from grasping dread's omnipresence. We see the fearful where we *expect* to see it but are by and large insensitive to its call in circumstances we deem familiar and safe. Poe's losers fail due to their blindness: following the comparison between 'The Purloined Letter' and the dynamics of fear, it could be argued that humiliating defeats are in store for anyone unwilling to extend their field of vision and detect the workings of fear in quotidian and apparently stable situations. As a metaphor for the unanchored signifier, the letter symbolizes an absence, a lack. Even when it is present on the scene, its value, like that of Desdemona's handkerchief, depends entirely on its ability to evoke something that is missing: an imponderable, a harrowing doubt, an unspeakable fear. Allusions to the pervasiveness of dread through the colluding agencies of horror and terror, such as those typically proffered by dark fiction, likewise operate as floating signifiers. They point to the overwhelming materiality of the forces that unremittingly loom over individual and collective sanity. Yet, they constellate those threats not as presences but as reminders of an abiding sense of loss which no available symbolic system, either verbal or visual, may ultimately heal. (Poe's aesthetic principles are also discussed in 'The Frame of Reference' and in **Chapter 6**.)

A further example of the interaction between words and visions, textuality and spectral forms, is supplied by Charlotte Perkins Gilman's *The Yellow Wallpaper* [1892]. Here, the physical and psychological reality of the protagonist's incarceration by her husband in an attic, justified on the grounds of her presumed insanity, is encapsulated by the walls of her prison as sites of both writing and haunting. The walls gradually become a text whose shifting patterns resemble an idiosyncratic handwriting as 'up and down and sideways they crawl'. The text tells a story of Gothic entrapment hinging on the patriarchal victimization of women, a message reinforced by the fact that when the heroine struggles to organize the wallpaper's sliding signifiers into an intelligible image, the vision she perceives is that of 'a woman'. Her ordeal, as she painfully endeavours to negotiate words and visions, is replicated by the predicament of another spectral female. It is also significant that the narrator lacks confidence in her ability to write. This feeling does not merely result from a general sense of insecurity and self-dispossession. It is also related to the notion that what she is attempting to bring to life on 'dead paper' is a ghost, the phantom of both her silenced self and the fleeting vision on the wall. *The Yellow Wallpaper* seems to confirm the hypothesis, advanced earlier, that words and visions partake simultaneously of presence and absence: words erode the materiality of the real by translating presences into absences while visions, in turn, question the reliability of perception by intimating that there is often a discrepancy between what is there for us to see and what we ideate in its absence. However, both verbal and visual discourses frequently challenge us to find coherence in their elusive operations. The protagonist of Gilman's story could be said to pursue this very aim in her search for a pattern in the wallpaper's disconcerting hieroglyphics. Yet she fully recognizes that such a quest is 'pointless' (1981:16, 26, 10, 19). This, arguably, is the story's most potent message. It suggests that both words and visions, though they relentlessly provide clues to meaning, are not disposed to deliver meaning as such.

The distinctive open-endedness of dark texts inspired by a Gothic vision entails that the meanings constructed by authors and narrators are inevitably provisional. The precariousness of authorial power places the responsibility for producing more durable messages upon the reader. However, the interpretive task is ultimately as inconclusive as the narrative itself, and rendered ambiguous by the fact that readers are concurrently encouraged to detect the text's intrinsic shape and warned about the viability and desirability of doing so. This ambiguity is foregrounded by Henry James's 'The Figure in the Carpet', a short story explicitly concerned with the function of criticism (James 1962–4). The 'figure' of the title refers to the ultimate structure or pattern sought by critics eager to glean a consoling image of order beneath the text's surface and, by extension, beneath the bustling anarchy of the phenomenal world. James intimates that the figure may simply amount to a figment of the decoding imagination, a shifting mirage pathetically invoked to exorcize the demons of linguistic arbitrariness. The phantasmatic character of the Platonic design pursued by much traditional criticism is often irreverently exposed by dark narratives that ask us to accept their status as bundles, or perhaps catalogues, of riddles which elude structural ordering. The recurring formal and thematic preoccupations evinced by the Gothic vision could indeed be mapped out as clusters of hypothetical and enigmatic propositions whose truth value remains imponderable due to the simultaneous applicability of a statement and of its opposite, of a visual image and of its specular alternative, as contrapuntal forces unrelentingly whirled into collision with their own duality.

— 8 —

𝕿extual 𝕴dentities

REPLICATING THE PROCESSES which they assiduously dramatize – the ongoing emergence and unresolved unfolding of fear – narratives of darkness are fundamentally open-ended. Gothic tropes of fragmentation, psychological and physical disarray, and hesitation could be regarded as the discursive repertoire underlying the representation of the polymorphousness of fear and its affects. The most memorable plots tend to leave things somewhat unfinished or to round them off in perfunctory ways, by merely paying lip service to ethical and aesthetic conventions. Sometimes the denouement is so preposterously rapid as to appear farcical. For example, Matthew Lewis's *The Monk* [1796] terminates its protagonist's crime-laden exploits in ways which, far from offering a conclusive moral ending, draw the reader back to the horrors that fill the main body of the book and to their arguably perverse *frisson*. (*The Monk* is also discussed in **Chapters 1** and **3**.) Precluding the plot from reaching completion is also a means of eroding the characters' possible plenitude. Splintered narratives go hand in hand with fragmented subjectivities.

This idea is foregrounded by a number of narratives of darkness which consist of multi-layered texts intent on flouting the ethos of authorial omniscience. Mary Shelley's *Frankenstein* [1818] reads as an essentially composite narrative, resulting from the interweaving of letters, memoirs, and both autobiographical and descriptive accounts rendered from different viewpoints. This novel will be discussed later in this chapter. (See also Chapter **14**.) Emily Brontë's *Wuthering Heights* [1847] hinges on the interplay of disparate voices, none of which is ultimately capable of fully rationalizing the tale's events, despite both Lockwood's and Nelly's different attempts to do so. (*Wuthering Heights* is examined in greater detail in **Chapter 11**.) Bram Stoker's *Dracula* [1897] is another paradigmatic example of compound textuality: it draws together letters, diaries, newspaper clippings and medical case notes, without any of these forms gaining definitive priority over any other. The text's composite nature reflects metaphorically the vampire's identity as an aggregate of various incarnations of otherness. Sexual, racial, physiological, political and economic forms of degeneration and abomination coalesce in the depiction of the blood-drinker. (See also **Chapter 13.**)

These prismatic narratives stress that the text's composite identity on the formal and structural planes duplicates the identities of its characters on the physical and psychological planes. Charles Robert Maturin's *Melmoth the Wanderer* [1820] exemplifies this notion: the text sets up consistent correspondences between narrative structure and the convolutions of the Gothic personality by conjuring up varyingly deranged and benighted subjects in a tapestry of phantasmagoric intricacy. The book's extravagant proliferation of characters, episodes and interlocking tales, with their cornucopian abundance of violent and inexplicable deaths, hauntings, demonic possessions, unlawful unions and Faustian pacts, serves to convey a pervasive atmosphere of Gothic excess. Moreover, dark fiction unremittingly ideates the self as inevitably plural and divided, an offspring of the interaction of disparate and indeed often contradictory and warring forces. This condition, made famous by R. L. Stevenson's *The Strange Case of Dr Jekyll and Mr Hyde* [1886], is also vividly dramatized by Emma Tennant's reinterpretation of this text in *Two Women of London* (1990) (see also **Chapter 1** for a discussion of these related narratives), as well as by Peter Ackroyd's *Hawksmoor* (1985) with its almost obsessive handling of *doppelgangers*. (*Hawksmoor* is examined in some depth in **Chapter 4.**)

Narrative and the self are interdependent insofar as the pivotal features of texts and those of their characters mirror one another. As Lucie Armitt observes, 'the body of the text is also the body within the text and the language is embodied by the forms it inscribes' (1996:9). It is also noteworthy that while a patchwork text reflects its characters' mixed emotions and sense of confusion, it also has the effect of producing feelings of dislocation in its readers. Often, the distinction between real people and fictional personae is blurred. This idea is vividly expressed by J. L. Borges in 'Partial Magic in the *Quixote*': 'Why does it disturb us that Don Quixote be a reader of the *Quixote* and Hamlet a spectator of *Hamlet*? I believe I have found the reason: these inversions suggest that if the characters of a fictional work can be readers or spectators, we, its readers or spectators, can be fictitious' (1970:231). Readers' identities, then, are as textual as those of the characters whose ordeals they amuse themselves with. However, the phrase 'textual identities' carries further connotations. It does not merely suggest that a story's structure is capable of drawing attention to the nature and constitution of its personae. It also intimates that texts have a propensity for constructing identities. Specifically, shadowy and aberrant selves are effects of textuality: narratives construct monsters *as* monstrous by inscribing their alterity in the supposed authority of the written word. This is typified by the belief that books have the power to frame and explain the deviant other. In Anne Rice's *Vittorio, The Vampire*, for instance, the protagonist states: 'I had to find texts . . . that defined the demons' (2000:226–7). This strategy is reminiscent of the project, documented by Edward Said in 'Crisis (in orientalism)', whereby the West constructs the supposedly exotic East as alien against a corpus of both fictional and historiographical texts. Said emphasizes the textual dimension of alterity by proposing that the imaginary subject of orientalism comes into existence 'when a human being confronts at close quarters something relatively unknown and threatening and previously distant. In such a case one has recourse not only to what in one's previous experience the novelty resembles but also to what one has read about it'. The Other is accordingly evaluated in relation to narratives because human beings have a tendency 'to fall back on a text when the uncertainty of travel in strange parts seems to threaten one's equanimity' (1988:295). In the domain of dark fiction the textual production of identity is often geared towards the definition of otherness as a phenomenon replete with ideological connotations, the villains, monsters and lunatics evoked by the Gothic vision encapsulating everything which a culture deems latently or overtly outlandish and hence menacing.

The quintessentially Gothic text, to sum up the propositions advanced in the preceding paragraphs, could be described as a composite entity wherein disparate narrative strands parallel the split subjectivities of both characters and readers. No less significantly, however, the notion of textual identity refers to the corporeal status of the narrative itself. Texts are bodies which, in being fashioned by their writers and readers, simultaneously construct the readers' identities by incarnating their most inveterate desires and fears. If it is the case that human subjects articulate ideas and emotions in linguistic form, it is also the case that they, in turn, are spoken and written by language.

On the structural level, texts may be conceived of as bodies constituted by the combination of recurring formal and thematic components. Narratives of darkness, specifically, can be explored in the light of typical plot formations whose employment of particular devices contributes vitally to endowing the story with one kind of body or another. In *The Philosophy of Horror*, Noel Carroll proposes a generic typology of recursive plot structures that might help us identify some of the most prominent textual configurations produced by dark fiction. Carroll posits the 'complex discovery plot' as a structure based on four fundamental 'functions': 'onset, discovery, confirmation, and confrontation'. The onset usually takes one of two forms: the identity of the threat may be immediately revealed, which is generally the case with 'thrillers', or else only its destructive effects may be displayed, in which instance we would be in the presence of 'mysteries' (1990:99). Discovery refers to the realization that the menacing agent belongs to the ranks of either the unnatural or the supernatural: such knowledge is often resisted by the champions of enlightened common sense. In the subsequent movement, confirmation, 'the discoverers of or the believers in the existence of the monster' (101) endeavour to make the sceptics accept the actual nature of the threat. The confrontation function, finally, defines the processes through which the offending Other is attacked and, ideally, vanquished. These actions are hardly ever conclusive and hence require reiteration, the annihilation of the destructive force being, by and large, a matter of hypothesis rather than a foregone conclusion. If the complex discovery plot can be regarded as a sophisticated textual organism, there are alternative and more elementary narrative bodies to be taken into consideration. Thus, Carroll argues that 'by *subtracting* various of the functions or plot movements from the complex discovery plot', we may arrive at the '*discovery plot*', where 'the confirmation function' (108) does not feature; the '*confirmation plot*', where confrontation does not occur; and the plot that 'lacks discovery' insofar as the threatening creature is 'already known to exist' (110) and where this knowledge guarantees further permutations of the menace in the form of sequels, reworkings and parodies.

Not only is the dark narrative endowed with pointedly physical attributes, it is also a specifically gendered body. As E. J. Clery argues, the climate of opinion surrounding early Gothic literature is coursed through by insistent suggestions that there is an intimate connection between 'female readers and improbable, unimproving fictions'. This belief was, at least in part, responsible for a 'confounding of books and female bodies'. Circulating libraries added weight to the argument by intimating that a link could be traced between the cheap and dirty volumes passing through many anonymous hands and women as 'machines for reading' likewise tainted by their 'voracious consumption' of trifling and licentious images (1999:96–7). (See also 'The Frame of Reference'.) While the monstrous body produced by the collusion of Gothic fiction and avid female readers is an eminently patriarchal fabrication, it is nonetheless important to appreciate the identity of all bodies as texts inscribed by both personal and collective histories. Clive Barker graphically conveys this idea in 'The Book of Blood', the opening tale in the first volume of *Books of Blood* [1984]. A young man, pretending to be able to hear the voices of the dead and to transcribe their stories, fills the walls of the attic of a reputedly haunted house with narratives which he claims to receive directly from the Beyond. Ultimately, the dead take their revenge upon the mendacious youth by turning his own thriving body into a gory palimpsest of wounds and indelible scars. Barker's story vividly depicts the concept of the body-as-text: 'He was to be used to record their testaments. He was to be their page, their book, the vessel for their autobiographies. A book of blood. A book made of blood. A book written in blood' (1999a, vol. 1:8). It is hard to imagine a more fitting record of lives steeped in violence and sorrow, indeed of identities shaped by unutterable pain, than a text formed by 'hieroglyphics of agony' inscribed 'on every inch' (9) of the cherubic adventurer's face and limbs: 'There were minute words on every millimetre of his body, written in a multitude of hands . . . here it was: the revelation of life beyond flesh, written in flesh itself' (10–11). Barker equates not only the tangible body but also the psyche to a written text. In 'Pig Blood Blues' (*Books of Blood, vol. 1*), for example, he describes 'minds' as 'scrawls . . . sprawling splashes of graffiti, unpredictable, unconfinable' (1999a, Vol. 1:64).

In order to elucidate the mutual mirroring of narrative and the self in the realm of dark fiction, it seems appropriate to examine a selection of texts that varyingly articulate the interplay of multi-layered textual structures and correspondingly composite identities. Turning to the early Gothic, one finds that Mary Shelley's seminal anatomy of monstrosity provides precisely one such text. As pointed out earlier, *Frankenstein* stands out as a veritable quilt of narrative forms and methods which make the novel a quintessentially hybrid assemblage comparable to the creature upon which the tale revolves. It is also, however, a paradigmatic instance of the pluri-gendered body to which the Gothic vision insistently returns. *Frankenstein* simultaneously exposes the exclusion and victimization of women and asserts the dominance of images of disunity and darkness conventionally associated with femininity, in contrast with masculine and specifically humanistic fantasies of unity and light and with the male desire to produce life without female interference. As a corporeal entity in its own right, moreover, the novel displays an ambiguous gender identity. It is starkly male in its prioritizing of Promethean ambitions. It is female by virtue of its multi-climactic narrative rhythms and shape which, in defying definitive framing, brings to mind 'the body of woman' as 'fluid and undifferentiated' (Nead 1992:17). At the same time, the text is traversed by allusions to homoerotic attachments: powerful bonds obtain between Frankenstein and Walton as alternative variations on the theme of Faustian overreaching; between Frankenstein and Clerval as pursuers of truth by recourse to varyingly extreme ethical and scientific creeds; and between Walton and Clerval as explorers eager to penetrate and colonize remote lands. Furthermore, Frankenstein expects unconditional love from his creature, a feeling ostensibly intended to be filial but concurrently replete with physical connotations. The monster himself exhibits bisexual traits since, while demanding the production of a female companion, he craves above all else the recognition and love of another man, his creator.

The multi-facetedness of Shelley's novel is underscored by what Fred Botting describes as 'patterns of doubling and reversal' (1996:104). The early epistolary section in which the polar explorer Robert Walton communicates with his sister Margaret Saville informs us of the presence of a giant in the Arctic floes and then of the rescue by Walton and his crew of a dying man in pursuit of the giant. The explorer and Victor Frankenstein are thus structurally linked and it is this early connection that gradually leads to the delivery of the creator's and the creature's narratives. However, as indicated, the text's presentation of its characters' relationships in ambiguous terms shows that the interlocking of narrative strands affects psychology no less deeply than structure. Above all, the doublings produced by Shelley converge into a picture of shattered idealism, the visions pursued by its personae suffering catastrophic reversals that transform the noblest aspirations into aberrant and indeed monstrous fantasies.

Another instance of Gothic doubling is supplied by James Hogg's *Private Memoirs and Confessions of a Justified Sinner* [1824], where Robert Wringhim's nefarious actions could equally well be ascribed to his subjection to a diabolical alter ego or to a fanatical religiosity conducive to the ideation of a malevolent spirit igniting the protagonist's criminal passions. These two interpretations, by splitting the narrative into simultaneously conflicting and complementary perspectives, mirror each other without ultimately merging into a unified textual body. As Douglas Gifford points out, 'in part one the rational minds of the reader *and* writer struggle to impose a logical explanation for the events therein; while in part two the reader tends, temporarily at least, to allow himself to be carried by the subjective account of supernatural events'. However, 'this is not a total separation', for in the third part, consisting of the editor's comments, the two readings are further assessed 'with new evidence on both sides, which significantly comes to no final resolution of both or either decision' (1976:145). Whether Wringhim is a self-deluded eccentric or a religious maniac remains a moot point: the text's double structure yields an imponderable identity. 'The text refuses,' as Carroll states, 'to say which alternative is most compelling, and the reader is left in a state of suspended judgment' (1990:149).

Moving to the contemporary Gothic scene, we find that the composite nature of narratives and selves alike is frequently conveyed by recourse to the concept of intertextuality. In stressing the interdependence of disparate texts, this notion proposes that no story can be ultimately regarded as autonomous and self-contained, for texts unrelentingly absorb and transform other texts. All narratives are, more or less explicitly, fashioned out of traces and echoes left by other tales and voices and can therefore be conceived of as galaxies of quotations or mosaics of allusions. Barker vividly conveys this idea in 'Son of Celluloid' (*Books of Blood, vol. 3*). The cancer which, having ravaged Barberio's body, acquires independent life is a bestial collage built from the cross-narrative fantasies of cinema audiences. Though crudely and repulsively corporeal, this creature/text also partakes of the hyperreal logic of the simulacrum since the icons it successively embodies, from Marilyn Monroe to John Wayne, from Peter Lorre to Greta Garbo, are illusions which do not merely simulate or imitate the real but actually replace reality itself. They succeed in doing so not only by virtue of their verisimilitude as textual identities but also, more significantly, because they are capable of feeding vampirically on their spectators' desires. Thus, the amoeboid son of celluloid depends, both ontologically and epistemologically, on the willingness of its viewers to acknowledge its intertextual incarnations by projecting their own emotions onto the latter's illusory screens.

Barker also highlights the existence of a crucial connection between textuality and weaving which harks back to the very etymology of *text*, the Latin word *texere* 'to weave'. This idea plays an especially prominent role in *Weaveworld* [1987], a paradigmatic example of intertextuality in which Barker states that the narrative's 'threads can always be traced back to some earlier tale, and to the tales that preceded that' (1999b:5). In the novel, the magical Seerkind, forced to flee the human Kingdom of the Cuckoo and its ruthless persecution, are woven into a carpet containing stylized versions of their origins. The carpet is the supreme object of Seerkind Immacolata's desire: having remained in the Kingdom, she feels hostility against the exiles and is determined to destroy their otherworld. Cal and Suzanna, conversely, endeavour to guarantee the carpet's safety. The struggle on which the text hinges is fundamentally a struggle for power, for possession of the alternative domain regularly conjured up by the woven artifact and the textual identities forming the weft and warp of its fabric. However, the yearning for such possession remains unfulfilled for it is inherent in the intertextual status of the world of the weave, also significantly referred to as the *Fugue*, that, lacking a single point of origin, it should consequently frustrate all attempts to define its final destination.

Suzy McKee Charnas's *The Vampire Tapestry* [1980] corroborates the link between textuality and weaving posited by Barker. The novel makes the author's production of the narrative weave coterminous with the text's own construction of plural identities for both its characters and its readers and, at the same time, with the coming into being of the story itself as a body. In delivering a polyphonic constellation of tales, Charnas concomitantly offers a composite image of subjectivity by characterizing the vampire as an eminently decentred and fragmented self. Weyland's displaced consciousness is, in turn, echoed by the feelings of disorientation and alienation experienced by other characters with whom he comes into contact. In Part 1, for example, Katje de Groot, having discovered Weyland's vampiric nature, finds herself empathizing, albeit unwillingly, with the monster because she recognizes that they are both strangers, that 'if he was a one-way time traveller, so was she': as an expatriate, Katje is no less pointedly aware than Weyland is of what it means 'to lose one's world' (1983:44). Moreover, she is led to identify with the vampire by the realization that if Weyland is a predator, so, in a sense, is she, as long as she remains committed to hounding down the blood-drinker: *'I am myself a hunter!'* (50). Thus, in weaving a multi-stranded tapestry, Charnas simultaneously constructs complex identities that resist both generic and humanist definitions by underscoring their plurality and porousness, and by intimating that affinities exist where undiluted difference may at first seem to hold sway. A process of doubling analogous to the one discussed in relation to Shelley and Hogg can therefore be detected in *The Vampire Tapestry*.

The mechanism of reversal also plays an important role. This is evident in Part 2, where Charnas inverts the somewhat stereotypical equation between blood-sucking and the sexual violation of a helpless victim by a virile attacker, either a literal male or an erotically voracious and hence metaphorically masculine woman. (This notion is discussed in some detail in **Chapter 13** with reference to Bram Stoker's *Dracula*.) Weyland, in fact, is deprived of his potency and figuratively feminized. As Anne Cranny Francis observes, in this segment of the novel, 'Charnas shows the vampire stripped of his power, a victim to the greed and voyeurism of others . . . what is revealed is not the monster, the bio-logically different, the "other", in the woman, but the woman in the monster. Bereft of power, Weyland is placed in the traditional female role' (1998:140). In Part 3, the association of a feminine or feminized textual identity with power-lessness is reinforced by the suggestion that when Weyland becomes emotionally and sexually engaged with a woman, the psychoanalyst Floria Landauer, he loses his predatory instinct. This section thus also intimates that the erotic import of vampirism, with its proverbial violence and brutality, stems from patriarchal conventions insofar as at the point where the blood-drinker is willing to enter a non-exploitative partnership, the rapacious urges fade away. Yet, Weyland cannot cope with the extreme threat to his monstrous identity posed by his involvement with Floria and, having left her, feels compelled to kill again. However, by now, he finds himself taking lives 'without need, without hunger' (Charnas 1983:220). This predicament bears disturbing simi-larities to the situation in which both writers and readers participate when their ideological conditioning leads them to produce and consume texts unre-flectively, as though the meanings and values conveyed by a narrative were a matter of common sense rather than fleeting effects of arbitrary decisions. The actions of the vampire, which destroys mechanically and pleasurelessly, symbolize the moves through which the symbolic systems that shape us prey on our psyches and cause us to leave both texts and the identities they spawn dangerously unquestioned. Charnas's articulation of the relationship between narrative and the self thus points to the inextricable intertwining of the iden-tities of texts as prismatic fictional bodies, of those of their characters as multi-faceted constructs, and of those of their readers as offsprings of ambiguous ideologies, capable of simultaneously sustaining and depleting their subjects.

The written word is by no means the sole vehicle through which complex textual identities are produced. The closing part of this chapter offers a case study of a visual text that vividly dramatizes the interplay of narrative and the self through both its themes and its compositional techniques: Pablo Picasso's

Guernica (1937). The painting supports the proposition, central to this study, that in representing fear human beings simultaneously express contingent cultural concerns and tap into a reservoir of archetypal symbols. Indeed, while inspired by a specific event, the bombing of the ancient Basque capital by Franco's Nazi allies in 1937, *Guernica* draws on myth as the most ancient and enduring means of grasping and organizing reality: the epitome of the 'poetic wisdom' (*sapienza poetica*) theorized by Giambattista Vico in *The New Science* (1725). Picasso does not resort to this time-honoured form of knowledge to suggest merely that myths are timeless and universal bodies of ready-made metaphors. In fact, in utilizing archetypal images to give expression to a contemporary occurrence of catastrophic proportions, he draws attention to the plastic resilience of myth and, by implication, to the protean flexibility through which dread manifests itself.

Guernica embodies two apparently contrasting emotions at one and the same time. On the one hand, there is the profound sense of disruption brought about by a military orgy of sadism and fury: starkly defined shapes that either absorb or negate the vitality of colour through the exclusive adoption of white, black and grey combine with jagged and criss-crossing lines to convey feelings of intense bewilderment and anguish. The sensation of fear surges unnervingly through the juxtaposition of disparate experiences of horror and terror. The barbarity of warfare, torture, sexual rape, infanticide and bullfighting come together in a symbolic configuration. On the other hand, we witness a sense of structure, which Picasso conveys by depicting the city's shattered fabric as a paradoxically harmonious interweaving of diverse scenes of suffering, and by presenting the agonizing characters as flat and clearly outlined shapes that nonetheless overlap and metamorphose into one another. Distraught women, murdered children, dazzled and stricken animals, a house in flames, the flashing eye of the electric light, the lamp pathetically brought to shine upon a scenario of impenetrable darkness, the broken sword, the absurdly surviving flower coalesce into a disquieting aporia: ruptured continuity. Thus, despite its emphasis on fragmentation, *Guernica* also evinces a commitment to form, thereby suggesting that a sense of pattern may be perceived in even the most intractably chaotic situations. In this respect, the painting mirrors the dynamics of fear as a similarly ambivalent phenomenon, seemingly based on what is most inchoate in the psyche and yet endowed with a structure by its pervasiveness and by its function as a latent organizer of experience.

According to Dorothy Koppelman, *Guernica* 'shows that, even as it takes on the cruelty and seeming non-sense in the world, there is form, there is organization, there is something larger than man's "inhumanity to man"'. This statement reflects the ethos of Aesthetic Realism as theorized by Eli Siegel in *Is Beauty the Making One of Opposites?*, where it is argued that 'in every work of art' one may detect 'a certain progression . . . a design which makes for continuity' and, at the same time, 'the discreteness, the individuality, the broken-ness of things: the principle of discontinuity' (Koppelman 1999). Robert Hughes similarly proposes that what makes the painting's fractured forms tolerable is precisely its sense of structure: 'The spike tongues, the rolling eyes, the frantic splayed toes and fingers, the necks arched in spasm: these would be unendurable if their tension were not braced against the broken, but visible, order of the painting' (1991:110). In viewing *Guernica* as a major instance of the collusion of continuity and discontinuity, Koppelman also maintains that the painting is able 'to make the ugliness of things bearable' and 'to show those things as continuous with what we see as beautiful', and thus demonstrate the interdependence of appalling brokenness and life-affirming progression (Koppelman:website). If this hypothesis is accepted, then *Guernica* could be said to reflect the operations of fear by virtue of its ability to function simul-taneously as a paralysing record of intolerably sinister forces and as an illuminating reminder of the omnipresence of darkness and of the need to come to grips with it.

It can be argued that there is an analogy between the fragmentary and open-ended forms of dark fiction and the split and decentred identities of its characters, and indeed of its readers, insofar as the readers' points of reference are constantly brought to trial and found deficient. Moreover, the text's own identity consists not merely of its contents but also of its body. Just as fear reveals itself through plural incarnations, so dark narratives take on diverse bodies in order to articulate human emotions revolving around dread, its causes and its effects. *Guernica* exemplifies this argument as a text whose composite nature replicates and is replicated by the identities of both its characters and its viewers, and as a body capable of expressing the polymorphous quality of fear through a visual narrative of both symbolic and documentary value.

— 9 —

𝖲𝖙𝖔𝖗𝖞𝖙𝖊𝖑𝖑𝖎𝖓𝖌 𝖆𝖘 𝕿𝖍𝖊𝖗𝖆𝖕𝖞

DESCRIBING STORYTELLING as a therapeutic activity is not tantamount to framing it as a merely consolatory practice. Indeed, narratives of darkness operate therapeutically by capitalizing on disquieting feelings of uncertainty and hesitation, on ambiguity and on the blurring of neat demarcations between the safe and the risky, the logical and the bizarre. These disorienting sensations can be regarded, according to Tzvetan Todorov, as the most salient attributes of the 'fantastic', a genre with which dark fiction is inextricably intertwined. The fantastic is a borderline phenomenon, a frontier region precariously poised between the 'uncanny' and the 'marvellous', whose indeterminacy challenges the tendency to seal and contain texts through strict generic classification (Todorov 1975). This definition is applicable, in various degrees, to the Gothic vision at large, as testified by its emphasis on irresolution, the suspension of principles of verisimilitude and its concomitant commitment to discourses of psychological and ideological transgression. If storytelling can be deemed therapeutic, in this context, it is not because of its propensity to comfort either the narrator or the narratee but rather because of its ability to trespass the boundaries of subjectivity and language by quizzing the validity of legion conventions and the restrictions imposed upon the imagination by deeply-ingrained societal taboos. Resorting to Roland Barthes's distinction between the text of *plaisir* and the text of *jouissance*, it could be argued that the dark narrative embodies the latter's ethos. The pleasures it yields are not conducive to complacent feelings of fulfilment and resolution and it does not, therefore, provide 'a *comfortable* practice of reading'. In fact, it is continually traversed by intimations of rupture and unrest: it 'imposes a state of loss', it 'discomforts' and it 'unsettles the reader's historical, cultural, psychological assumptions' (1990:14).

One of the most influential attempts to theorize the therapeutic import of narration can be found in Sigmund Freud's writings on art and literature. In 'Creative writers and day-dreaming' (1908), in particular, it is argued that creative writers behave analogously to both day-dreamers and children at play, and that their urge to phantasy proceeds from unhappiness: both authors and readers are drawn to stories by a sense of lack and unfulfilled desire. Thus, Freud constructs the phantasies yielded by narrative as compensatory pleasures that enable writers to share their anxieties with others through the culturally acceptable medium of narration and, in so doing, play a healing role. What is proposed in this chapter is that narratives of darkness call for a more comprehensive approach to the concept of storytelling as therapy than the one advocated by Freud. Indeed, while often corroborating the Freudian model, those texts simultaneously interrogate it. This is because, though indubitably intriguing, Freud's argument ignores two elements of the creative process which dark texts insistently throw into relief. Firstly, in equating storytelling to a form of consolatory therapy, it does not adequately take into consideration the possibility of salutary effects ensuing not so much from the evocation of a sense of security as from the disruption of rational certitudes inherent in the notion of *jouissance*: it is the ego bent on fortifying the edifices of its personality by disavowing the unknown that dominates the Freudian scene, even when its phantasies patently emanate from unconscious sources. In this respect, consciousness as portrayed by Freud is always on the verge of falling into the trap described by Clive Barker: 'the danger' that ensues 'from the merely human who define life too narrowly, who seek a kind of deathly purity by destroying whatever they do not recognize' (1987b).

Secondly, Freud reductively concentrates on the author's perspective and his/her licence to create alternative realities. The reader's own role is accordingly minimized. Narratives of darkness, by contrast, emphasize that storytelling's potentially therapeutic properties consistently rely on the reader's responses and active participation in the production of the fiction no less than they depend on the subversion of common sense. This point gains prominence in Todorov's evaluation of the fantastic: at the point where a story resists containment by marking a threshold territory, it is its recipient's responsibility to negotiate its evanescence and elusiveness. 'In a world which is indeed our world,' states Todorov, 'the one we know, a world without devils, sylphides, or vampires, there occurs an event which cannot be explained' (1975:25). The author may well have given expression to such an occurrence in order to come to terms with her/his own troubled emotions and to deal self-therapeutically with the inexplicable. Yet, ultimately, the narrative only comes to life as a result of its effects upon a reader because it is through the latter's interpretative efforts that the tale's pivotal lessons are embodied and perpetuated. Such messages repeatedly foreground the imperative to embrace dread as an ongoing condition, since it is to that theme that we constantly and compulsively return in the most disparate circumstances. As Barker observes in the opening paragraph of 'Dread' (*Books of Blood, vol. 2*):

> If it were possible to sit, invisible, between two people on any train, in any
> waiting room or office, the conversation overheard would time and again circle
> on that subject. Certainly the debate might appear to be about something
> entirely different; the state of the nation, idle chat about death on the roads,
> the rising price of dental care; but strip away the metaphor, the innuendo, and
> there, nestling at the heart of the discourse, is dread. (1999a, vol. 2:1)

These ideas can be conveyed by means of numerous strategies. Outlined below are a few examples of the ways in which storytelling provides scope for the articulation of both personal and communal apprehensions of darkness. These include the medical approach to narration as a means of coping with the threat of bodily and mental dissolution; the commitment to recounting as a form of self-assertion required by ideological pressures that endanger the subject's reality; the parallel need to find sense and form in ostensibly meaningless and amorphous situations. In all cases, dark tales can be said to both confirm and question the Freudian approach.

The therapeutic value of storytelling has frequently been acknowledged by modern medicine. Surgeon and critic Cecil Helman, for example, maintains that medicine is a world of narratives, more or less *dark*, insofar as the patient's predicament is encrypted in a labyrinth of both verbal and non-verbal languages. Most importantly: 'All illness and unhappiness generates its own, very special types of tale. This is because telling a story is one of the most basic human ways of organizing experience – and of shaping suffering into a form, in order to give it meaning' (1992:8–9). Scheherazade in the *One Thousand and One Nights* [1704–17] employs storytelling precisely along these lines as a means of staying alive. In Jeanette Winterson's *The Passion* [1987], characters in the grip of unspeakable deprivation likewise realize that 'Stories were all we had' (1988:107). Moreover, the ailing body and the healing trajectory are steeped in language and narrative for 'Just as medical diagnosis involves the constant process of turning the body from flesh into metaphor, so medical treatment seems to consist partly of turning metaphor back into flesh' (Helman 1992:10). Dark texts repeatedly underline the interdependence of corporeality and symbolic systems of signs by positing identity as an effect of concurrently material and intangible factors. The discursive operations of horror and terror corroborate this point by showing that fearful occurrences impact on the self and bring some of its dormant elements to life through the deployment of both intensely physical, horrifying images and impalpably elusive, terrifying sugges- tions of dread. Furthermore, narratives of darkness stress the human propensity for couching experience in narrative form as a corollary of the fact that identity itself is an offspring of textuality: we are texts. Turning once more to the medical domain, one finds confirmation of this thesis in Oliver Sacks's writings. 'If we wish to know about a man,' the neurologist and case-study writer maintains, 'we ask . . . "what is his story – his real, inmost story" – for each of us *is* a biography, a story. Each of us *is* a singular narrative, which is constructed, continuously, unconsciously, by, through, and in us – through our perceptions, our feelings, our thoughts, our actions; and, not least, our discourse, our spoken narrations' (1986:105).

The medical approach echoes Freud's theories by positing narration as a means of assuaging the anxieties of a troubled self. At the same time, however, it implicitly casts a shadow of doubt on the viability of a unified ego by reminding us that both the patient's identity and the doctor's identity are predicated upon shifting constellations of signs. An analogous message is conveyed by fictions that concurrently present writing as an instrument for self-realization and indicate that the pleasure granted by this state is constantly overshadowed by the phantoms of the selves that have been sacrificed or repressed for the sake of its attainment. The intertextual relationship between Charlotte Brontë's *Jane Eyre* [1847] and Jean Rhys's *Wide Sargasso Sea* [1966] exemplifies this point. Brontë's novel shows that telling one's story is a way of appropriating a his/herstory that other, ostensibly more powerful, individuals may have presumed to write on our behalf. The text's autobiographical dimension aims precisely at making the dispossessed heroine speak in her own voice as an autonomous author. Nevertheless, the ownership of a voice and of the right to tell tends to benefit its owner to everybody else's disadvantage. This is brought home by Jean Rhys's fictional interpretation of *Jane Eyre* from Antoinette (Bertha) Mason's point of view, where it is emphasized that the appropriation of an independent narrative voice by Brontë's heroine still leaves plenty of other narratives and tribulations untold. The idea that the self brought into being through narration is a provisional entity predicated upon the erasure or misrepresentation of other identities is also central to Margaret Atwood's *Lady Oracle* [1976], where the protagonist's struggle to negotiate a psychologically and physically divided self is embodied by a literally split narratorial identity: she is concurrently the writer of cheap popular romances and an acclaimed poet. Any gain in one area entails a loss in the other, for over both roles hovers the shadow of an abused childhood identity. (*Lady Oracle* is examined further in **Chapter 15**.)

Freud's model is most explicitly validated by narratives that suggest that the need to tell proceeds largely from the longing to give shape to baffling experiences and may exhibit the traits of a repetition compulsion, as famously exemplified by the self-persecuted narrator of Samuel Taylor Coleridge's *The Rime of the Ancient Mariner* [1798]. At the same time, that need stems from the desire to identify reliable anchoring points in otherwise shifting and deceptive worlds. A written narrative cannot, of course, be regarded as a definitive statement, record or testament inseparable from the author that has penned it, however laboriously, due to the metamorphoses it is bound to undergo as a result of its encounter with successive generations of readers. Nevertheless, there is something uncannily seductive about the myth of the written word as a putative guarantee of continuity and stability and therefore a means of revolting against the threats of oblivion and dissolution. This is borne out by Edgar Allan Poe's *The Narrative of Gordon Arthur Pym* [1837–8], where Pym's psyche equates the chasm-riddled landscape of Tsalal to an archetypal scene of writing and, gazing anxiously into their abysmal darkness, finds that horror coexists with the latent promise of relief. These mixed emotions can be attributed, as J. G. Kennedy argues, to the fact that Pym is dominated by 'the unconscious desire to fall into writing, to surrender his mortal being to the timelessness of the inscribed text' (1987; quoted in Bloom 1998:192).

Accessing the realm of writing is not exclusively a means of indulging in a fantasy of immortality. At times, the page comes to constitute the therapeutic space wherein one may articulate tormenting perceptions and concerns that would otherwise stand out as unspeakable. For example, the narrator in Stephen King's *The Green Mile* [1996], admits to having accepted participation in the most atrocious tasks and situations somewhat uncritically as part of his job. On the one occasion in which he has found his professional duties questionable, he has been led to find explanation for them by committing his memories to the page: 'There was only one time I ever had a question about the nature of my job. That, I reckon, is why I'm writing this' (1999a:5). Susan Hill's *The Woman in Black* [1983] proceeds from a comparable desire to share with the reader a deeply unsettling experience: 'I should tell my tale . . . set it down on paper, with every care and in every detail . . . Then perhaps I should finally be free of it for whatever life remained for me to enjoy' (1998:22).

However, while echoing the theses put forward in 'Creative writers and day-dreaming', texts that equate the longing to narrate to the urge to make sense of disconcerting experiences often quiz those theses in the same movement. Dean Koontz, for example, harks back to Freud in intimating that writing horror novels is a means of exorcising one's own demons and of purging one's own fears. At the same time, Koontz radically questions the possibility of constructing a durable ego by drawing attention to the incidence of multifarious phobias likely to shatter the bastions of selfhood. The manacles that constrain numerous psyches in often devastating manners tend to assume a bewildering variety of forms. Commenting on his novel *False Memory* (1999), Koontz opines that 'human beings can devote . . . much energy to small and unlikely fears', such as 'anthrophobia' (a fear of flowers), 'genuphobia' (a fear of knees) and 'pogonophobia' (a fear of beards). Over and above these apparently preposterous phobias, however, looms the phantom of 'autophobia': namely, 'a fear of oneself' that may lead the sufferer to become 'afraid of his very shadow, of his reflection in a mirror, of his hands' (Koontz:website). Robert Bloch, like

Koontz, relates horror fiction to murky experiences likely to leave indelible traces in the writer's identity, with particular emphasis on the part played by childhood traumas:

> On the basis of personal belief and observation, I'd say that those of us who direct our storytelling into darker channels do so because we were perhaps a bit more mindful than most regarding our childhood confusions of identity, our conflicts with unpleasant realities and our traumatic encounters with imaginative terrors. (1998: 77)

Once again, the desire to harness storytelling to the imperative of self-consolidation is countered by an understanding of subjectivity as a haphazard collage of disruptive and not always consciously apprehensible experiences.

Finding a structure in which disturbing experiences may be accommodated, however temporarily, often requires a willingness to *let go*, to become someone else or, as Stephen King points out, to become oneself at a different stage in one's life. 'The act of writing,' he maintains, 'is very hypnotic. It's like dreaming awake . . . If I say in a book . . . that I want to write about what it was like to be a kid, my first thought is, "Gee, I really don't remember that much." But if you start, little by little you are able to regress, and the more you write the brighter the images become' (*Salon*:website). King's confident statement stems from his faith in the ability of writing to save the day in the face of apparently intractable obstacles. His fictional authors may be blocked, as exemplified by the protagonists of *Bag of Bones* (1999b) and *The Shining* (1977), or may be working under duress, as in *Misery* (1987), where the writer is kidnapped by a mad fan and forced to write what *she* wishes to read while he is physically powerless. However, one gets the recurring impression that as long as the author Stephen King himself is in a position to map out those characters' ordeals and as long as the writing itself continues unabated, opportunities remain for a therapeutic resolution. All this seems to militate in favour of Freud's argument. Yet, King also undermines the Freudian definition of writing as a recuperative activity by reminding us that no compensation is ever definitive. He does so by returning with almost uncanny regularity to the representation of some of humanity's most abiding anxieties and especially to the fear of isolation and solitude. (See also 'The Frame of Reference' for further comments on this idea.)

The writer himself is only partially in control of the narrative and, relatedly, of the disquieting feelings that this evokes. Thus, King admits that although he is by and large able to keep fear at bay, he is nonetheless vulnerable to the unexpected eruption of troubling emotions. Asked whether his stories frighten him, he states: 'Well, if you're ticklish, can you tickle yourself in those ticklish spots? And most people can't tickle themselves – it has to be from an outside source. So I don't generally scare myself. I feel I'm in control; I feel like I'm behind the monsters that I create, where I can more or less see the zippers that run up their backs'. Yet, in the same interview, he concedes that

> There have been a few occasions when I have scared myself. There's a scene in *Bag of Bones* where the main character, Mike Noonan, goes downstairs to look for something in the cellar and the door shuts behind him . . . I found myself visualizing our stairway in our home . . . . So that now, whenever I go down the stairwell, I'm immediately reminded of that scene in the book, and I'm afraid that the door's going to swing shut behind me.

These words are redolent of the idea, put forward in *Bag of Bones* itself, that much of what eventually materializes on the page is the result of subconscious operations. (See **Part 3**, Introduction.) If writers can be frightened by what they themselves have produced, it is because behind the act of conscious construction lie multiple layers of subliminal ideation. What proves scary is, in a sense, the offspring of something *other* than the author as a singular and neatly defined entity. This is corroborated by the intimation that writing 'is not an exact science. A lot of times I feel like a guy who is shooting a missile from a silo in Iowa, and you wanna land it down a chimney in Iraq, you know, on Jihad Street . . . So I don't feel entirely in control of the endings' ('Love, Death, and Stephen King'). King's position encapsulates many of the most salient traits of the concept of storytelling as therapy both as codified by Freud and as problematized by the Gothic vision. Principally, it stresses that while the act of narrating may endow writers with a sense of authority and indeed with the illusion of an impregnable identity, it simultaneously exposes their limitations by highlighting their susceptibility to the raw reality of fear and to the troubling inevitability of irresolution in fiction and reality alike.

The closing segment of this chapter takes a leap back in time and, echoing the reference to the *Arabian Nights* made in the opening part, proposes that the notion of storytelling as a therapeutic process can be traced back to the fairy tale tradition. This can be attributed, on one level, to the fantastic character of the stories in question, their disregard for the laws of physics and logic, and their penchant for drawing the reader or listener into a domain that enables her/him to reconfigure experience in the image of atavistic desires. To this extent, fairy tales would seem to confirm Freud's argument by supplying compensatory frameworks for both their characters and their readers. On another level, the narration of fairy tales constitutes a kind of therapy insofar as it allows the narrator to couch cultural terrors and horrors, both inveterate and contingent, in allegorical terms and hence vocalize preoccupations that might seem unendurable if expressed literally but become palatable once they are articulated through an entertaining medium. Yet, making critical issues tolerable is not tantamount to resolving them: many traditional tales foreground the idea that the most troublesome concerns tend to be insoluble or else amenable to merely temporary resolution. In this respect, fairy tales depart from the Freudian schema by drawing attention to unresolved tensions and crises which the ego cannot presume to survive totally unscathed.

According to Marina Warner, 'Fairy tale offers a case where the very contempt for women opened an opportunity for them to exercise their wit and communicate their ideas' (1995:xix). Of course, storytelling is not 'an exclusively female activity' (21). Indeed, there is plenty of evidence that evening gatherings whose participants shared news, gossip and stories, often while performing household tasks such as spinning, weaving and mending, were an important feature of early modern cultures, at least since the sixteenth century, for members of both genders. If it is in the case of women that the therapeutic dimension gains special significance, this is because narration allowed them to comment, more or less elliptically, on the realities of motherhood, a mother's or a stepmother's relations to husbands and children, domestic labour, social oppression and other cognate issues.

Furthermore, the connection between women and storytelling as a means of self-expression is pregnant with ideological implications since it is not the narrative voice generally but the *female voice* specifically that has repeatedly come under attack over the centuries. It could be argued that it is largely as a result of the recognition that storytelling entails salutary potentialities likely to benefit silenced individuals that women's tongues have been persistently demonized. According to Warner, this is borne out by the gradual deterioration of the semantic import of *gossip*, a term that has shifted from signifying a 'godmother or -father' (eleventh century) to denoting a female friend 'invited by a woman to the christening of her child' (fourteenth century) and, further down the line, to meaning, in an explicitly derogatory fashion, 'a person, mostly a woman, especially one who delights in idle talk; a newsmonger, a tattler' (33). This pejorative definition became established in the sixteenth century. Gossip, at this point, emplaces itself linguistically and ideologically as the label for 'a woman's derided instrument of self-assertion' (xix). The satanization of gossip, based on the idea that female speech is not only pointlessly garrulous but also tainted by Eve's tongue-inspired sin, points to a political agenda intent on devaluing women's narratorial authority, thereby depriving the act of storytelling of its positive connotations as a healing instrument. Concurrently, it casts a sinister shadow on the character of the traditional narrator: the proverbial old woman who is acceptable insofar as the young are allowed to visit her and listen to her tales but also marginalized by being placed on the outskirts of the village. There are even intimations that the ancient teller may have the power to seduce children into entertaining illicit fantasies. This type lies behind the characterization of the granny in *Little Red*

Riding Hood and her symbolic equation to the sexually predatory wolf. Thus, it is imperative to realize that the curative powers of narration have been resisted and ostracized no less than they have been celebrated. It is in the light of this ambiguous legacy that dark fiction goes on articulating its own variations on the theme of storytelling as therapy. (Fairy tales are also discussed in **Chapters 5** and **6**, and in the Introduction to **Part 4**, with an emphasis on their contribution to the socialization of the young.)

Storytelling is a means of structuring and publicly articulating inveterate human fears and its principal aim, be it consciously recognized or instinctively sensed, is to provide arenas wherein an otherwise intractable Beyond may be grappled with. If narration is a form of therapy, this is not merely because of its usefulness as a vehicle for articulating the traumatic experiences of individual authors. More importantly, storytelling is salutary insofar as it reminds us that it is in the production and sharing of fictions, especially those that represent symbolically the ubiquity of fear in both the phenomenal world and its imaginary variations, that humans might begin to accept the omnipresence of darkness in their daily lives rather than opt for the ostrich approach to crisis management. Just as the tales woven by patients in order to establish or restore a sense of selfhood in the face of radical infringements of their identities would seem quite meaningless were they not grounded in suffering, so dark texts only rise above the status of ephemerally escapist dreams to the extent that they are able to posit pain as the substratum of consciousness. The forms which such texts impart upon traumatic experiences vary hugely over time and space, ranging from the representation of what could be considered no more than a mildly aggravating affliction to the portrayal of life-shattering calamities. The degree of distress depicted by the narrative and the intensity of the fear induced by such suffering are important factors. More significant still, however, are the urge to fashion sickness and grief into stories and the willingness to recognize that whilst no one text will ever manage to encompass the complexity of those phenomena, refraining from storytelling would amount to a selfish act of repression. Indeed, as the narrator of Anne Rice's *Vittorio, The Vampire* observes, even if we are not eminent artists, we have not merely the right but also something of an obligation to convey to others our perception of pain, our apprehension of fear:

> I am not saying I am a great painter. I am not such a fool. But I say that out of
> my pain, out of my folly, out of my passion there comes a vision – a vision
> which I carry with me eternally and which I offer you. It is a vision of every
> human being, bursting with fire and with mystery, a vision I cannot deny nor
> blot out, nor ever turn away from, nor ever belittle nor ever escape. (2000:338)

— Part 4 —
Child and Adult

Introduction

'. . . Ugh, Serpent!'

'But I'm *not* a serpent, I tell you!' said Alice. 'I'm a – I'm a – '

'Well, *What* are you?' said the Pigeon. 'I can see you're trying to invent something!'

'I – I'm a little girl,' said Alice, rather doubtfully, as she remembered the number of changes she had gone through that day.

'A likely story indeed!' said the Pigeon in a tone of the deepest contempt.

(Lewis Carroll, *Alice in Wonderland*)

Narratives of darkness tend to construct the child as an ambivalent creature. On the one hand, children are associated with innocence, simplicity and lack of worldly experience. In the Romantic ethos, in particular, they are often ideated as exemplary beings, unsullied by the murky deviousness of socialized existence. On the other hand, precisely because children are not yet fully encultured, they are frequently perceived as a threat to the fabric of adult society: they retain a connection with a primordial and inchoate world that does not respect rigid codes and fixed patterns of meaning. The latent sense of menace associated with childhood as a realm of undifferentiation is reinforced by the Freudian notion that children's sexuality is polymorphously perverse and hence likely to transgress the dominant sexual mores. Recently, an even more sinister light has been cast upon child sexuality by intimations that nearly 50 per cent of the sexual abuse suffered by children is inflicted by other children. This makes them into little monsters and fuels the desire to codify the rules for proper sexual behaviour amongst the very young.

It could be argued, however, that the demonic child is an ideological construct resulting from the tendency, widespread in Western culture, to simultaneously idealize and deprive the younger generations. According to Marina Warner, contemporary society 'loves children' in hypocritical ways,

by stimulating their desires, by exploiting their vulnerability and suggestibil-
ity, by finding them irresistibly cute, by staging, in any number of
advertisements, films and infant beauty pageants, the performance of their
seduction. Yet, at the same time, material measures taken to improve children's
lives – their play, their care, their education, their health, their nutrition, their
prospects – remain paper promises. (2000:386)

It would be quite preposterous, in this scenario, to conceive of the child as a
figure of light. If human beings of all ages feel impelled to protect and even
secrete facets of their existence which they deem private from inquisitive eyes,
this is pointedly the case with children due to the greater vulnerability of their
physical and psychological territories to intrusion and violation. As the
narrator of Peter Høeg's *Miss Smilla's Feeling for Snow* observes,

> There's a widespread notion that children are open, that the truth about their
> inner selves just seeps out of them. That's all wrong. No one is more covert
> than a child, and no one has greater cause to be that way. It's a response to a
> world that's always using a tin-opener on them to see what they have inside,
> just in case it ought to be replaced with a more useful type of tinned foodstuff.
> (1994:44)

Numerous strategies have been deployed by diverse cultures in order to
socialize children. The codification of play and the institution of a canon of
didactic fairy tales are two of the most significant. Play is often considered a
vital part of the process through which children develop into adults through
the understanding and application of rules within given parameters. According
to D. W. Winnicott, for example, 'play and playing . . . form the basis of cultural
experience in general' (Winnicott *et al.* 1989:205). Moreover, as Lucie Armitt
observes, play does not constitute a free and utterly spontaneous activity since
it is at all times 'determined by an implied prohibition that says it may only
take place within certain temporal and spatial constraints (between but not
within lessons, and within the playground not the classroom)' (1996:4). Concurrently, play is implicated in 'a prohibitive structure held in place by firm,
territorial demarcations', as testified by terms such as 'playground' and 'play-
pen' (6). Furthermore, it often aims at moulding the child in the image of the
adult 'as owner, as user' (Barthes 1973:60), which suggests that it is a product
of adult fantasies no less than it is the child's prerogative. Particularly, grown-
ups often construe it as a form of regression to a time and place preceding
ethical, sexual and economic responsibilities attached to maturity. Nevertheless, it is hard to quantify what adults really know or remember about such
circumstances and there are reasons to suspect that it may not amount to
much. Indeed, their indulgence in mythologized conceptions of play as a carni-

valesque, unrestrained and infinitely protean practice are radically contested by the reality of children's games with their restrictions and often monotonous repetitiveness.

However, play is not merely a means of either disciplining the young or allowing adults to seek gratification in edenic dreams. In other words, it is not a monolithically regulatory discourse, for it is also capable of challenging adult principles of sense and purpose by virtue of autotelic proclivities that implicitly undermine its functional objectives. Echoing Martin Heidegger, Allen Thiher (1987:159) observes that a child plays, ultimately, just in order to play. Moreover, to paraphrase James Joyce, children may as well play as not: the ogre will come in any case. According to Gregory Bateson, the ambivalent character of play adumbrated by such positions is one of its most beneficial, creative and revitalizing attributes:

> play and its paradoxes . . . prevent the organism from being trapped within one
> set of interpretive procedures . . . Without these paradoxes the evolution of
> communication would be at an end. Life would then be an endless interchange
> of stylized messages, a game with rigid rules, unrelieved by change or humour.
> (1972:193)

There is something simultaneously tantalizing and disturbing about play's propensity to subvert existing structures of meaning through its imaginative manipulation of symbolic signs since it intimates that no system is unproblematically stable.

The unsettling connotations of play are thrown into relief by the ambiguous status of anthropomorphic toys, especially dolls, which combine the attributes of innocent and timeless beauty with darker qualities related to their artificiality, their utilization by black magic and their representation of humanity as a gallery of more or less grotesque dummies. After all, dolls only came to be regarded as playthings relatively recently, most probably in the nineteenth century. Traditionally, they were objects to be taken quite seriously – as fetishes, religious icons and images endowed with metaphysical properties. Moreover, the sadistic victimization of children presented by many narratives of darkness (an issue examined in detail in **Chapter 11**) has an ominous correlative in children's own often ferocious treatment of dolls. This is documented, for example, by Dea Birkett's account of her handling of one of the most iconic dolls ever designed: 'As a child, I liked to torture Barbie. . . . I enjoyed doing damage to Barbie . . . I wanted to deconstruct her' (1998:13). The designer Diego Fortunato, for his part, keeps his Barbie in the freezer of his Barcelona home (Carro 1999:129). If it is the case that play is a vital way of learning how to become an adult, and that having a charge, in particular, prepares kids for the task of caring, there is something more than just a trifle chilling about this whole picture.

Let us next consider the function of fairy tales in the socialization of the young. Those stories, regardless of their more or less overtly dark themes and images, are implicated in hegemonic programmes that often aim at consolidating the status quo by prescribing standards of exemplary conduct for children and, by extension, for the adults into which they are expected to grow. Jack Zipes has persuasively demonstrated the sociopolitical significance of the fairy tale discourse by arguing that although the stories have become enshrined in cultural history as 'universal, ageless, therapeutic, miraculous, and beautiful' (1991:1), they are actually entangled with contingent ideological agendas. In their complex metamorphoses, the narratives have proved immensely resilient in adapting themselves to the requirements of specific contexts and their ethical priorities. The momentous role of fairy tales in the enculturement of the young began to assert itself in seventeenth-century France, a society in which both the traditional aristocracy and the emerging bourgeoisie had a vested interest in inculcating the imperative of self-control and the importance of curbing natural instincts. Significantly, the socialization of children goes hand in hand with the domestication of the darker aspects of the traditional stories from which modern fairy tales stem. This entails a transformation of 'the crude peasant tales' into a '"civilized" literary form' (Teaching gender roles:website). Charles Perrault's *Histoires ou contes du temps passé* [1697] epitomize this trend: here, folk materials have been edited not only by excising their murkiest elements but also by commending the ideal of self-discipline in explicitly gender-inflected terms: 'Gone are the blood, gore and rape of the traditional folk tales . . . Gone as well are all semblances to a strong and resourceful female character. In the perfect universe constructed by Perrault's pen, the women are inevitably beautiful, industrious, obedient, passive, meek, dependent, silent and nameless' (Female roles in the fairy tales of Charles Perrault:website). Fairy tales thus prescribe different roles for boys and girls, the 'female locked in a tower for a hundred years' finding a counterpart in the male expected to 'battle dragons and trick his opponent' (The psychology of sexuality in fairy tales:website). Such roles are further problematized by the fact that the tales often rely on double-bind mentalities. In several stories based on the Beauty-and-the-Beast theme, for example, the Beast symbolizes both animal urges to be eradicated from the young and the forces of male reason to which Beauty must yield if she is to overcome her own desire for physical gratification. However, fairy tales are ultimately comparable, for both sexes, to 'initiation ceremonies' concerned with 'killing the infantile ego' (Campbell 1988:168). Males and females alike are locked in the ideological obligation to secure 'the harmonious existence of family and society at large' through marriage as the means of purging girls and boys of potentially unruly sexual drives (Seifert 1996:109). (The connection between the regimenting of children and gender relations is discussed in **Chapter 10**, with an emphasis on the analogy between the persecuted child and the dis-possessed Gothic heroine.)

Narratives of darkness respond to the child's menace in three main ways: they engulf children into varyingly oppressive family structures; they ostracize children by abandoning them to a rootless condition; they associate children with enslaved people. (This theme is addressed in **Chapter 12.**) In all three cases, the child becomes a scapegoat, callously delivered into perilous situa-tions, sacrificed so that the sins of adult society may be redeemed and its so-called certainties may be allowed to thrive unabated. Eduardo Sanchez and Dan Myrick's film *The Blair Witch Project* (1999) is a good example of the tendency to let children wander off into a Beyond from which they cannot protect themselves and from which adults have no intention of protecting them. Wes Craven, himself the casualty of a strict Baptist upbringing, associ-ates darkness with the abuse of parental power: Freddie Krueger is 'the ultimate bad father'. As Suzie Mackenzie points out in her commentary on Craven's views, 'we use our kids to uncover uncomfortable truths that we don't dare to look at ourselves'. However, while many children of darkness are destroyed by their parents, literal or metaphorical, many others succeed in conveying a basic lesson: their ability to live and interact with the unnameable while their adult counterparts blunder by striving to explain and contain it. For Craven, children are capable of undermining paradigm authority figures because they know that 'the nightmare is real' and 'are much more prepared to confront these issues than adults' (1999:16).

The abused, immolated or alienated kids of dark fiction could be regarded as Morality Play characters whose ordeals serve cautionary agendas by intimating that a baleful fate lies in store for anyone ill-disposed to conform to the requirements of the adult world. Yet, as long as the young retain a connection with play, especially in its autotelic guise, and thus invite the older generations to cultivate that link for themselves, disciplinary measures will remain only partially effective. This is because play, despite its enculturing function, ulti-mately defies ideological closure by paradoxically bracketing pleasure and fear together. According to Warner, this is attested to by children's propensity to 'make fun of intimidation, and turn its threats hollow', nourished by an osten-sibly instinctive tendency 'to play the bogeyman and scare themselves into fits. The pretence appears to match the observed pleasure in fright that children take: it defies fear at the very same moment as conjuring it. It exemplifies a defensive response that is frequently adopted in real experience: internalizing the aggressor in order to stave off the terror he brings' (2000:168–9).

If the Janus-faced character of games can benefit children, it is feasible that it will also sustain adults. Narratives of darkness inspired by a Gothic vision represent a metaphorical variation on the play model, with its coalescence of dread and delight, through which socialized grown-ups may be encouraged to capitalize on evocations of fear as simultaneous sources of anxiety and illumination. The adult presented with a frightening narrative may find it entertaining and hence be able to introject its disquieting import. Introjection will not automatically be conducive to the attainment of a sense of power, if what is meant by power is the vanquishing of the other by an oligarchic self. It might, nonetheless, lead to an understanding of mastery as a corollary of self-dispossession and of the inevitability of our coexistence with forces that relentlessly threaten our plans.

—10—

𝔉amilie𝔰

𝕿HE THESIS THAT REPRESENTATIONS OF FEAR articulate both singular and communal concerns is strikingly brought home by tales that explore darkness with reference to familial structures wherein members of different generations can be regarded simultaneously as individuals persecuted by private anxieties and as incarnations of collective mentalities haunted by cultural ghosts. The themes of the cursed family, ancestral rivalries and legal vicissitudes pervade Gothic fiction. They are the lenses through which the abiding fears of individuals and groups, subject to the often ungenerous demands of socialization, may be explored. In many classic Gothic novels, the family is portrayed as a dominant and intractable system. Horace Walpole, Ann Radcliffe, William Beckford, Matthew Lewis and their con-temporaries were among the first to foreground the corruption and deceit upon which traditional dynasties nefariously relied for the perpetuation of their specious prerogatives. Uncannily, the sickness of families addicted to the main-tenance of their inviolable status is no less prominent a theme in contemporary dark literature than it was in the eighteenth century. One example is William Gibson's depiction, in *Mona Lisa Overdrive* [1988], of cyberaristocrats who, with the benefit of biotechnology and orbital displacement, go on making the same old claims to the excellence of their 'labyrinth of blood' (1995:133). The families depicted by many narratives of darkness – classic, modern and contemporary – are invariably nests of vipers. Moreover, the serpentine genealogies presented by various texts abound with instances of transgenerational haunting. (See also **Chapter 7** for an evaluation of this phenomenon.) Family secrets are passed on unknowingly to children by both blood relatives and figuratively parental cultural structures. The children, in turn, are not conscious that this is the case. Such encrypted secrets come to form volume upon volume of an unspoken history counterpointed by the theme of infantile sacrifice.

Although narratives of darkness, in making the child the emblematic victim of familial crimes and deceptions, may appear to suggest that the family is an all-powerful conglomerate, they also consistently present it as vulnerable to alien intrusions that threaten to rescind its authority at a moment's notice. The penetration of the familial space by disruptive forces has asserted itself as a familiar topos of suspense and horror cinema over the past few decades. Stanley Kubrick's *The Shining* (1980), Martin Scorsese's *Cape Fear* (1991) and Peter Hanson's *The Hand That Rocks the Cradle* (1992) constitute some emblematic cases. Arguably, families, like nations, would not need to resort to strategies of victimization if they were stable structures confident about their power and legitimacy. If the archetypal Gothic family's main casualties are frequently children, this is because it is around children that the pressing issue of legitimacy pivots. Gothic ancestries abound with illegitimate children and accordingly unlawful claims to power, with semi-legitimate or even legitimate, yet deviant, young members, and with aberrant acquired relations, often young wives, likely to plant in their midst the seeds of discord and eventual catastrophe. As Anne Williams has shown, the Gothic discourse itself has been critically categorized by recourse to familial metaphors. First, it has been branded as an illegitimate offspring, relegated to the status of 'a skeleton in the closet' (1995:2) by the Leavisite canon. Second, it has been dismissed as a 'black sheep' throwing the spanner into the works of High Romanticism by failing to engage with profound philosophical and ethical issues. Third, it has been equated to a 'madwoman' (8) contaminating the patriarchal home and the House of Fiction alike.

It is noteworthy, however, that the Gothic family's favourite victims are not always actual children. Often they are young women who, although they are no longer children in a literal sense, are treated as such by patriarchal power structures. This draws attention to the fact that the treatment of the family is virtually inseparable from the exploration of gender politics. At the time when Gothic novels were enjoying maximum popularity, the bourgeois commitment to an architectural code of comfort, privacy and control tended to go hand in hand with the advancement of a philosophy of domesticity which pivoted on the feminization of space – the relegation of woman to the walled-in realm of the home, hypocritically dubbed as a celebration of woman's maternal and matrimonial authority. Woman's confinement infantilized her. Ironically, while the aristocratic, barbarian Gothic is supposed to embody women's oppression by presenting its female characters as captives of aristocratic male persecutors, it is the bourgeois home itself that does its best to devalue women by confining them to the claustrophobic environment of supposedly civilized housing. Arguably, Gothic fiction is neither an attack on the evils of archaic feudal buildings nor a celebration, by implication, of bourgeois architecture and ideology. Rather, it could be said to comment, in a displaced fashion, on the perpetuation by new regimes of the infamies of the old. According to Avril Horner, 'The heroine's attempts to escape [from the Gothic prison] indicate a desire to subvert a domestic ideology which was beginning to tyrannize the lives of middle-class women within a capitalist, newly-industrialized society; in such a society the bourgeois home was becoming uncomfortably like the castle or prison of the Gothic text in the way it constrained its female inhabitants' (1998:116–17). Actual children and women weakened by their infantilization are the archetypal victims of the Gothic building and of its villainous master but they are also victimized by the middle-class residence. Ultimately, they seem to have no choice but to come to terms with the walls that encircle them, to learn to negotiate the crimes and traumas they secrete, while also making the most of those weak spots where the stone unexpectedly yields or shifts to reveal concealed passages or openings. The pages that follow examine a few illustrative examples of familial oppression revolving around the disenfranchisement of young and female characters and, subsequently, the collusion of this theme with architectural symbolism.

The theme of filial deprivation plays a conspicuous role in Horace Walpole's *The Castle of Otranto* [1764], where the young labour vainly against fate within a framework of domestic perverseness and misappropriated power. (See also **Chapter 1**.) The romantic dimension does not provide any authentic relief because it is unremittingly undermined by the concern of vicious parents with the transmission of property and titles. The Matilda–Theodore–Isabella triangle does not yield a rosy picture of innocent love but rather demonstrates that youthful passions and attachments are inexorably benighted by adult intrigues. What is most disturbing about this child–adult dynamic is that even benevolent parents often prove instrumental to their offspring's extreme afflictions. This is further corroborated by Ann Radcliffe's *The Mysteries of Udolpho* [1794], where Emily is simultaneously strengthened and crippled by her father St Aubert's ethical teachings. Indeed, her unquestioning respect for the deceased parent verges on masochism as, in submitting to his order to destroy certain documents, she renounces the right to solve the mystery that haunts her entire existence.

The frequent conflation of children and heroines as likely candidates for persecution is partly a corollary to the ambiguous handling of gender relations evinced by the Gothic vision. Corrupt patriarchs are most often the principal villains in Gothic families hell-bent on the repression and exploitation of the young. However, mothers, both biological and adoptive, insistently prove as obnoxious as the patriarchs themselves. The Grimms' *Snowdrop* [1810–12], a classic narrative of darkness informed by Gothic motifs, exemplifies this idea by demonstrating that totalitarian dispensations based on spurious claims to legitimacy use rivalries between women as self-perpetuating ruses. By extension, the female child and femininity itself come to be associated with evil as both the perpetrators and the victims of extreme atrocities. Furthermore, as Sandra Gilbert and Susan Gubar argue, the tale articulates the theme of conflict between 'mother and daughter, woman and woman' around the image of the 'mirror' as a symbol of entrapment that 'frames' the wicked Queen, compelling her 'to be driven inward, obsessively studying self-images as if seeking a viable self' (1984:36–44). In the Grimms' story, the mirror carries ambivalent connotations by operating as a metaphorical door to an alternative realm on the one hand, and by imprisoning the subject in the cage of her own narcissism on the other. This ambivalence echoes the Lacanian concept of the mirror stage, where the infant jubilantly identifies with a coherent and autonomous specular image, by far preferable to its uncoordinated body, and is thus caught in a circuit of misrecognition and self-division (Lacan 1977). *Snowdrop* vividly dramatizes this condition by presenting the Queen's specular image as an illusory self and by ultimately making the image projected by the mirror literally and devastatingly alien. The fact that the threatening reflection takes the semblance of the abhorred stepdaughter suggests that although the Queen may deem herself safe once the flesh-and-bone child has been abandoned to a dire destiny, the child, like the repressed, is nonetheless capable of resurging in virtual form. In beholding the child's countenance where she would expect to find her own the Queen is figuratively infantilized since, on the symbolic level, her aim was not only to annihilate a potential rival but also to transcend her own childhood, with its connotations of weakness and dependence, and to assert her uncontested authority. Snowdrop's specular appearance acts as a disquieting reminder that such an ambition is patently incompatible with the patriarchal system in which she is inscribed. The tale intimates that at the same time as dark families thrive on the oppression of the literally young, they concurrently endeavour to disqualify adult members considered illegitimate and unfit to rule by demoting them to a childlike status.

Fairy tales often aim to inculcate into the child principles of exemplary behaviour by recourse to submissive and self-abnegating heroines. (See also **Chapter 5** and the Introduction to **Part 4**.) In much Gothic fiction, the collusion of childhood and femininity is reinforced through the positing of analogies between the vulnerability of the young and the helplessness of female characters persecuted by patriarchal authority. Arthur Hughes's *Ophelia* (1852) epitomizes this idea visually through its representation of the doomed Shakespearean heroine as a pubescent girl crowned with green reeds, watching the drifting of the petals she distractedly drops into the stagnant water as a premonition of her impending fate. Immersed in an eerie setting, the childlike figure stands out as an icon of physical and mental sickness whose psychological anguish and even insanity are graphically echoed by her emaciation. In this respect, the painting reflects the Victorian stereotype of woman-as-child, an ideal that aptly encapsulates male notions of female dependence and, at the same time, the cult of invalidism, whereby an infantile woman's surrender to illness constitutes the final form of self-obliteration and evidence for her self-sacrificial proclivities. These are supposed to symbolize both her virtue and her inferiority, just as obedience in the socialized child signifies at once propriety and subjugation to the adult world. In classic manifestations of the Gothic vision, passivity in both women and children is frequently construed as an index of purity, self-restraint and the sublimation of sexual impulses, which serve to confirm the adult male's right to indisputable dominance. Concurrently, passivity is supposed to demonstrate children's and women's lowly status in the chain of being. The late nineteenth-century evolutionist ethos, specifically makes infantilism and femininity interchangeable as likewise base and feeble-minded categories. As Bram Dijkstra points out with reference to Charles Darwin's *The Descent of Man*, evolutionism as preached by several anthropologists and psychologists stressed that 'a mother and her children were essentially coextensive and formed a "primitive and natural unity"' (1986:173).

In twentieth-century narratives of darkness, the topos of filial dispossession plays no less prominent a role than it does in classic Gothic novels. Anne Rice, for example, repeatedly portrays vampires as rejected children par excellence: rootless beings painfully incapable of communicating with the one creature they are, in principle, most intimately bound up with – their maker. Indeed, while vampires are generally able to read one another's and mortals' thoughts, makers and fledglings cannot access each other's minds due to their very closeness: they are 'divided by intimate blood' (1998:9). It is this unresolved tension between feelings of intimacy and alienation, compounded with the conflict between the need for love and the aversion to companionship, that insistently draws Rice's vampires into a vain search for origins. When Amadeo/Armand pathetically declares to Marius 'We must come from somewhere' (222), or Louis reaches out for Armand 'seeking so sadly the answers to the terrible questions of why we are here, and for what purpose' (269), what these creatures are attempting to find is a genealogy, a mythical family that may grant them a sense of belonging. The theme of infantile victimization is most overtly typified by the ordeals of a literal child-vampire, Claudia. In the version of her misadventures presented in *Interview with the Vampire* [1976], Claudia is subject to a twofold punishment: she is trapped forever in a doll-like body when what she most desires is the shape of a fully grown woman, and she is destroyed by forced exposure to the sun in retaliation for her attempted murder of her metaphorical father, Lestat. In *The Vampire Armand*, Claudia's plight is given a more sinister twist still through disturbing references to Armand's manipulation of her body by means of 'Satanic surgery' that instantly brings to mind Frankenstein's Promethean enterprise. Whereas in previous accounts of the child-vampire's experiences, she never abandons her childlike body, in Armand's rendition an alternative story comes to light: 'I tried to grant her fondest wish, that she should have the body of a woman, a fit shape for the tragic dimension of her soul. Well, in my clumsy alchemy, slicing heads from bodies and stumbling to transplant one from another, I failed', the result being a 'writhing jerking catastrophe' (1998:271). (Anne Rice is also discussed in **Chapters 1** and **13**.)

The pervasive mood of filial deprivation evoked by Rice's *Vampire Chronicles* is also a salient aspect of Poppy Z. Brite's own treatment of vampirism. In *Lost Souls* [1992], the child Nothing, the biological offspring of the male vampire Zillah and the mortal female Jessy, is vampirized by Zillah and willingly subjects himself to multifarious forms of physical and emotional violation in order to belong to a family of sorts. Nothing resents Zillah's exploitative conduct: 'You don't treat me like your son,' he complains, 'you treat me like I'm half sex slave and half lapdog . . . you never explain anything to me. What kind of a father are you, anyway?' (1994a:288). Yet, he is willing to live in the tormenting awareness of self-degradation if this can yield at least an illusion of filial and parental companionship: Nothing

> told himself: *For a week now you have been fucking your own father. His tongue has been in your mouth more times than you could count. You've sucked him off . . . you've swallowed stuff that could have been your brothers and sisters!* But he could not disgust himself . . . He knew that now Zillah would not leave him, would not abandon him . . . And he would never have to be alone. (232–3)

When Zillah is finally killed, a victim of his own greed and megalomania, and Nothing is once again forsaken by an irresponsible parent, he still pitiably consoles himself by speculating that 'his father had loved him in his way. In the way of decadence and self-gratification' (347). Brite concurrently elaborates the Gothic interweaving of the theme of the dispossessed child and that of the abused female by intimating that the despotic and proprietorial proclivities exhibited by preternatural fathers like Zillah are also widespread among natural fathers. Both Jessy and Anne, eventually destroyed by Zillah's selfish lust, are in the first place dominated by possessive patriarchs. Anne's father Simon, in particular, controls his daughter's life by systematically aborting her plans for development and self-fulfilment, largely by recourse to an intrusive rhetoric in the face of which she feels 'as if she were trying to wind up earthworms on a spoon' or 'drive a nail through a blob of mercury' (260). A similar case is presented by James Herbert's *The Fog*, where Casey's father, 'by overcompensating for the lack of his wife', has 'tied the daughter almost irrevocably to him' (1975:34). Although Anne's and Casey's fathers are not literally, or at least explicitly, incestuous, the pathological intensity of their attachments to their female children symbolically carries connotations of not exclusively psychological abuse. (Poppy Z. Brite is also discussed in **Chapters 1, 3** and **13**.)

Moving on to consider the utilization of architectural motifs, we find that in the realm of Gothicity, the family and its dwelling are often coterminous. (See also **Chapters 1** and **6.**) Familial sins, passions and sorrows are projected onto the body of the house. Gaston Bachelard's reflections on the affective properties of space are particularly useful, in this respect. He argues that the home is the point of departure for our negotiations between the inner realm and the circumambient universe. The parental residence may seem safe and comforting in comparison with the mysterious outside but its protective enclosures tend to breed not so much security as anxiety, since they emphatically assert the outside world's irreducible alterity. Thus, although we may 'feel calmer and more confident when in the old home, in the house we are born in' (1994:43), it is in the very heart of this ostensibly invulnerable environment that we become increasingly likely to perceive the external world as a malicious enemy eager to penetrate our nest and hence develop our deepest and most abiding preoccupations. Fears revolving around images of confinement, of exclusion, of abandonment and of invasion meet and merge in a tangled psychodrama of which the parental abode is the characteristic stage set. The home's ambiguous role is thrown into relief by narratives of darkness where the familial dwelling's aura of security is not merely punctured by its propensity to conjure up a menacing outside but is also rendered ominous by its coexistence with evil forces of an internecine nature. Realizing that their spaces are polluted from within, the inhabitants of dark homes are forced to confront the precariousness of all enclosures and, consequently, of any form of safety supposedly granted by them. Moreover, as Kate Ferguson Ellis stresses, 'the literary use of the home as a place of security and concord' is unremittingly overtaken by images of the family dwelling 'as a place of danger and imprisonment' (1989:x).

The Gothic vision emphasizes that family mansions are fundamentally ideological constructs designed to both embody and protect the status, authority and secrets of privileged, albeit frequently illegitimate, individuals. Towers are often presented as the supreme icon of power, to the point that their symbolic import surpasses their practical function and their ability to overawe the beholder gains priority over their defensive utility. (Tower symbolism is examined in **Chapter 1** in relation to William Beckford.) The primacy of architectural symbolism over function is further demonstrated by the fact that eighteenth-century patrician families often shunned the grandly solitary castles and country mansions with which Gothic fiction tends to associate them in search for the mundane pleasures and gregariousness of the city. Image and conduct are not, therefore, automatically coextensive. Architectural symbolism, in the context of Gothicity, also serves political purposes on the national level. Indeed, the cultivation of neo-Gothic styles in the eighteenth century stems largely from a desire to counteract the Palladian style imported from Italy in the wake of the Renaissance and thus celebrate a specifically English aesthetic. The taste for mediaeval ruins and buildings inspired by the feudal past is itself motivated by the yearning to revive and assert a national ancestry.

It is also worth observing that the intimate interrelation of dynastic and architectural themes does not feature exclusively in the domain of fiction. It is also grounded in social reality. For example, an historical illustration of the collusion of family politics, Gothic architecture and the abuse of the young is provided by the Gothic Revival castle of Mitchelstown in County Cork. Its owners, the Kingsboroughs/Kingstons could indeed be regarded as incarnations of stereotypical Gothic villains whose spurious claims to power are interwoven with a sordid hankering to control children's destinies and crudely violate defenceless young girls. The darkness of their political and sexual pursuits is appropriately mirrored by the family residence. Worthy of consideration for immediate purchase by any self-respecting ogre, Mitchelstown Castle exhibits all the features traditionally associated with forbidding Gothic buildings: disconcerting size, unrelieved desolation, severe gloom, damp and deep solitude, and a spooky labyrinth of subterranean caves.

A classic example of the interweaving of a Gothic family and Gothic architecture centred on the predicament of a child is supplied by Mervyn Peake's *Gormenghast Trilogy* [1946–59]. Moreover, the body of the narrative itself, with its profusion of eccentric characters and intricate subplots, mirrors the complexity of both familial and architectural structures. The adventures of the seventy-seventh Earl of the dynasty of Groan, Titus, whose right to the inheritance of Gormenghast Castle is challenged by the devious kitchen boy Steerpike, are inextricable from the sprawling geography of the decrepit castle itself – an embodiment of Gothic excess conveyed by the proliferation of ruins resistant to rational mapping. As the young Earl's vicissitudes unfold, in a meandering fashion, through an ever-growing accretion of complications and threats, their setting evinces analogous traits as a 'circumfusion' of quadrangles, cloisters, stairwells and dungeons stretching for mile upon mile of stone and mortar. Considerable emphasis is placed on the effects of temporal deterioration: upon the 'irregular roofs' of Gormenghast's buildings invariably fall 'the shadows of time-eaten buttresses, of broken and lofty turrets' (1992:7). The erosion of an imposing architectural structure alludes symbolically to the young generation's subjugation to cobwebbed, decaying systems reliant, for their perpetuation, on the obsessive enactment of ancient and macabre rituals. Indeed, Titus is described as 'Heir to a crumbling summit: to a sea of nettles: to an empire of red dust: to rituals' footprints ankle-deep in stone' (373). At the end of the third novel, *Titus Alone*, the hero leaves the ancestral home. This is partly a triumph marking Titus's escape 'from Ritual' and its commitment to the preservation of a seemingly immutable power; yet, it is also something of a defeat attended by a painful sense of 'separation' (761). Titus may have cause to rejoice in the discovery that he has 'no longer any need for home' (953) as indicative of a newly found autonomy. However, by fleeing Gormenghast's suffocating stasis and preposterous grotesqueries, and entering a larger world that is potentially even more baffling and bizarre than his birthplace, he also pathetically relinquishes any viable aspiration to belong anywhere. Titus is haunted by dynastic pressures as long as he remains in the castle and bereft of parental models when he eventually flees.

Loneliness is thus writ large over Peake's character as the fate which the Gothic vision insistently reserves for children and, more often than not, for the adults into whom they are doomed to grow. Solitude is indeed a primary ingredient of the experience of fear as an ongoing condition that obstinately haunts us as we relentlessly, and often blindly, crawl from the babble of infancy to the babble of senility. Even narratives of darkness that seem to offer relatively compensatory or reparative endings ultimately cannot and will not exorcize the knowledge of certain loneliness any more than they could or would ever obliterate the knowledge of certain death.

—11—

The Abandoned Child

N THE AGE OF REASON, children were by and large dismissed as undeveloped adults, as irrational and only randomly sentient beings. Romanticism rehabilitated childhood as a time of metaphysical wisdom superior to the worldly knowledge available to the socialized self. However, the Romantics themselves were eager to point out that the blessings of early life are transient and that adaptation to the demands of adult society is an inevitable fate. The Victorian era promoted different interpretations of childhood. On the one hand, the young were associated with innocence and goodness. On the other, they were deemed to be intrinsically soiled by the original sin, and consequently requiring submission to often drastic disciplinary measures designed to humanize them. The Victorian approach has played a crucial role in advancing the notion of the child as a potentially innocent yet incomplete creature, an entity in need of enculturement. That same approach has also contributed to the growth of the theme of the abandoned child. Western culture abounds with harrowing intimations of a conviction that if the young cannot be comprehensively socialized and thus impelled to leave their childhood behind, the only viable alternative is to forsake them, on the basis of a flawed presocial and latently antisocial identity that stigmatizes them beyond redemption.

It is noteworthy, however, that when adults claim to own children and to be able to control them, they implicitly voice their own longing for unattainable gardens – the Garden of Eden, the Hanging Gardens of Babylon, Alice's Garden in Wonderland. What makes the recovery of such imaginary sites impossible is the fact that they are aesthetically and, by extension, ethically incompatible with the mores of encultured adulthood. In embodying the spirit of the sublime rather than the beautiful, they are effervescently chaotic and therefore in excess of anything which adult society may be willing to countenance. Arguably, the image of the abandoned child recurs so obstinately in narratives of darkness because it symbolizes what adults have to keep on repressing in order to hold themselves together. Children are rejected, more or less explicitly, as a means of stressing the adult world's ability to disavow its own inherent and still alluring infancy. However, although the retrieval of idyllic worlds (which have plausibly never existed except in the imagination), is an impossibility on the practical plane, those realms may nonetheless be conjured up and enjoyed through the medium of narrative, especially fantastic texts. As Sarah Gilead argues, the fictional evocation of idealized situations linked to a mythical notion of preadult freedom proceeds precisely from the desire to 'recuperate' the 'lost wholeness and stability of an imagined (and largely imaginary) past'(1991:288).

Among the philosophical and ideological explanations most frequently proffered in order to justify the desertion of children, particularly prominent is the notion that children are somehow tainted by their proximity to prenatal darkness and, by implication, primordial chaos. No less widespread is the belief that the young are essentially untrustworthy due to their connection with alternative fantasy worlds, such as the universes created through storytelling and play. It should be noted, however, that the imaginary realms associated with children, though they may not be instantly associated with a sense of threat or images of abuse, often revolve precisely around putting the fate of the young in peril. This is evinced, for example, by Lewis Carroll's *Alice in Wonderland* [1865] and *Through the Looking Glass* [1872]. Some critics have romanticized these narratives as unproblematic confirmations of youthful stamina. Ann Donovan embraces this position by claiming that 'in chapter after chapter, incident after incident, [Alice] extricate[s] herself from nightmare-like situations with complete aplomb' (1987:28). While Carroll's heroine is undoubtedly clever and plucky, it is nonetheless hard to deny that what makes her adventures tantalizing is not so much her nerve as her repeated exposure to danger, to a darkness pervaded by harrowing images of haunting, excess and mutilation. Moreover, Alice's very assertiveness, intelligence and courage are potentially damning marks of alterity in a cultural milieu that would automatically expect young females to adopt the inert doll as an ideal role model. Alice's otherness is corroborated by her association with alien forms, more or less explicitly monstrous, grotesque or hybrid.

It is also noteworthy that the worlds through which Alice travels, even when they are not explicitly threatening but ostensibly hospitable, are fundamentally narrative and rhetorical fabrications reflecting adult notions of what should constitute an infantile fantasy realm. Just as Alice's environment is linguistically constructed, so is her very identity, as she is alternately addressed as 'child' (Carroll 1986:221; 232; 272), as 'little goose' (262), as monstrous 'serpent' (75), as 'mad' (88) and as 'not real' (245). These variable appellations suggest that names are not stable possessions for they can be imparted and taken away at random and, by extension, that the same destiny pertains to the self's integrity. Indeed, Alice senses that the scariest prospect consists of the loss of one's name since, as she speculates upon entering the wood 'where things have no names', were that to happen one would most probably be given 'another' name which 'is almost certain to be an ugly one' (229–30). The fact that Alice's adventures take place in a region demarcated, albeit hazily, by adult fantasies is corroborated by the theme of play. When this is introduced, it always operates with reference to thoroughly formalized and ritualistic games (cards in *Alice in Wonderland* and chess in *Through the Looking Glass*) which emphasize the dominance of rules, strategic moves and strict hierarchies.

Several influential accounts of the child's place in the adult world construe the young as strangers. Of course, strangers can be perceived as fascinating by virtue of their latent mysteriousness, in spite of the threat of invasion of familiar territories which they generally pose. However, more often than not, they tend to be ideologically framed not merely as alien but also as intellectually inferior or defective in comparison with the sensibilities evinced by their host cultures. This approach to foreignness frequently colours adult perceptions of the younger generations, as testified, for example, by Bruno Bettelheim's assessment of children's dreams and responses to fiction. While adults are presented as competent analysts, capable of experiencing complex fantasies and visions both worthy of and amenable to thorough investigation, the young are consigned to a realm of unanalysable simplicity: 'Children's dreams are very simple: wishes are fulfilled and anxieties are given tangible form'; concurrently, the 'child's dreams contain unconscious content that remains practically unshaped by his ego' and 'for this reason, children cannot and should not analyze their dreams' (1991:54). Bettelheim may seem to be doing children a favour in suggesting that their fantasies and dreams elude rational dissection insofar as his position could be interpreted as respectful of presymbolic instincts. Nevertheless, when he categorically asserts 'do not attempt to analyze the child's unconscious fantasies, for harm can only result' (155), he is effectively insulating the young from the sphere of symbolic language and, relatedly, depriving them of the powers which this bestows upon the adult subject. As Lucie Armitt points out, 'the truth behind this over-protective dynamic is that withholding information is one of the most effective and duplicitous ways of maintaining superiority (as fairy tales themselves so often remind us)' (1996:44).

Fairy tales (see **Chapters 5** and **6** for the link between fairy tales and the socializing process and **Chapter 9** on the consolatory function of the genre), even the ones most explicitly intended for children, do not provide young readers with fictional replicas of their own worlds but actually churn out endless variations on the theme of a very adult universe in which children are captives well before they can hope to become heroes or heroines. When they are allowed to aspire to freedom, the models they are required to emulate are also set by adults and accordingly pivot on the imperatives to succeed against all odds, to annihilate monstrous enemies, to grow to gigantic proportions. Above all, they are expected to internalize the mores of socialized existence, and are insistently reminded of the dire fate in store for those who dare contravene those laws. Carlo Collodi's *Pinocchio* [1883] (see also the Introduction to **Part 1**) epitomizes this cautionary approach: as Jack Zipes observes, 'Collodi torments and punishes the puppet each time Pinocchio veers from the norm of accept-able behaviour' (1997:81). If the wooden puppet's adventures amount, as it has often been contended, to a *Bildungsroman* of sorts, then the narrative's central message would appear to be that the learning curve entails a great deal of suffering. One way of summarizing Pinocchio's ordeals suggests graphically that while the story may concern the reformation of a naughty child, it is, above all, a harrowing depiction of sustained abuse. Pinocchio is indeed:

Abducted by a nomadic company under the aegis of an ominous leader
Burned, when his wooden legs are devoured by the flames
Unmasked, whenever he lies, by the grotesque growth of his nose
Swallowed by a colossal shark and by the greed of midnight assassins
Exploited, as a donkey, as a watchdog and as a substitute son
Drowned, in both the literal sea and the depths of culturally imposed guilt

The theme of abuse features prominently in the fairy tale tradition, its specific association with the plight of the young being attributable, at least in part, to the pervasiveness of legion forms of maltreatment and victimization in the early lives of real children. This notion is corroborated by the theories of the psychologist Alice Miller (1981, 1983), who argues that all children are exposed to some kind of abuse and thereafter grow up dreading the prospect of further impingement upon their physical and psychological integrity. However, once they have reached adulthood through multifarious humanizing processes, human beings tend to become complicitous with various cultural strategies intended to efface or, at any rate, minimize the ubiquity of infantile abuse, and are thus likely to go on transmitting a sinister legacy. According to Zipes, the Brothers Grimm's 'Hansel and Gretel' (best known in the form in which it appeared in 1857, though repeatedly reworked from 1810) exemplifies precisely the effort to play down the extent of child persecution. It does so by articulating two contrasting agendas: 'It is a soothing, pacifying tale that touches on issues of abuse and abandonment and provides hope that security and happiness can be found after a traumatic episode.' At the same time, 'it is also a tale that reinforces male hegemony and exculpates men from a crime against children'(1997:58). This reading is reinforced by the fact that female characters are blamed for the desertion of Hansel and Gretel, and that their nefarious agency has gained momentum through each successive reworking of the narrative, most notably by means of the metamorphosis of what is initially just an old woman into a witch, and of the biological mother into a stepmother – someone less likely to care naturally for the welfare of her charge. The father's horrible deed is excused while woman is cast in the role of either a greedy demon or a self-seeking exploiter incapable of Christian compassion.

Gothic fiction has consistently elaborated the themes of abuse and abandonment with an emphasis on female deprivation. The paradigmatic incarnation of the forsaken child is arguably the eponymous heroine of Charlotte Brontë's *Jane Eyre* [1847]. (See also **Chapters 9** and **12**.) Jane is a maltreated and lonely orphan who only stands to receive further humiliations from any adoptive family or institution intended to look after her. Even when she is no longer a literal child, she goes on carrying her dispossessed infantile self with her, as exemplified by the recurring dream in which she is burdened by the weight of a baby. Jean Rhys's rereading of Brontë's novel in *Wide Sargasso Sea* [1966], while modifying the perspective from which the story is told, preserves the theme of the abandoned child as its principal concern. Regardless of age, Antoinette is anchored to a condition of emotional deprivation that strikes its roots in childhood and in her rejection by family and friends alike. (See also **Chapter 9**.)

Emily Brontë's *Wuthering Heights* [1847] (see also **Chapter 8**) provides one of the most enduringly disturbing dramatizations of the theme of the deserted child, by articulating two interrelated motifs. First, the novel intimates that children are not only abandoned by their parents by being literally discarded: in fact, they also feel emotionally and psychologically abandoned within the family. Second, having to negotiate an identity out of the awareness and reality of having been forsaken breeds a vindictiveness which not even death is able to satisfy. *Wuthering Heights* offers a gallery of abused and abandoned children that stretches across the intersecting destinies of two apparently very different families, the Lintons and the Earnshaws. While the conduct and physical environment of the Lintons connote luxury, comfort and a sense of civilized restraint verging on iciness, those of the Earnshaws evoke a raw and elemental world traversed by fiery passions. As members of the two families are brought together in varyingly inadequate matches, their offspring tend to embody one or the other set of proclivities, thus standing out as either 'children of calm' or 'children of storm' (Cecil 1948:3). Regardless of their association with either pole, all the children portrayed in the novel are subjected to physical violence, mental cruelty and emotional torture. The theme of infantile brutalization is introduced as dominant early in the story, as Lockwood heartlessly rubs the wrist of Catherine's childlike ghost against the broken glass of a window pane. Subsequently, virtually all the other unfledged characters are presented as objects of merciless mistreatment. The principal causes of their afflictions are their entrapment in uncongenial matings, as exemplified by the union of Catherine and Edgar, and their manipulation by Heathcliffe as instruments of his revenge. He marries Isabella, ruthlessly exploiting her infatuation, led only by the wish to destroy the Lintons, whom he deems responsible for his separation from Catherine, and symbolically seals the doomed matrimonial pact by hanging her puppy. Indeed, not only human children but young animals are repeatedly subjected to violence throughout the novel. Catherine's brother Hindley, once the victimizer preventing his young sister and Heathcliffe from amicably sharing a bed, is tyrannized into self-destruction and his son Hareton is degraded to the level of an illiterate uncouth beast. The second Catherine, in turn, is punished by being forced to marry the wasting Linton, the pathetic product of a loveless conception, shortly before his death, and then by forced cohabitation of the haunting rooms of Wuthering Heights with the animal-like Hareton and the despotic Heathcliffe.

A paradigmatically Gothic hero–villain, Heathcliffe invites compassion and repugnance at one and the same time. (Heathcliffe's ambivalent status is also examined in **Chapter 3**.) Many readers have sympathized with his implacable hatred of stifling conventions and his striving for a union that transcends common ethical boundaries, while simultaneously recoiling from his satanic commitment to vengeance and persecution of the young. Heathcliffe's character is made especially enigmatic by his obscure origins and implicit association with distant, possibly savage, lands. All we know about him is that he has been discovered by Mr Earnshaw as a 'dirty, ragged, black-haired child' (Brontë 1969:77) in the streets of Liverpool. Given this city's economic role as a nodal point in the colonial and slave trade involving the Far East, West Africa and the West Indies at the time when the novel was written, it is tempting to surmise that Heathcliffe is not merely an incarnation of the dispossessed child, who then proceeds to torment other children, but also an icon of racial and ethnic alterity. (The collusion of childhood and alterity is examined in detail in **Chapter 12**.) This reading casts a sinister light on the narrative as a whole, by intimating that the direst forms of abuse can be expected to ensue from the dark Other. Perhaps Emily Brontë, having portrayed infantile violation as rampant, felt the need to delimit its boundaries and presumed to be able to do so by demonizing an alien agent as the perpetrator of the most heinous crimes. The desire, whether conscious or unconscious, to tame ostensibly uncontrollable energies is also borne out by the text's own split identity. While thematically *Wuthering Heights* throws chaos and wildness into relief, it is painstakingly structured around a starkly symmetrical interweaving of genealogical trees.

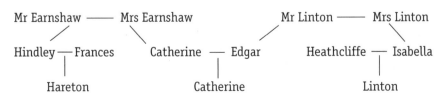

Both the attribution of diabolical proclivities to an alien interloper and the domestication of the plot could ultimately be seen as ways of paying lip service to hegemonic requirements that were inevitably beyond the author's power to dissolve. This does not mean, however, that *Wuthering Heights* does not carry subversive connotations. Indeed, the novel brings to the fore the iniquity of familial obligations and the monstrosity of the restraints which they place upon the young. Even though Emily Brontë's reasons for making child abuse one of the story's recurring motifs cannot be conclusively ascertained, borrowing the concept introduced by T. S. Eliot in his 1919 essay on *Hamlet* (Eliot 1999), one could regard the novel's sadistic imagery as something of an *objective correlative* for its central preoccupation – the devastating effects of boundless passions that shun the normalizing structures of family, marriage and dynastic propagation. It is because children, and young animals generally, are conventionally associated with the inchoate substratum of human nature that they are insistently oppressed in an effort to keep those destabilizing energies at bay. Even when children biologically turn into adults, they remain liable to be branded as pariahs as long as their behaviour bears the vestiges of infantile unruliness. Nelly says of the adult Heathcliffe: 'I did not feel as if I were in the company of a creature of my own species' (Brontë 1969:197), and of Catherine: 'Far better that she should be dead' (199). The young are here implicitly presented as victims of adult preconceptions, imprisoned in the cage of the older generation's self-concern.

The idea that familial environments dominated by parents who are too wrapped up in themselves and their own ambitions and dark yearnings to recognize their offspring's needs are likely to breed profound feelings of dispossession still plays an important part in contemporary fiction. This is borne out, for instance, by Joyce Carol Oates's 'The Ruins of Contracoeur'. In this story, a father 'disgraced and defeated' (1999:24) by 'former associates' who have 'betrayed him for political reasons' (28) relocates the family to a crumbling ancestral mansion in a remote region. While he is concerned exclusively with redeeming his reputation and restoring his wealth, and his wife is busy mourning the loss of the glamorous life of the capital, their children are abandoned to their own resources and forced to confront, without adult assistance, both natural and supernatural threats. The most bereft of the children is Graeme, who roams the 'old house as if it were a tomb in which, his father's son, the child of a man in exile, he was unjustly confined' (25). He is also the first to be exposed to the dark forces surrounding the decrepit dwelling in the form of 'a thing-without-a-face' (27), his experience paving the way to a long chain of ominous occurrences. The children suddenly find themselves trapped in a time warp causing new and expensive objects, such as their cutting-edge bikes, to deteriorate at a preposterous pace or get 'unaccountably lost' (39). Forsaken by self-centred parents, they soon discover that their predicament is not an isolated event but actually the latest chapter in a long history of ruthless abuse of the young, traceable back to the builder of their home, the textile mill owner Moses Adam Matheson – a tyrannical and murderous exploiter of his workers, many of whom were children. A correspondence is suggested between Matheson's murky past and the situation of the present-day father, as it gradually transpires that his implication in numerous scandals and intrigues questions his self-depiction as 'an innocent victim of others' malevolence' (64). The analogy is symbolically reinforced by the fact that the appearance of the thing-without-a-face shortly after the father and his family have settled in the ancestral home echoes one of old Matheson's most atrocious crimes: an inexplicable conflagration that destroyed his young labourers and indeed reduced them to 'bodies without faces' (52).

In examining the topos of the abandoned child, it is also necessary to evaluate its grounding in myth and folk narratives. It is especially noteworthy, in this respect, that legends across the world featuring preternatural creatures whose lives are dominated by the urge to prey upon children suggest that the victimization of the young proceeds from adult insecurities. (See also **Chapter 12** for a discussion of this theme with a focus on the phenomenon of cannibalism.)   According to Marina Warner, the symbolic message implicit in the proverbial covetousness of many mythological figures is that 'they have lost a baby or cannot have one and feel the lack. So they can be "boo-baggers", who carry bags in which they stow away babies and their other victims, principally children.' They may also be witches adept at sacrificing infants 'in a sacrilegious imitation of the Eucharist'. Very real fears lie behind some of these stories – fears to do with the fate of dead children, the curse hanging over their parents, the incidence of infantile death and the dire urge to dispose of unwanted babies. Before the introduction of the 'state of limbo', sheer dread attached to the destiny of 'miscarried, still-born and hence unbaptized babies' and, by implication, to the sorrows that might befall the unfortunate soul's family. Moreover, while the 'loss of infants may have been expected in times of high mortality', there have been insistent attempts to explain the loss of the very young through stories that put their disappearance down to the appetites of imaginary beings yearning for the newly born, such as the Irish 'Tuatha De Danann' and the Scottish 'Lammikin' (2000:27). If preternatural creatures can be invoked to account for the vanishing of infants or children, and hence cope with the experience of loss, it would seem that they can also be exploited to ratify deaths that have been caused by human agents. The legends are not always unproblematically consolatory for they may well serve as

a justification for neglecting babies with birth defects or other problems. A changeling could be discreetly made to disappear, as an evil gift of the fairies, or even of the devil; to dispose of a human child on the other hand, however

unwanted or damaged at birth, lay beyond the frontiers of acceptable conduct
. . . Infanticide, in cases where there was nothing untoward, could thus be
concealed. (29)

When the young are not literally exterminated, they are nonetheless insistently regimented by recourse to predatory spirits such as the wolf, the
bogeyman, the sandman, the man-in-the-moon, the *coco* (Spain) or *l'uomo
nero* (Italy). Using terrifying monsters to discipline the young could be interpreted as an unpardonable form of abuse. It is also conceivable, however, that
when adults resort to dark creatures in the service of a repressive educational
policy, they open themselves up to unsettling reminders of what it was like to
be a child susceptible to supernatural fears, of what it was like to climb a dark
staircase on one's own, to go to sleep in the midst of muffled, inexplicable
noises, or to walk home from school in midwinter pursued by weird shadows. In
subjecting children to imaginary threats, adults concurrently, albeit subliminally, reexperience their own nascent dread and are thus impelled to
contemplate the extent to which fear still dominates their lives in muted guises
as a pervasive dimension of embodied existence. Children, despite their
exposure to prospects of abuse and abandonment, may ultimately play the
upper hand in the terrorizing game orchestrated by adults since, whereas adults
often lack material referents for the anxieties that unrelentingly assail them,
the young seem capable of giving visible faces to their apprehensions of
darkness and, ideally, of rendering them tolerable in fantasy and play. Ogres,
spectres, goblins, giants, witches, metamorphic creatures, elves and polter-
geists may even be considered friends.

This idea is consistently conveyed by J. K. Rowling's *Harry Potter* series
(1997–2000) (the series is also mentioned in **Chapter 5**) through an extensive
gallery of abandoned children who, notwithstanding their persecution by
varyingly unscrupulous and corrupt adults, ultimately prove immensely
resourceful and resilient even when the magic wand is unavailable. Some of
Rowling's characters are literally bereft; the half-giant Hagrid and the clumsy
pupil Neville fall into this category. Harry himself is doubly deprived. While
labouring under the constant threat of extinction at the hand of the Dark
Wizard Voldemort, whose assault he has survived as a tiny infant but has left
him an orphan, he is simultaneously abused by the Dursleys, the *muggle*
relatives who have reluctantly adopted him. (Muggles, incidentally, are people
without the vaguest trace of magic in them, keen only on safeguarding their
greyness through the worship of narrowly bourgeois notions of normality.)
Other characters are less explicitly but no less deeply affected by their
childhood experiences. One of Harry's best friends, Ron, belongs to a full-
fledged wizard family but feels disadvantaged in comparison with his brothers
and sisters; Harry's other principal pal, Hermione, is discriminated against due

to her muggle background in spite of her amazing knowledge and refined skills; Dudley Dursley, regardless of his parents' total devotion to his grossly inflated self, comes across as a freakish outsider; Voldemort himself, finally, is largely driven by a poisonous hatred for his father. Villainous figures who associate themselves with the supposedly adult world ultimately fail due to their commitment to an ethos that allows no room for playful mobility and that is only prepared to accept the relationship between good and evil in starkly binary oppositional terms. Children, conversely, are by and large able to survive the severest trials by virtue of their willingness to adopt flexible sets of rules that require them to acknowledge the shifting qualities of light and darkness and, by extension, the potential omnipresence of horror, terror and fear in their lives.

At the same time as grown-ups exploit the young's subordinate status as a means of both exorcizing and reenacting their own primordial anxieties, children confront the dark on their own terms in an endeavour to comprehend and define fear. This frequently requires a disposition to interact imaginatively with frightening entities and with attendant indications of danger, and to establish a creative interaction with one's potential foes. It is on this basis that children may begin to grasp, however tentatively, abstract concepts such as darkness, evil and destruction, by correlating them symbolically to ludic contexts peopled by menacing forces. Having glanced at 'the table where his monsters rested in tableau', the child Mark in Stephen King's *Salem's Lot* observes: 'Understand death? Sure. That was when the monsters got you' (1977:167).

—12—

Childhood and Otherness

NARRATIVES OF DARKNESS consistently resort to the theme of familial repression in order to foreground infantile exploitation by the adult world. In much Gothic fiction the persecuted child is often equated to a doomed young heroine. Generational and gender politics become closely interrelated. A major way of keeping at bay the anxieties raised by childhood is to forsake the young, by either expelling them from a family or by making them feel like exiles within that structure. Children are also victimized by so-called mature subjects on the basis of their connection with a putatively primitive, uncivilized Other.

One of the most potent and enduring instances of the association of childhood with menacing alterity is the figure of the aggressive, sadistic and cannibalistic infantile ego. This creature plays an important role in the psychoanalytic theories of Melanie Klein. She proposes that children, initially unaware of their separateness from other people and objects, gradually develop the concept of difference by splitting entities into 'good' parts perceived as supportive of the ego and 'bad' parts seen to threaten the self's unity. The splitting process is fundamentally triggered by the child's apprehension of destructive urges within the self and by the concomitant desire to erect a barrier between what it cherishes and what it abhors, what should be allowed into the self and what should be expelled. The developmental trajectory outlined by Klein comprises two principal stages. In the first, the 'paranoid-schizoid position', the child experiences intensely cannibalistic urges. It yearns to incorporate the objects which it is starting to sense as separate and to establish its own mastery over them by symbolically devouring them. In the second, the 'depressive position', the child begins to feel anxious about the possibility that the introjected objects might retaliate, and guilty about the damage that might have been inflicted upon them. It seeks to make reparation (Klein 1988).

The voracious tendencies of the monsters of myth and legend are located by the Kleinian psychodrama in the child itself. An intriguing example of the young's association with monstrous entities is supplied by Maurice Sendak's *Where the Wild Things Are* (1963), where the feral beings both warn Max that they will devour him and welcome him as their king. If Max in his wolf suit is not exactly a terrifying ogre, his connection with a monstrously primordial breed highlights the link between childhood and wild drives. These gain baleful connotations in contrast with the supposed security of home where a hot meal awaits the hero upon his return from the land of the Wild Things. The Max who shouts at his mother 'I'LL EAT YOU UP!' and is therefore sent to bed with no supper exemplifies the child in the throes of the paranoid-schizoid position. The Max who, having 'tamed' the Wild Things, having enjoyed his power over them in an orgy of games and dances, and having finally consigned the monsters themselves 'to bed without their supper', discovers that he now feels 'lonely', typifies the second-stage creature – the child disempowered by his newly found sense of responsibility.

Max is demonized and accordingly reformed as a result of adult apprehensions of his latent monstrosity. Paradoxically, however, traditional narratives insistently posit the child as the victim, not the perpetrator, of crimes hinging on the consumption of human flesh. The image of the uncivilized, gluttonous young is hence not so much a reflection of a documented state of affairs as an imaginary, indeed hyperreal, construct designed to efface the pervasiveness of predatory drives at the very core of grown-up society. (This idea is linked to the issue of child abuse as discussed in **Chapter 11**.) This reading is corroborated by the realization that cannibalism is frequently coupled with infanticide in myths, legends, folk tales and fairy tales. In some stories, as in the myth of Kronos, fathers eat their progeny in order to deny the latter's autonomy. As Marina Warner points out, 'The ogre who eats babies . . . embodies a monstrous and anomalous paternal response to the anxiety that his offspring would supplant him; his wicked folly makes plain the social and human imperative that the young must be allowed to thrive and grow' (2000:77). Ironically, the one of Kronos's descendants whom the Titan is unable to ingest, Zeus, survives to become not only the ruler of Olympus but also a flesh-eater himself, as testified by the tale of Metis, Athene's mother. Appraised by an oracle that Metis, a Titaness he has surreptitiously impregnated, would 'bear a son fated to depose Zeus' (Graves 2000:52) were she to conceive once more, the father of the Olympian deities proceeds to swallow her. In due course, Athene triumphantly emerges, fully equipped for battle, from Zeus's very skull. In this myth, the theme of paternal anthropophagism is interwoven with two further traditional motifs – the vanquishing of the Other and the curbing of childhood. The annihilation of Metis symbolizes the quintessential patriarch's victory over a dark breed whose dominance predates his own ascent to power. His appropriation of the unborn daughter, relatedly, represents a successful effort to extricate her from that sinister background of pre-Olympian alterity. It is no coincidence, moreover, that Athene should spring forth as a fully developed creature and hence proceed to became the patron of war, science and craftsmanship. Zeus's cannibalistic act, while cleansing her of ominous connections with the Titans, purges her of the stigmata of childhood. The Other and the infant are rendered coextensive in this narrative and equally deserving of drastic suppression.

In several myths, paternal cannibalism is interwoven with the theme of revenge, as evinced by the narrative in which Thyestes is perfidiously lured by his brother Atreus into feasting on a meal consisting of his brood's flesh. Revenge also plays a major part in the legend of Zagreus, a further instance of the connection between Zeus's ongoing struggle against the Titans and of infantile victimization centred on the ingestion of young flesh. The boy–child begotten by Zeus upon Persephone is said to have been torn to shreds and consumed raw by the vengeful Titans. This myth bears remarkable affinities with that of Dionysus, a deity whom many indeed consider interchangeable with Zagreus. Here, once again, Zeus exhibits all the salient traits of a megalo-maniac patriarch. Having appeared to his mistress Semele, pregnant with the prospective Dionysus, as thunder and lightning and thus utterly destroyed her, Zeus then has the six-month-old foetus sewed up inside his thigh so that the child may enter the world when ready to do so. Like Zagreus, Dionysus is torn apart by the perfidious Titans who, having possibly developed more sophisti-cated culinary habits by the time this myth takes shape, boil the morsels in a cauldron.

In several well-known tales where the young are not literally ingested, food items still play a prominent role as figurative correlatives for the fate of the alienated child: the apple in 'Snow White', the pumpkin in 'Cinderella', the apple and the berries in 'The Juniper Tree', and onions and spices in 'The Sleeping Beauty in the Wood'. What is most intriguing about these narratives is that, in spite of their pervasive darkness and in spite of the ghastly trials and tribulations to which they subject their unfledged protagonists, they finally allow children to survive and even triumph. A tension is set up between grotesque and terrifying attempts at infantile violation intended to suppress the young's menacing alterity, and the drive to celebrate the continuity of life. That tension is thrown into relief by the association of eating or otherwise physically using another person's body with the process of consuming. This term can be ubiquitously adopted to refer not merely to the act of absorbing and disposing of an object but also to a passion, especially an erotic one, and hence to the urge to procreate. The child thus stands out as an aporetic figure that supposedly stimulates a perverse desire for consumption tantamount to the longing to annihilate life, and yet emerges from an engrossing instinct to reproduce which fosters the perpetuation of life. Therefore, at the same time as both children and adults are alternately depicted as actual or potential cannibals, their destructive impulses are counteracted by an equally potent imperative – the impetus to assert the human proclivity to endure in the face of the malevolent phantoms spawned by indomitable and omnipresent fears. It is nevertheless noteworthy that whereas children may be symbolically associated with cannibalistic drives, as in the case of the Kleinian paradigm, the actual flesh-eaters are adults intent on physically engulfing the child's baffling otherness. If the reproductive impulse ultimately gains priority over its destructive counterparts, this is often at great cost for the dispossessed party. The restoration of harmony proposed by many traditional endings cannot completely efface the import of the horrors which one has witnessed along the way.

The connection between childhood and otherness is explicitly indicated by numerous Gothic narratives in which the theme of infantile brutalization is consistently interwoven with the topos of racial alterity. This trend can be traced back to William Beckford's *Vathek* [1786], where those motifs are articulated in tandem in the context of a Faustian pact that enslaves the intemperate Vathek to the whims of a repugnant stranger. (This text is also discussed in **Chapter 3**.) Multiple layers of otherness proliferate throughout Beckford's novel. Vathek himself is depicted as Other due to his connection with an Oriental world of forbidden pleasures; the pagan Giaour requesting him to immolate innocent children is even more patently constructed as an alien due to its demonic powers and physical monstrosity; the sacrificed children are presented as the ultimate Other, insofar as they are the products of a culture of exotic overindulgence and can be mercilessly disposed of for the advancement of the caliph's aspirations, regardless of their social status. The notion of the Other as a threat to be tamed or, at least, normalized is paradigmatically documented by Beckford's recreation of the Orient as a world of decadence, egotism and excess, capable of accommodating the most extravagant extremes of the Gothic vision. The idea of the child as a disposable Other meant to feed the insatiable desire of a tyrannical adult goes hand in hand with the notion of the East as the West's Other: a depraved, irrational, sultry incarnation of both the Western fear of and fascination with cultural and geographical alterity. Important ideological and economic factors contributed to the emergence of the orientalist construct in Beckford's days. (See **Chapter 8** for an evaluation of this concept with reference to the writings of Edward Said.) As Michael Franklin points out, 'The East had always connoted expensive consumer items from silks, spices, and sandalwood to porcelain, coffee, and tea; European familiarity with these colours, textures, and scents was complicit in the voyeuristic invasion of the fragrant and forbidden spaces of the serail, where conspicuous consumption entailed appealingly abominable debauchery' (1998:168). (The paradoxical interweaving of fascination and repulsion is examined in detail in **Chapter 15**.)

In the tyrant Vathek's hands, doomed children to be sacrificed in the name of his self-advancement become akin to consumer items such as those cited by

Franklin and, like them, can be regarded as symbolic spyholes allowing voyeuristic glimpses into an outlandish fairground erected upon the oxymoron of titillatingly detestable thrills. Moreover, far from protecting Vathek's intended victims, their unparalleled beauty and patrician status only serve to make them more desirable and hence more vulnerable. They are no more in control of their destinies than the outsiders, dwarfs, eunuchs, genii and mutes that people Beckford's orientalist cabinet of curiosities. In staging an apocalyptic instance of infantile victimization in an appropriately distorted Orient, Beckford simultaneously exculpates the putatively civilized West from any possible implication with barbaric forms of abuse and establishes a harrowing connection between alienated children and alienated cultures. Age and race become almost interchangeable indices of primitiveness and savage dispositions.

However, the young hold a modicum of power within the text signalled by their centrality to the development of the plot and, by extension, to *Vathek's* overall structure. Unable to affect their own lot, they are nonetheless granted the ability to influence the story's narrative trajectory. Indeed, it is from the point at which children become the ferocious caliph's ceremonial scapegoats that the novel begins to darken. Earlier on, Vathek's crimes appear boisterously farcical, products of the machinations of a clownish dictator. With the introduction of the theme of infantile massacre, the mood palpably deteriorates; various villainous parties, overwhelmed by the atrocities they have hitherto nonchalantly perpetrated, begin to turn against one another. Although the children are powerless to resist their persecutors, the cruelties of which they are the primary victims initiate the villain's descent into catastrophe. This would seem to suggest that the figure of the brutalized, oppressed child, though physically helpless, retains an active rhetorical function as an instrument of Nemesis.

Vathek voices a colonial/imperialist ethos echoed by later Gothic narratives. In Charlotte Brontë's *Jane Eyre* [1847] (see also **Chapters 7** and **11**), for instance, the masterful Rochester relies on wealth obtained through colonial exploitation. The young governess herself, though initially infantilized by her economic dispossession and thus put on the same level as her young charge Adele, eventually inherits a substantial legacy the provenance of which is foreign trade. Jane, moreover, is the alter ego of a literal victim of colonial abuse, the madwoman considered hardly more valuable than chattel. In different ways, Jane, Bertha and Adele are all children at the mercy of a ruthless economy that thrives on the other's disempowerment. Charlotte Perkins Gilman's *The Yellow Wallpaper* [1892] (discussed in some detail in **Chapter 7**) corroborates the association between femininity, childlike defencelessness and colonial exploitation: the central characters inhabit a colonial mansion that has become available as a result of 'some legal trouble' (1981:11).

If Charlotte Brontë's heroine eventually becomes the beneficiary of a colonial heritage, the young characters that people her sister Emily's novel *Wuthering Heights* [1847] are, conversely, the victims of a dark presence implicitly associated with distant dependencies: Heathcliffe. His status, moreover, is redolent of the situation of a colonized subject since, despite his apparent power, he is no less a casualty of socialization than the children he maltreats. Heathcliffe is essentially a cultural construct whose putatively natural 'passions' are, as Fred Botting observes, actually 'produced: he is found in the city and then miserably domesticated by a hostile middle-class family whose criticisms, exclusions and prohibitions of his progress towards the properly bourgeois ends of marriage make him wild and vengeful' (1996:130). (See also **Chapters 3** and **11** for further analysis of this character.)

A profoundly distressing parallel between the violence perpetrated upon children and fierce racial exploitation is supplied by Toni Morrison's *Beloved* (1987). (*Beloved* is also examined in **Chapters 1** and **4**.) In this text, infanticide is posited as a horrific yet somewhat ineluctable form of release from a destiny of unutterable degradation. However, the child's violent death cannot relieve the historical burden which she carries in her genes, any more than the transition from slavery to freedom is capable of anaesthetizing the reality of the black holocaust. The relationship between childhood and racial abuse also features prominently in Jane Campion's *The Piano* (1993). The film sets up a whole series of intriguing correspondences between childhood as a literal state, exemplified by the character of Flora; childhood as the state to which dispossessed women are forced to revert by oppressive patriarchal dispensations, as typified by Ada's predicament; and the metaphorical childhood of remote, non-industrial and economically deprived lands. It also comments on the West's abhorrence of infantile eroticism by graphically suggesting the polymorphous sexuality of the young Maori population, in contrast with the self-restraint expected of white children.

The collusion of childhood and otherness is most overtly dramatized by texts that entangle the persecution of the young and the brutalization of ethnically and racially disenfranchised people. In Stephen King's *Bag of Bones* (1999b) (see also **Chapter 2** and the Introductions to **Parts 2** and **3**), for example, the curse that hangs over generation after generation of children conceived through unions associated with a particular geographical location results from the persecution and eventual extermination of the black community that was once settled there. The novel links the predicament of the blacks, demonized as intruders with lax mores, to the suffering of the young characters who, across various generations, become the impotent victims of either racial discrimination or postcolonial vengeance. Peter Høeg's *Miss Smilla's Feeling for Snow* (1994) also intermeshes the themes of colonial oppression, bigoted segregation and economic exploitation – of Greenland by Denmark – with the plight of deprived children: the little boy Isaiah whose death the plot pivots upon, and Smilla herself as the casualty of a sexual/cultural clash between her mother, a Greenlander and a hunter, and her father, a Dane and a surgeon.

Paul Bryers's *The Prayer of the Bone* articulates an analogous theme by relating the vicious murder of a young woman and the ensuing ordeals of her sister and little daughter, both prey to present-day treachery and greed, to the vicissitudes experienced by the land's aboriginal Souriquois Indians and tribal shape-shifters, known as the Bear People, a civilization branded as irredeemably savage that has, in fact, been savaged by mass slaughter and by the desecration of its holy sites by unscrupulous settlers. Maddie, an adventurous young woman working on an archaeological dig in Northern Maine, is brutally killed by someone, or something, that uncannily harks back to the place's traditional and supposedly bestial ancestry. Observing the 'curious regularity of the wounds, as if she'd been *raked*', a man points out that the only time he has seen anything comparable before, a 'bear' had been the cause of death (2000:1). If Maddie is a primary instance of the physically violated child elliptically connected with vestiges of ethnic alterity, her nine-year-old daughter Freya typifies the case of the child traumatized and emotionally drained by grief. Maddie's sister, Jessica, though apparently more in control of this intractable situation, is also a dispossessed child rooted in dark otherness, deprived of vital knowledge by the persistent obfuscation of her mother's Native American heritage. The main characters' afflictions are made particularly ominous by their association with a long history of ethnic and racial violation. Indeed, in spite of repeated attempts to cover up the truth about Maddie's death by means of tall tales featuring shamans and followers of the bear cult, the murder turns out to have been motivated by crude financial interests linked to a colonial massacre performed three centuries earlier.

In Geoff Ryman's *Was* (1999), similar preoccupations emerge, the tribulations of the Kansa Indians, with their submerged baggage of rituals and values, paralleling the travail of subsequent generations of abused children. The lives of various characters are intertwined around *The Wonderful Wizard of Oz*, both Frank Baum's novel [1900] and the iconic 1939 movie. Central to Ryman's plot is Dorothy Gael, an orphan living with her grossly abusive aunt and uncle on a Kansas frontier settlement, and the story of the life she could have had, as told by a kindly, yet ineffectual, supply teacher named Frank Baum. A paradigmatic instance of infantile brutalization culminating in madness, Dorothy Gael's life story consistently overlaps with that of the fairy-tale Dorothy (whose surname is actually Gale) and with that of Judy Garland, the female lead in Victor Fleming's musical. The atmosphere evoked by *Was* may seem at odds with the utopian vision projected by Baum's story and the comparably hopeful message conveyed by the 1939 movie. However, as Jack Zipes points out, there is already 'a tragic side to Baum's concept of Oz' for 'the book and its sequels emanate from the sensibility of a naive writer who was disturbed by the Gilded Age, which glossed over the desperate economic plight of farmers and workers, especially in the Midwest. And the film, too, arose against the background of the great economic Depression of the 1930s' (1991:122). Utopias may seem to promise desirable change as long as the ideal situations they propose are deemed likely to take shape in the real world. They become symbols of hopelessness, however, once they are identified as containing what reality lacks and will never feasibly gain. Indeed, Baum eventually consigns Dorothy to 'permanent exile', in the belief that the American dream will never actualize what Oz potentially guarantees. Already in *The Emerald City* [1910], the sixth of the thirteen tales following the first book, Dorothy is portrayed as leaving Kansas behind never to return.

In emphasizing the pervasiveness of poverty, frustration and disappointment among joyless labourers, Ryman explicitly draws attention to the dark dimension of Baum's project alluded to by Zipes. At the same time, it relates the suffering and victimization of the young not only to an ominous past of racial discrimination but also to a present of economic dispossession. Like Ryman, Salman Rushdie throws into relief the more sombre aspects of the Oz story, with specific reference to the 1939 movie, by suggesting that '"There's no place like home" . . . is the least convincing idea in the film' (1992:14) for it is never conclusively explained why one should want to return to a world of uniform drabness: 'The Kansas described by L. Frank Baum is a depressing place, in which everything is grey as far as the eye can see – the prairie is grey and so is the house in which Dorothy lives'. 'And *this* is the home that "there's no place like"? *This* is the lost Eden that we are asked to prefer (as Dorothy does) to Oz?' (16–17). The film's positive message may ultimately consist of its representation of the child as resourceful and tenacious in the face of life-threatening dangers. However, it is noteworthy that even this optimistic picture ensues not so much from a confident acknowledgment of childhood stamina as from a disturbing recognition of 'the inadequacy of adults, even of good adults' (10).

The illustrative cases offered in this chapter have drawn attention to the persistent tendency to yoke childhood and alterity together on the basis of perceived affinities between supposedly unfledged humanity and monstrous, predatory, brutalized and dispossessed incarnations of the Other. If those cases can be presumed to share a message of sorts, this is likely to amount to a recognition of the paradoxical status of the young as cultural entities that are both enabled and disabled by their association with darkness, specifically prenatal darkness. The narrator of Clive Barker's 'Hell's Event' (*Books of Blood, vol. 2*) stresses the empowering import of the submerged wisdom connected with that state and accordingly describes the mature response of the young to the demonic: 'Children, knowing the nature of the dark having been so recently touched by it, were the least troubled. They took their parents' hands and led them away from the spot like lambs, telling them not to look behind them, and their parents half-remembered the womb, the first tunnel' (Barker 1999a, Vol. 2:55). Conversely, 'Rawhead Rex' (*Books of Blood, vol. 3*), in stressing the young's association with primordial darkness, foregrounds their sense of dispossession: while 'the old lay awake working out the geography of the ceiling . . . children dreamt of the womb, and babies mourned it' (Barker 1999a, Vol. 3:60).

— Part 5—
Monstrosity

Introduction

He who fights monsters should look to it that he himself does not become a monster. And if you gaze for long into an abyss, the abyss also gazes into you.

Nietzsche, *Beyond Good and Evil*

The multi-faceted figure of the monster acquires its most starkly negative connotations in the eighteenth century, as a result of a neo-classical aesthetic devoted to notions of unity and harmony, and hence inclined to brand anything which might fail to fulfil these criteria as irrational, immoral and viciously ugly. Monstrosity is further constructed as the Enlightenment's principal enemy due to its penchant for challenging the subordination of the material body to the cognitive self. Indeed, it reminds us that thoughts, emotions, fantasies and fears are not incorporeal and ethereal states but rather living entities affected deeply by the bodies they inhabit. Monstrosity has also been associated by the champions of Reason with the demonic, the preternaturally subversive energy which, harking back to Milton's Satan, threatens to undo the socio-ethical fabric. Narratives of darkness repeatedly quiz the idea that the aberrant emanates from a metaphysical realm by projecting it onto human, all too human, characters: Montoni in Ann Radcliffe's *The Mysteries of Udolpho* [1794], Heathcliff in Emily Brontë's *Wuthering Heights* [1847] (also examined in **Chapters 3, 11** and **12**), Mr Hyde in R. L. Stevenson's *The Strange Case of Dr Jekyll and Mr Hyde* [1886] (see also **Chapter 1**) and, in more recent times, the supposedly possessed characters in films such as *The Exorcist* (William Friedkin, 1973), *Rosemary's Baby* (Roman Polansky, 1968) and *The Omen* (Richard Donner, 1976).

The Western notion of the monster as a creature whose intellectual and moral aberrations are mirrored by its physical deformities or, in some cases, concealed beneath a seductive and charismatic facade, is closely related to ideological agendas committed to the identification and curbing of degenerate drives. The fact that monsters are not unequivocally hideous but may actually evince a charming countenance and gallant conduct, as testified by characters such as Hannibal Lecter and various incarnations of Count Dracula, makes the task of detecting the detested enemy arduous. In the face of this difficulty, many societies tend to warn their subjects to look out for monsters everywhere, since the threat of degeneracy cannot be confined to some dark cave but actually traverses the cultural environment in its entirety. This idea gained considerable weight in the nineteenth century at the behest of Max Nordeau, whose *Degeneration* [1892] argues that the urban context itself breeds depraved creatures by forcing humans to live in a state of unremitting nervous excitation. Most vulnerable are those who 'allow aesthetics to prevail over the useful', as pointed out by George Mosse in his preface to the text (Nordau 1993:xxi), for these are the very people whose susceptibility to flickering and unreliable impressions is likely to turn their brains into decaying monstrosities. The ideological implications of these positions are pretty obvious: Nordau is encouraging the reader to distrust the senses in favour of a 'tense vigilance of the judgement' (313). At the same time, the economic metaphors which run through *Degeneration* suggest that relinquishing rational control amounts to a form of dissipation, to a mental bankruptcy conducive to 'deformities' (60) and 'violent decomposition' (63). It could be argued, however, that in its exhortation to define and vanquish the threat of hideous deterioration and its insidious repercussions, Nordau is emitting nervous signs of red alerts. As Jane Goodall observes, 'It is the rationalizing processes surrounding the anxieties themselves . . . that are the real noxious influence' (1996:77). In attempting to frame and domesticate the aberrant, human beings often end up constructing yet more monsters, the fear of wastage and pollution repeatedly supplying the raw materials for this enterprise.

Paradoxically, although monstrosity may be at odds with the ethos of the Enlightenment, it is by no means at odds with the concept of enlightenment. Indeed, its etymology points to its illuminating potential: the Latin *demonstrare* means 'to show', 'to reveal', 'to disclose'. Therefore, like the fear it so often induces, the troubling prodigy holds not only blinding but also awakening and strengthening potentialities. J. B. Twitchell corroborates this idea by arguing that to expose ourselves to horror, especially in fiction and cinema, is 'to practise controlling one of our primary impulses – the impulse to flee' (1988:5). From prehistoric cave-paintings produced around 15,000–10,000 BC to the present, fear has been recursively embodied by bestial, hybrid and grotesque forms that serve to remind us of our puniness. However, those shapes do not numb consciousness, much as they may scare us, but actually alert us to our vulnerability and need for self-protection: 'Night visitors prepare us for daylight' (7). The aberrant plays a vital role in the evocation and exorcism of fear upon which many popular festivities and rituals hinge. Events such as Hallow'een, ceremonies associated with patron saints in several Catholic countries, pageants, processions and carnivals all utilize and indeed enthusiastically flaunt monstrous shapes, costumes and masks. According to Marina Warner, these displays are predicated upon a desire to assert in symbolic and ritualistic form the human determination and ability to survive danger: 'The magical attempt to secure safety takes two predominant forms: either the participants impersonate the danger itself, as in the carnival masks and fancy dress of Hallow'een, and thus, cannibal-like, absorb its powers and deflect its ability to inflict harm; or they expose themselves and by surviving the ordeal, prove their invulnerability' (2000:112).

Arguably, one of the most stupendous things about deviants is their protean multiformity. Defining the monster is a very tall order when one considers the amazing diversity of forms which physical and psychological abnormality is capable of taking: zombies, trolls, gremlins, creatures from outer space, aliens, werewolves, demonically possessed people, slug-like or blob-like creatures, deformed and unbounded bodies. The monstrous body is not fixed, despite its persecutors' attempts to frame it as conclusively evil, demonic or simply repugnant. In fact, it has a proclivity to undergo baffling metamorphoses that are frequently literal, as testified by the penchant for self-transformation evinced by various shamanic and vampiric creatures. Yet, such metamorphoses are also occasioned by rhetorical interpretations of the anomalous: monsters are shape-shifters to the extent that we read their anatomies differently, depending on whether we wish them to conform to a regulatory discourse of order or to a carnivalesque narrative of excess. Particular cultures and ideologies decide, both consciously and unconsciously, which pole to be drawn to.

On the one hand, we witness the urge to define and contain sprawling apprehensions of the fearful as a means of fostering an illusion of order. Societies unrelentingly endeavour to classify and explain the abnormal so as to reassert by implication their notions of normality and stability. As Stephen King points out,

> almost every physical and mental human aberration has been at some point in history, or is now, considered monstrous – a complete list would include widows' peaks (once considered a reliable sign that a man was a sorcerer), moles on the female body (supposed to be witches' teats), and extreme schizophrenia, which on occasion has caused the afflicted to be canonized by one church or another. Monstrosity fascinates us because it appeals to the conservative Republican in a three-piece suit who resides within all of us. We love and need the concept of monstrosity because it is a reaffirmation of the order we all crave as human beings . . . it is not the physical or mental aberration in itself which horrifies us, but rather the lack of order which these aberrations seem to imply. (1993:55–6)

On the other hand, we discover that monstrosity is not easily classifiable since it cannot be unproblematically connected with negative versions of humanity. In fact, as Warner observes, it is not uncommon for ostensibly commendable figures such as heroes to be associated with deviant shapes: 'Even the occasional major Christian saint begins in monstrous form, with paganism written on his body. St Christopher, patron saint of travellers, had a dog's head before his conversion. According to early Byzantine legend, he came to his humble occupation as ferryman in repentance for a rampaging career as this cynophelus giant' (2000:99). Not surprisingly, Christian scholars felt rather uncomfortable about the association of one of their most eminent saints with pagan folklore, hence the elimination of Christopher's bestial physique. Yet, the fact remains that in many traditional monstrous creatures, elements of barbarity and of Christianity coexist.

Moreover, monstrosity eludes conclusive categorization insofar as it embodies what we concurrently dread and hanker for most intensely: the transgression of dividing lines meant to separate one body from another, one psyche from another, and, at the same time, the pure from the impure, the delightful from the gruesome, virtue from vice, good from evil. It implicates us in structures of fear and desire wherein pleasure and horror constantly map themselves on each other; the prospect of boundary dissolution is both alluring and frightening. Forms of physical and psychological deviance also resist compartmentalization as a result of their orchestration by narratives of darkness that are proverbially fluid, rhetorically extravagant and open to conflicting interpretations. They challenge any normative measures designed to put the monster definitively into place. (The relationship between monstrous figures and narrative form is examined in detail in **Chapter 8**.) This idea is emphasized by the sense of ambivalence surrounding our cultural approaches to monstrosity and by the crisscrossing of diverse discourses – medical, philosophical, commercial – over the territory of presumed abnormality. It is far from clear, for example, by what routes societies come to label serial killers as monsters. One of the principal characters in Poppy Z. Brite's *Exquisite Corpse* assesses the situation as follows:

> Some may think killing is easy for men like me, that it is a thing we murderers
> do as casually and callously as brushing our teeth. Hedonists see us as
> grotesque cult heroes performing mutilations for kicks. Moralists will not even
> grant us a position in the human race, can only rationalize our existence as
> monsters. But *monster* is a medical term, describing a freak too grossly
> deformed to belong anywhere but the grave. Murderers, skilled at belonging
> everywhere, seed the world. (1997:66)

Although Andrew Compton's evaluation of the serial killer's social and existential status could simply be dismissed as a by-product of his own psychotically distorted vision, it nonetheless throws vividly into relief the multi-accentuality of the supposedly deviant personality.

Furthermore, although many cultures associate monstrosity with physical defects, these are often rendered ideologically coterminous with intellectual and moral flaws. This sinister propensity is confirmed by traditional Western perspectives on disability. Medical definitions of disability have repeatedly coloured popular approaches to the anomalous body resulting in discrimination, disempowerment and abuse. Western history abounds with cases in which the disabled body has not only invited feelings of repugnance and dread but also the desire to ostracize, domesticate or utterly destroy its image. This is testified, for instance, by the practice of infanticide in ancient Rome as a means of disposing of frail infants, and by the mediaeval apprehension of invalids as evidence for the workings of Satan. Various idealizations of the body perfect over time have served to perpetuate the bias against somatic difference well into the present day. At the same time, through a puzzling shift of logic, monstrosity has been increasingly linked not so much to phenomenal surfaces as to the dark recesses of putatively degenerate psyches. This notion has led many thinkers and critics into convoluted debates about the precise composition of abnormality.

Donatien Alphonse François, Marquis de Sade (1740–1814) is indubitably a key figure in virtually any discussion of monstrosity, and it is with a brief assessment of his case that this introduction will end. What makes the Marquis's example especially intriguing is that there is no consensus of opinion as to where Sadeian monstrosity actually lies. Is Sade himself the monster? Are his characters aberrant? Or is the entire culture he depicts the receptacle of rampant deviance? Given that the Marquis's ideas have been either suppressed or distorted throughout history, answering such questions is an arduous task. What is blatantly clear, however, is that the vehement condemnations of Sade that feature to endemic proportions in both nineteenth-century and twentieth-century thought appear to be grossly hypocritical when one considers that the Marquis's own society was violently abusive and, consequently, that the appalling scenarios he portrays are more of an incarnation than a vicious misrepresentation of his culture's prevailing trends. The atrocities presented by texts such as *Justine* (1791) could indeed be read as allegories of a monstrous power system in which the spectacular display of pain sanctioned by judicial codes played a very prominent part, and supposedly noble principles constituted a hyperreal facade intended to mask the ubiquity of corruption and perversity.

According to Angela Carter, what has made Sade the object of consistently fierce censorship is the fact that his writings do not allow the reader to indulge in timeless fantasies of erotic satisfaction, which is generally the purpose of pornography, but actually 'comment on real relations in the real world' (1979:19). The Marquis's representation of 'the last years of the ancien regime in France', she argues, conjures up 'not an artificial paradise of gratified sexuality but a model of hell, in which the gratification of sexuality involves the infliction and the tolerance of extreme pain. He describes sexual relations in the context of an unfree society as the expression of pure tyranny', thus constructing 'a diabolical lyricism of fuckery' that 'makes of sexuality itself a permanent negation' (26). Following this premise, Carter views Sade as a 'moral pornographer' able to 'use pornography as a critique of current relations between the sexes' potentially conducive to 'the total demystification of the flesh' (20). The political relevance of Sade's corpus is also stressed by Roland Barthes, who maintains that its 'adventures are not fabulous: they take place in a real world, contemporary with Sade's youth, i.e. the society of Louis XV' and 'the corrupt practices of despotism' (1996:130).

The idea that Sade's work does not commend cruelty but unashamedly highlights its pervasiveness and, relatedly, maintains that the apparent upholders of virtue embody monstrosity far more starkly than the writer himself, notwithstanding his reputation, is explicitly corroborated by Philip Kaufman's cinematic fictionalization of the Marquis's last days in *Quills* (2000). In spite of its emphasis on Sade's charisma, the film does not attempt to deny the character's dark proclivities and passions or indeed the monstrous megalomania driving him to fill page upon page and, when paper, ink and quills are taken away from him, bed linen, walls and his own clothes with tales of sexual perversity. However, the ultimate and finally triumphant monster is the eminent doctor, Royer-Collard, the luminary sent by Napoleon himself to the lunatic asylum in which Sade is imprisoned to ensure that he will be prevented once and for all from smuggling his lurid stories into the outside world. As the Marquis is gradually reduced to a naked, chained and tongueless animal, the doctor asserts his authority by treating mental patients with devices that would have made the Inquisition itself salivate in anticipation, and accordingly scorns any human attempt to help the sick by engaging them in self-therapeutic activities, which is what the Abbé in charge of the institution is committed to. Royer-Collard also brutally and repeatedly ravishes his child bride and locks the door, sadistically indeed, behind which the heroine Madeleine is being lethally assaulted by the madman Bouchon. When the doctor becomes the sole and omnipotent controller of the asylum and its inmates (Sade and Madeleine are now dead and the Abbé incarcerated on charges of incurable insanity), the ultimate irony lifts its monstrous head. We discover that Collard is raising funds for the restoration of the infirmary by publishing the Marquis's ultra-censored writings through the efforts of the patients who, while busy setting, printing and binding, might at least temporarily keep their manias at bay.

Monsters as diverse as mythological hybrids, blood-suckers, grotesquely deformed semi-humans, serial killers and pornographers varyingly embody a Gothic ethos of excess, disorder, and physical and psychological disturbance. Their cultural pervasiveness mirrors the ubiquity of the phenomenon of fear which narratives of darkness are unremittingly eager to articulate and which common responses to the deviant subject epitomizes. It is noteworthy, however, that not all beings presumed to defy socially accepted notions of normality are exposed to uniformly severe strategies of regimentation and repression. Aberrant subjects may indeed be everywhere and, in principle, equally free and equally entitled to give vent to their unorthodox predilections. However, as the case of Sade illustrates, it could be argued, in an adaptation of George Orwell's famous dictum, that *some monsters are more equal than others*.

—13—

𝔙ampires

𝕿HE NIGHTMARISH FIGURE of the undead blood-sucker has haunted humanity since prehistory, and tales, legends and case histories revolving around that figure have steadily proliferated from antiquity to the present. It is vital to acknowledge, however, that the vampire's cultural endurance does not make it timeless, for the myth has a proclivity to adapt itself with extraordinary versatility to the particular fears and beliefs of each specific age and society in which it manifests itself. The vampire myth is inseparable from a deep-rooted fascination with blood as simultaneously symbolic of a life-sustaining stream and of the dark abyss into which one is pre-cipitated by its loss, of strength if undiluted and of impurity if mingled, and it is largely in an attempt to negotiate this ambiguity that people all over the world have incorporated sacrificial offerings of blood in their ceremonial practices. The meanings of blood are ultimately as fluid as the substance itself.

The early Church Fathers realized that in symbolically emphasizing the regenerative powers of blood, the Christian Eucharist risked encouraging a regression to pagan rituals. Piero Camporesi's 'The Consecrated Host: A Wondrous Excess', where the Holy Communion is linked to the sacrificial slaughter of a child by a heaven-sent angel, states that it was common for early Christians to regard 'God's sacrifice as a prodigy of abominable grandeur' and to be physically aware of 'the bloody fragment of divine flesh that descended into their stomachs in the guise of the Host'. The image of the child dissected by the angel graphically dominates the more abstract concept of the coalescence of the human and the divine, reflecting a 'profound attraction-repulsion toward the sacrificial mystery' (Straub 1999:4). In spite of persistent attempts by the Church to dispel these superstitions, a powerful connection survived between Christianity, the consumption of flesh and blood and, by implication, vampirism. With specific reference to the Middle Ages, J. B. Twitchell comments: 'What the mediaeval church found in the vampire legend was not just an apt mythologem for evil, but an elaborate allegory for the transubstan-tiation of evil. The reason this was so important was that the vampire myth

explained the most difficult concept in the last of the sacraments to be introduced – the Eucharist. It explained the doctrine of transubstantiation in
reverse' (1998:108).

Moving on to consider specific incarnations of the blood-drinking monster,
we find that there is ample evidence, supported by both archaeological and
literary sources, for the pervasiveness of vampire mythology across the globe,
from Western and Eastern Europe to China, India, Malaysia and Polynesia, from
the Aztecs to the Eskimos. Some of the most popular figures are the Russian
Vurdulak, the Eastern European *Vampyr* or *Oupir* or *Nosferatu*, and the *Vryko-
lakas*, the latter bearing witness to the vampire's shifting connotations
throughout history. Originally denoting the werewolf, this Slavonic term subsequently came to signify both the harmless undead, deemed so due to their
burial in unconsecrated ground, and blood-thirsty monsters. Greek mythology
features vampiric entities such as the *Empusae*, described by Robert Graves as
'filthy demons' begotten by Hecate, the nocturnal deity said to rule Tartarus
and to symbolize the moon's insidious effects. Those creatures 'disguise themselves in the forms of bitches, cows, or beautiful maidens' and 'lie with men by
night, or at the time of midday sleep, sucking their vital forces until they die'
(2000:182). The hapless *Lamia* joins this nefarious breed by seeking retaliation
for the murder of her own children by Hera and hence slaughtering the
offspring of others. The association of sleep with a dangerous relinquishment of
rational vigilance is a recurring topos in Western literature and folklore. In the
Christian tradition, the monsters described by Graves reappear as night-time
demons – female *succubi* and male *incubi* – adept at preying on defenceless
mortals when they are asleep. The *Empusae* probably made their first appearance in Palestine and in Babylonian mythology as children of *Lilith*, the deity
being connected with the draining of infants' blood. She is also reported by
ancient Hebrew sources left out of the Old Testament to have been Adam's first
wife and to have rejected him on the grounds of his sexual ineptitude, thereby
becoming the queen of diabolical spirits.

The fear of the predatory undead, often regarded as a corpse whose sinful
soul is animated by fiendish powers, was fuelled in the early modern period by
tales hinging on the blood-lust of real people: for example, the late fifteenth-
century Wallachian prince Vlad Dracul with his grisly military exploits; Gilles de
Rais (1400-40), a Bluebeardish alchemist who, in pursuit of the philosopher's
stone, killed between two and three hundred children; the seventeenth-
century Hungarian aristocrat Erzsebet Bathory, said to have bled to death
scores of young girls so as to bathe herself in their invigorating substance.
Thereafter, vampirism proved a tantalizing subject for some of the most
eminent Romantic poets. In 1797, Johann Wolfgang Goethe produced the
seminal vampire poem *Braut von Corinth*, where a dead woman returns from the
grave to stop her promised husband from marrying her younger sister. The

dread of contamination plays a prominent part in Goethe's poem, as does the explicit association of blood-sucking with eroticism. The dark sexual connotations carried by vampirism are also central to Samuel Taylor Coleridge's *Christabel* (1816), where the irresistibly beautiful, albeit reptilian, Geraldine seduces the young heroine in the very heart of the paternal home. Sexuality also plays a key role in John Keats's own version of the Greek myth referred to earlier in *Lamia* (1819). The relevance of vampirism as not only a sexual but also a political metaphor is highlighted by Percy Bysshe Shelley's sonnet 'England in 1819', where blood-drinking is compared to the conduct of abusive and exploitative 'Rulers' who drain their countries in a 'leech-like' fashion until they themselves 'drop, blind in blood' (Gardner 1999:581).

Literary and filmic images of the vampire summoned by the Gothic vision indicate that this monster is a context-bound fantasy which alters through time as the creature is required to incarnate different ideological messages. Not all vampires are alike: some are portrayed as enemies, others as intimate friends or even lovers; some as rebels against society, others as power-hungry beasts. Before Stoker's *Dracula* [1897] (see also **Chapter 8**), blood-drinkers are often depicted as close friends. Both Lord Ruthven in John Polidori's 'The Vampyre' [1819], a contemporary reworking of which is provided by Tom Holland's *The Vampyre* (1996), and Sir Francis Varney in James Malcolm Rymer's *Varney the Vampire* [1845–47] treasure their homoerotic friendships with humans. In Joseph Sheridan Le Fanu's *Carmilla* [1872], friendship develops into lesbian love: Laura and Carmilla share everything, including dreams. This novel is also a political allegory wherein Laura and her father's lifestyle recalls the 'isolated cultural self-consciousness' of a 'besieged Anglo-Irish gentry living in the hermetic world of the great house' and being 'only able to regenerate by a sort of legalistic vampirism' (Davenport-Hines 1998:254–5). The story's political relevance is reinforced by its treatment of the racial dimension: the vampire is an unequivocally foreign presence reminiscent of Charlotte Brontë's madwoman, a 'sooty-black animal that resembled a monstrous cat' (Le Fanu 1964:304) and is taken to her prospective victim's house by a 'hideous black woman with a sort of coloured turban on her head' (291).

Far from constituting a potential ally, the vampire as conceived by Stoker is a fundamentally solitary and hideous enemy embodying the quintessential phobias of Stoker's society: fears regarding the contamination of British blood by foreign, infectious intruders; the threat posed by a supposedly predatory female sexuality upon masculine integrity; the assault upon bourgeois values by the feudal aristocracy. Let us examine the implications of each set of anxieties. First, the vampire works as a metaphor for the eruption of alien diseases, especially venereal ones, since they, like vampirism itself, were believed by Victorian culture to originate in Eastern Europe. However, historical evidence indicates that, at least up to the sixteenth century, 'vampire-related superstitions had originated in Western Europe: Great Britain, France, Spain and Portugal' (Marigny 1994:39) and only then did they start spreading eastwards. One of the reasons behind the subsequent association of vampirism almost exclusively with Eastern Europe is, arguably, the latter's isolation from the modern world and, specifically, from the rationalist ethos ushered in by the Renaissance and the Enlightenment. It is precisely in the service of that worldview, conversely, that eighteenth-century Western Europe endeavoured to dissolve traditional fears surrounding the blood-drinker through a veritable deluge of tracts and dissertations penned by doctors, ecclesiastics and scholars claiming to be in a position to explain vampirism scientifically and not merely as evidence for Satan's accomplishments. However, the Age of Reason did not succeed in eradicating the fear of the vampire any more than it succeeded in vanquishing the dark and the inexplicable. Significantly, it is in a cultural context ostensibly devoted to progress, empiricism and Positivist common sense as the ideological foundations of order that *Dracula* itself originates.

Second, blood-drinking figuratively alludes to Victorian stereotypes of femininity based on the dread of woman's indiscriminate urges and erotic voraciousness. As David Skal observes, 'The Darwinian economic and social currents of the late Industrial Revolution placed an unprecedented competitive pressure on middle-class men, while opening new possibilities for women . . . As males grew anxious over their socioeconomic prowess, a cultural reaction-formation desexualized women' (1990:28). According to Peter Gay, 'To deny woman native erotic desires was to safeguard man's sexual adequacy. However he performed, it would be good enough' (1984:197). Women endowed with erotic urges, conversely, become 'life-draining killers, castrators . . . and vampires' (Skal 1990:28). W. J. Robinson's *Married Life and Happiness* confirms this notion: wives who are 'satisfied with occasional relations – not more than once in two weeks, or ten days' may be considered normal but 'there is the opposite type of woman, who is a great danger to the health and even the very life of her husband. I refer to the hypersexual woman, to the wife with an excessive sexuality. It is to her that the name vampire can be applied in its literal sense' (1922:90).

Blood-lust, hunger for semen and diabolically possessive powers are rolled into one in the portrait of the intemperate female, as they are in Charles Baudelaire's image of the woman vampire in 'Le Vampire' (*Les Fleurs du mal*, 1857):

> Toi qui, comme un coup de couteau,
> Dans mon coeur plaintif es entrée;
> Toi qui, forte comme un troupeau
> De démons, vins, folle et parée,
> De mon esprit humilié
> Faire ton lit et ton domaine . . .
> (Baudelaire 1961:37)

You invaded my sorrowful heart
Like the sudden stroke of a blade;
Bold as a lunatic troupe
Of demons in drunken parade,
You in my mortified soul
Made your bed and your domain . . .
(Baudelaire 1993:65)

In *Dracula*, Lucy and Mina represent respectively the failure and success of man's endeavour to civilize femininity and sever it from its troubling association with chthonian origins, the all-engulfing, all-devouring embrace of the earth goddess Cybele. While Mina obediently subscribes to nurturing and domestic obligations, Lucy becomes a symbol of the polyandrous and ultimately bestial female monster.

Third, *Dracula* dramatizes the struggle between the pillars of Victorian hegemony and the vampire as a battle between bourgeois values, with their inbuilt sense of self-righteousness, their nationalistic bias, philistinism and mediocrity, and the monster as a preindustrial despot bound to an aristocratic heritage. Although, as Franco Moretti (1997) argues, the endless circulation of blood which he fosters embodies the rhythms of capitalism, Dracula remains, by virtue of his isolation, an autocrat incompatible with the mores of the burgeoning mercantile classes and their hypocritical displays of gregariousness. Whether or not we are willing to read Stoker's novel as a story of cure and salvation based on the successful annihilation of the Other, *Dracula* insistently intimates that alterity is not an external dimension but rather a reality, however submerged, that is inside all of us, often in the form of repressed sexual longings. *Dracula* is largely about the explosive release of suppressed Victorian libido and oozes with eroticism: when the vampire bites, it penetrates the body in highly sexual ways.

The erotic import of blood-sucking is consistently emphasized by Anne Rice's *The Vampire Chronicles* (1976-98), where vampiric sexuality is conceived of as a polymorphous phenomenon capable of challenging conventional notions of dominance. Although the bite is a form of penetration and the sapping of the victim's energies a form of carnal possession, the emphasis is simultaneously placed on the attacker's loss of mastery with the surrender to the prey's own invasive powers. Marius's advice to the recently vampirized Armand indeed reads: 'Let the entire experience inundate you. That is, be both active and utterly passive' (1998:164). At the same time, gender positions are rendered fluid and unstable, as erotic *jouissance* encompasses an intricate circuitry of homosexual, bisexual and heterosexual relationships, involving mortals and immortals, adults and children, whereby the body becomes 'one great multipored organ for seeing, for hearing, for breathing . . . with millions of minute and strong tiny mouths' (153).

In the context of cinema, the tendency to subject vampirism to shifting interpretations is also evident. Early filmic vampires were set apart by their nature, not by dress, accent or mannerisms. Max Schreck in F. W. Murnau's *Nosferatu* (1922) was defined as a monster by his physical features: rat-like teeth, tentacle-like ears and fingers, luminous pallor. These attributes were retained in Werner Herzog's 1979 remake, *Nosferatu the Vampire*. The figure of the physically aberrant vampire returns in E. Elias Merhige's *Shadow of the Vampire* (2000). Max Schreck features as a real blood-drinker employed by F. W. Murnau in order to create the most realistic vampire movie ever. What is most striking about the film, however, is not so much the visible freakishness of the intemperate undead as the latent, yet no less ruthless, monstrosity of the fictionalized director's vision. Indeed, the film seems primarily concerned with conveying the vampirism of cinema as an art form, the psyche of a man consumed by his aesthetic ideals and the camera itself ultimately proving no less life-draining than the vampire.

The vampiric type immortalized by Murnau altered quite radically with Bela Lugosi, who acted in the 1931 version of *Dracula*, directed by Tod Browning. The reason Lugosi's Dracula is regarded as a monster is not that he is a blood-sucking beast: he is elegantly human, bears no overtly monstrous marks, and even wears his cape, tuxedo and medals in the coffin. Furthermore, while Stoker's Dracula was basically an animal and a rapist, Lugosi indulges in seductive rituals, enticing his women with promises of a glorious death. There is a romantic aesthetic at the root of his amorous exploits. Yet, Lugosi's Dracula is profoundly alien and displays his alterity ostentatiously: what makes him anomalous is the fact that the values he embodies are incompatible with those of the society he inhabits. He is exotic, unconventional and old-fashioned; he incarnates practically everything which a proper American would be expected not to be in the 1930s. As Nina Auerbach argues, Lugosi's Dracula, like his contemporaries King Kong and Frankenstein, articulates the connection between monstrosity and social crisis, with specific reference to the era of the American Depression: 'Not to be Dracula, foreign and formal; not to be Karloff's monster, abnormal and speechless; is to be American in 1931. The monsters' eccentricity confirms American authority' (1995:118).

Subsequent cinematic adaptations of the vampire myth include the immensely popular series produced by Hammer Studios in England between 1958 and 1970, by and large starring Christopher Lee. The first film in the series is *The Horror of Dracula* (1958), directed by Terence Fisher. In the Hammer Studios productions, the vampiric body and its environment undergo significant changes, which may again be interpreted in broadly cultural terms. Dracula's world is imbued with a spirit of 'modernity, speed, and above all, colour' which replaces 'the black-and-white gloom of 1930s America' (Auerbach 1995:120). Lugosi, despite his personal elegance, was surrounded by decay, rats and cobwebs. Lee's castle, by contrast, is spacious, modern, immaculate and expensively furnished. Sinuous columns and candelabra abound; the vampire's coffin is exquisitely carved. Lee even owns a white portable coffin for use in his travels. But at the same time as the vampire's world becomes increasingly comfortable and aesthetically refined, the vampire's own body becomes more and more vulnerable. Light comes to play a central role not merely as a symbol of progress but also, more crucially, as the vampire's greatest enemy. Schreck and Lugosi faded in sunlight but neither was exposed to the brutal searing of which Lee is the victim.

The tendency to foreground the blood-drinker's relative defencelessness has been gaining momentum in both fiction and cinema since the 1970s. Harking back to the corporeal agonies inflicted upon Lee's Dracula, several recent vampire narratives and films lay emphasis on the blood-sucker's physical weakness. In Kathryn Bigelow's movie *Near Dark* (1987), for example, 'the primary sensory experience is neither biting nor bloodsucking, but the sun's rending of tender vampire flesh' (Auerbach 1995:122). What is being emphasized is the vampire's body, its exposure to the dangers of physical existence. Arguably, this heightened sense of physical vulnerability is also a metaphor for the precariousness and helplessness which often characterize contemporary perceptions of embodied identity and is often explicitly linked to the phenomenon of AIDS, as testified, for instance, by Brian Aldiss's *Dracula Unbound* (1991) and Kim Newman's *Anno Dracula* (1992). In *Dracula Unbound*, vampires are sick by definition, and central to the narrative is the character of Bram Stoker himself as a decaying man ravaged by syphilis. The vampire's association with fatal illnesses is what calls for its destruction. In *Anno Dracula*, the vampiric body is linked with deterioration. Newman's vampires sicken and rot even when the sun is not shining.

Roderick Anscombe's *The Secret Life of Lazlo, Count Dracula* (1994) offers an alternative interpretation of the relationship between vampirism and medicine, by encoding Dracula as an eminent psychiatrist dominated by a fetishistic attachment to young women's blood which turns him into a serial killer: here, the supernatural is rationalized as crime and framed by scientific discourses. The themes of infection, physical agony and terminal illness feature prominently in Poppy Z. Brite's fiction. (See also **Chapters 1, 3** and **10.**) These gain especially harrowing connotations through their juxtaposition with mocking images of the vampiric world as a tableau of fashion-inspired stereotypes wherein Goth black cloaks, eyeliner and lipstick become ostensibly more significant than metaphysical issues. With her interweaving of sheer horror, irony and macabre humour, Brite stresses the vampire's loneliness and fear of extinction as the haunting feeling of belonging to a 'dying race' (1994a:247) that unremittingly darkens even the monster's most flamboyant exploits. The notion of vampirism as a lethal and slowly consuming disease is also foregrounded by John Carpenter's *John Carpenter's Vampires* (1998), a fusion of the horror and western genres revolving around the conflict between the vampire slayers led by Jack Crow and the 600-year-old Valek in search of the Berziers Cross that will enable blood-drinkers to tolerate daylight. The topos of corporeal deterioration revolves largely around the character of Katrina, the vampire hunter, whose impending metamorphosis into a blood-sucker makes her an ideal bait in the tracking of Valek by the Crow Team.

Anne Rice places considerable emphasis on vampires' both physical and psychological weaknesses. While foregrounding their vulnerability to mass destruction, especially in the case of the younger generations, *The Vampire Chronicles* also comment on the contemporary body as the victim of a crisis of authority. (Rice's writings are also discussed in **Chapters 1** and **10**.) Rice's main vampires are beautiful and lethal but often do not know what to do with themselves. When their bodies have had enough, they enter states of total inertia or even seek death through self-destruction. Though inhuman, they are tied at all times to the palpitating membrane of flesh and blood. The male body's power is also questioned. Louis and Lestat try to be fathers but fail miserably as, having made Claudia's body, they cannot control its desires or indeed comprehend what it may be like to have an adult mind imprisoned in a child's body. Moreover, the *Chronicles* emphasize vampires' emotional vulnerability as a concomitant of their inability to discover the sources of their tormenting condition. Rice's characters have the means of tracing the vampire body back to ancient history but cannot grasp their real sources. They find out that the first vampire, the Egyptian queen Akasha, was made into a vampire by a spirit, Amel, but there is no final way of knowing who or what produced the spirit in the first place. Although knowledge of the past is supposed to enhance the vampires' powers, it actually crushes them by frustrating all aspirations to discover their provenance, thereby intimating that looking back into the past is as futile as looking towards the future. *Interview with the Vampire* (1976) 'seeks the "truth" about vampires, and comes back empty-handed' (Gelder 1994:110). Claudia and Louis travel to Eastern Europe as the presumed cradle of vampirism but all they find is dazed incarnations of the undead, devoid of any principles or values, let alone glamour. Moving on to Paris, they encounter a hyperreal version of vampirism in the Théâtre des Vampires, where

> real vampires *act* as vampires for a mesmerized audience. The troupe presents
> the audience with an illusion (theatricality) of an illusion ('real' vampires); far
> from leading Louis and Claudia to the 'origins' of vampirism, they show it to
> have been (always?) a mode of representation, a *sign* of vampirism, a style or a
> posture. To be a vampire is, in other words, to *act* like a vampire . . . acting and
> being collapse into each other. (112)

The humanist notion of the quest as an enlightening journey is undermined as the vampire's own mission insistently leads to yet more obscurity: 'I wanted those waters to be blue. And they were not. They were night-time waters . . . a steady eye . . . seemed to fix on me from the depths and say, "Louis, your quest is for darkness only. This sea is not your sea. The myths of men are not your myths. Men's treasures are not yours"' (Rice 1994a:181). If the myth of origins is undermined, so is that of the authority of science. In *Dracula*, science is the primary means of destroying the monster: Van Helsing's handling of Lucy's body is a superstitious ritual but it is also a scientific experiment. Moreover, Stoker's fascination with technology is evidenced by his frequent references to 'up-to-date inventions', such as 'the Kodak camera, the telephone, the portable typewriter' and the 'phonograph diary', which place *Dracula* 'uniquely between the ages of Gutenberg and McLuhan' (Skal 1990:25). In Rice, by contrast, science is associated with modern technology, and technology with gadgets which may be fun but do not really improve life in significant ways. Whereas in *Dracula* the body is controlled by science as the supreme form of knowledge and power, in Rice's *Chronicles* the vampire embraces science but this is just an array of fashionable toys.

In Stephen Norrington's movie *Blade* (1998), vampirism and science also collude with an emphasis on the unlikelihood of either discourse being conclusively able to explain or supersede the other. As the half-mortal and half-immortal Blade is committed to avenging his mother's death and to cleansing the planet of a breed of blood-drinkers, the technologically enhanced vampires he aims at exterminating are, in turn, seeking to possess his unique blood type as a means of conjuring up a dark deity and hence annihilating humankind. Technology and mythology are locked together in an unresolved tension. Lack of faith in scientific progress is central to Kim Newman's 'Amerikanski dead at the Moscow Morgue', where the undead are presented as 'reanimated dead bodies', supposedly capable of developing into 'an entirely new species' (1999:9), produced as scapegoats upon whom the blame for all sorts of political, military and environmental calamities might be placed. A satire of international relations and their vicious distortion of history, the story also parodies the aims and procedures of science, by featuring professionals who are far more interested in playing with the dead and the undead than in advancing a scientific cause.

Vampires are frequently represented as not only physically but also emotionally vulnerable – the repository of a sorrow which humans have become too callous to comprehend. For example, the television movie *Bram Stoker's Dracula* (1973), directed by Dan Curtis and starring Jack Palance, portrays Dracula as a hero and a lover, rather than a tyrant, whose nefarious actions have been triggered by the slaughter of his beloved by the Turks. In Fred Saberhagen's novel *The Dracula Tape* (1975), Dracula tells his own story, emphasizing the depth of his love for Mina while exposing the stupidity of the vampire hunters. John Badham's *Dracula* (1979) likewise portrays the vampire, played by Frank Langella, as a commodious soul capable of profound feelings. Like Curtis, Francis Ford Coppola's own *Bram Stoker's Dracula* (1992) evinces a desire to frame the phenomenon of vampirism by relating it to an emotionally convincing etiology. These interpretations may elicit sympathy for the so-called monster but they also contribute to an explanation or rationalization of something which owns its enduring hold to irrational and inexplicable drives. However, these narratives simultaneously bear witness to the Gothic creature's exceptional versatility and adaptability to the changing requirements of different cultural and ideological scenarios. If Schreck was defined by his unearthly appearance, Lugosi by his eccentricity and Lee by his ambivalent relationship with modernity, more recent vampires are largely defined by their psychological afflictions. Further cases of vampires whose sickness is essentially affective are supplied by the film *The Vampire's Kiss* (Robert Bierman, 1989), where 'a smarmy yuppie convinced he's a vampire' becomes fatally 'immobilized in psychosis' (Auerbach 1995:166). Equally cheerless is Joel Schumacher's *The Lost Boys* (1987), where a bunch of West Coast high school students roam around the gaudy Californian town of Santa Carla, recklessly preying on mortals without experiencing any real pleasure.

In some narratives, the vampire's own ordeals are used as a means of exposing the monstrosity of humanity itself, the gaping and festering wounds of cultures and civilizations which may only perpetuate themselves through brutality and iniquity. In Chelsea Quinn Yarbro's Count Saint-Germain series of the 1970s, for instance, we are presented with a humane vampire who moves through history, from ancient Egypt to Nazi Germany, to reproach humanity for being only capable of mass murder. There are chivalric and romantic elements in the characterization of Saint-Germain, since his aim is generally to save a woman from patriarchal oppression by metamorphosing her into a blood-drinker. The vampire Weyland in Suzy McKee Charnas's *The Vampire Tapestry* (1980) is ostensibly the opposite of Yarbro's hero. (This text is examined in **Chapter 8**.) He is fundamentally an animal, with no time for aesthetic, let alone erotic, considerations. Yet in his exploits, as in Saint-Germain's, there is an implicit indictment of human history as a tangle of bestial drives. The interplay of the theme of vampirism and a pervasive sense of historical crisis is also central to Jonathan Aycliffe's *The Lost* (1996). When Michael Feraru leaves England to reclaim his ancestral castle in the heart of Transylvania, he becomes heir to a legacy darker than the Draculian building. He finds himself reclaimed, in turn, by the ghosts of undecaying forefathers driven by unquenchable blood lust, and eventually detects the same monstrous urge in himself. However, there is also an explicitly political dimension to the novel, the Gothic horror surrounding the undead *strigoi* being replicated by the darkness of post-Ceausescu Romania, with its bureau-cratic labyrinths and fake pictures of thriving social welfare.

The cultural adaptability exhibited by vampires as embodiments of a deeply ingrained fear and as appropriate vehicles for its fictional configuration mirrors the insistent resurgence of dark narratives themselves. Just as they continu-ously rework ongoing anxieties according to shifting historical circumstances, so vampires change over time and space to give contingent structures to the experience of fear. Joining forces with the transgressive propensities of the Gothic vision at its most creative, the vampire drastically undermines the unity and permanence of both individuals and collectivities.

—14—

Hybrid and Grotesque Bodies

HE TERM 'GROTESQUE' derives from the Italian *grotta/grotto*, a cave-like location beloved of Renaissance patrons and designers, and characterized by the use of bizarre ornamentation, a lavish profusion of sculptures and medallions and, above all, an extravagant admixture of human, animal and vegetable forms, distorted and caricatured to various degrees. Strictly speaking, the grotesque is amusing and, at times, even outrageously funny. However, it is also deeply disturbing, for its deformed shapes retain an element of verisimilitude. Its spectators are never allowed to forget that the human body is constantly implicated in the game of fantastical misrepresentation and that their own bodies, by extension, are at least potentially open to the incursions of preposterous and outlandish entities. The grotesque, by combining disparate and even logically incompatible elements, undermines the myth of corporeal unity insistently promoted by Western thought. Humanist philosophy, in particular, stresses the notion of the embodied subject as an enlightened and commanding presence whose authority is supposedly guaranteed by a unified and immutable form. Especially troubling for this ethos are hybrids that violate the dividing-line between human beings and other animals, since these challenge radically the presumed superiority of the rational, encultured self and ultimately compel us to wonder what being human really means.

In their irreverent violation of boundaries, the hybrid and the grotesque graphically remind us that the intrinsic nature of our own species is inconsistent and that any attempt to definitively quantify our affinities with, and differences from, other animals inevitably leads to intractable enigmas. Moreover, asserting our separateness from non-human species provides no ultimate guarantee of our excellence for it may well result in a sense of estranged loneliness, whereas fostering an understanding of our continuities with other creatures could yield a feeling of at-homeness on earth. Hybrid and grotesque bodies may help us rediscover an intuitive, albeit repressed, knowledge of life-sustaining energies: indeed, although they often denote disturbing phantasms forged by fear, they are also, as Mircea Eliade (1952) argues, manifestations of the sacred. This perspective brings to mind Carl Jung's speculations about the collective unconscious as the repository of archetypal symbols endowed with numinous attributes which, as sediments of an intersubjective accumulated memory, operate outside the will of the individual. The submerged spiritual dimension is posited by Jurgis Baltrusaitis (1977) as the ostensibly irrational and spectral, yet enduring and vividly real, substratum of affects underlying the Gothic vision. Attempts to bridge the gap between ghostly vaporousness and worldly solidity can be read as efforts to produce a more commodious approach to reality than strict logic and rationality allow for and hence to grasp latent relationships amongst apparently incongruous entities. The same attitude to the real underlies, according to Meri Lao, Picasso's endeavour, as suggested by his proclivity 'to explore all the intermediate stages between man and horse in the search for a more complete harmony' (1999:13). (See also **Chapter 8** on Picasso's *Guernica*.)

The awareness that bodies and identities are provisional and incomplete, despite humanist claims to the contrary, is signalled by the persistent resurgence of mythological and popular creatures based on the concept of the part-body as an amalgam of the human and the bestial, the biological and the artificial, the natural and the unnatural. Mermaids, sirens, hydras, centaurs, satyrs, sphinxes, chimeras, garudas, devils and angels are amongst some of the most familiar composite bodies populating folklore over the centuries. However, hybrid and grotesque bodies are also very real facets of ordinary contemporary existence. Transformations of the body initiated by both reparative and intrusive medical technologies, for example, often yield anatomies comparable to those of legendary creatures. Modern medicine may hide behind white coats, masks and cutting-edge machinery, yet, it also perpetuates corporeal metamorphoses reminiscent of ancient traditions. Prosthetic surgery, genetic manipulation and modifications of the immune system produce bodies that are reminiscent of the part-bodies of myth – the werewolf, Frankenstein's Creature, the fatefully contagious blood-drinker and the possessed subject. (See **Chapter 8** for a discussion of Mary Shelley's *Frankenstein*.)

In the light of the positions outlined above, it could be argued that what is most intriguing about both mythological and technological part-bodies is that they are not merely intended to document the recognition of human incompleteness but also to keep it at bay by endowing the amorphous Other with visible and latently playful, albeit monstrous, forms. It is by interacting, at least in fantasy and play, with alien beings that we may access a world in which partial and contradictory identities do not univocally elicit undiluted fear and the prospect of continuous self-disassembling and self-reassembling may be enjoyed. In keeping with their proclivity to highlight the ubiquity of fear and to emphasize the potentially stimulating qualities of that condition, narratives of darkness use the hybrid and the grotesque as both incarnations of ongoing anxieties and attempts to situate the latter in a fictional domain that may render the monstrous, if not safe, at least accessible.

One of the most comprehensive evaluations of the grotesque as 'The distortion of all ingredients, the fusion of different realms, the coexistence of beautiful, bizarre, and repulsive elements, the merger of the parts into a turbulent whole' (Kayser 1981:79) is provided by Mikhail Bakhtin in *Rabelais and His World*. This work maintains that several of the most ancient narratives of darkness configure monstrosity in terms of gigantic topographies. Underlying these stories is a mythological tradition that conceives of geological formations such as mountains, rocks and archipelagoes as the grotesque remainders of the bodies of dismembered giants. Bakhtin suggests that the earth as a whole could be ideated as a massive body, rendered hideously grotesque by the degradation of the environment caused by 'cosmic catastrophe' (1984:356). In some tales, the connection of titanic monstrosity with spatial motifs impacts not only on the natural sphere but also on the body of the city. This typically acquires monstrous connotations when it is anthropomorphically construed as the hybrid sum of its inhabitants.

Taking this notion to harrowingly preposterous extremes, Clive Barker's 'In the Hills, the Cities' (*Books of Blood, vol. 1*) depicts the urban organism as a monstrous giant produced by literally strapping together the bodies of its citizens by means of complex contraptions. (This story is also examined in **Chapter 2**.) The defeated city of 'Podujevo', whose collapse in the fight against 'Popolac' evokes 'childhood imaginings of Hell' amounting to 'a sight beyond sickness' (1999a, Vol. 1:135), is described as a gigantic structure consisting of bodies held into a grotesque whole by an 'extraordinary system of knots and lashings'. Commenting on the gruesome spectacle of its wreckage, the narrator observes:

> Some were yoked on their neighbours' shoulders . . . Others were locked arm in arm, knitted together with threads of rope in a wall of muscle and bone. Yet others were trussed in a ball, with their heads tucked beneath their knees. All were in some way connected up with their fellows, tied together as though in some insane collective bondage game. (136)

Popolac, assembled by analogous means, is victorious thanks to its faith in a bizarre perversion of the concept of the body politic and, by implication, in the 'irresistible command' of an identity-erasing totalitarianism: 'Locked in their positions, strapped, roped and harnessed to each other in a living system that allowed for no single voice to be louder than any other, nor any back to labour less than its neighbour's, they let an insane consensus replace the tranquil voice of reason. They were convulsed into one mind, one thought, one ambition' (139).

In hybrid and grotesque bodies, the overall monstrous effect frequently results from a familiar human feature being subjected to strategies of exaggeration and distortion. By recourse to popular motifs such as bulging abdomens, protruding eyes and penis-like noses, those bodies challenge drastically the visions of seamlessness, harmony and wholeness advocated by classical aesthetics, veering instead towards the sprawling, plural and penetrable organism. This idea is confirmed by Stallybrass and White's sculptural model:

> The classical statue has no openings or orifices whereas grotesque costume and masks emphasize the gaping mouth, the protuberant belly and buttocks, the feet and genitals. In this way the grotesque body stands in opposition to the bourgeois individualist conception of the body, which finds its image and legitimation in the classical. The grotesque body is emphasized as a mobile, split, multiple self, a subject of pleasure in processes of exchange; and it is never closed off from either social or ecosystemic contexts. The classical body on the other hand keeps its distance. In a sense it is disembodied, for it appears indifferent to a body which is 'beautiful', but which is taken for granted. (1986:22)

According to Bakhtin, the somatic element most likely to become a monstrous feature is the mouth due to its association with eating, on the one hand, and speech, on the other. Eating has been traditionally demonized since ingestion, mastication and swallowing are intensely physical acts that insistently foreground our animal natures and, in extreme cases, evoke the dark taboo of cannibalism. (See **Chapters 11, 12** and **15** for further discussion of this phenomenon.) Speech ought to extricate us from our purely bestial background by attesting to the civilized subject's powers of conceptual abstraction and symbolic encoding. However, words are treacherous and shallow and provide an inadequate medium for the expression of our most profound and abiding desires. Moreover, they insistently exhibit a penchant for misrepresenting reality by translating individual experiences into generalized pictures of an imaginary human condition, thus failing to mean what we say or indeed say what we mean.

If taken to pathological extremes, the sense of frustration generated by the ineptitude of verbal language may lead to a yearning to subvert violently the mouth's equation to the apparatus of speech and make it instead a close relative of the abdomen. In this respect, the oral urge underlying cannibalism can be seen as a longing to restore the lost haven of infantile plenitude preceding the entry into the symbolic and the related acquisition of language. According to Robert Ziegler, the topos of flesh-eating as dramatized by Thomas Harris's *The Silence of the Lambs* (1990) and its cinematic adaptation by Jonathan Demme (1991) points precisely to a deep dissatisfaction with the inadequacies of verbal language and to the related fantasy of a transgressive return to the imaginary realm (Ziegler 1993). Maggie Kilgour likewise maintains that 'knowledge as tasting and eating' (1990:9) is 'connected with the failure of words as a medium' (16). A close parallel is also established between the violation of corporeal boundaries precipitated by cannibalism and the serial killer Buffalo Bill's urge 'to breach the wall of skin that separates the killer from the victim. Rather than devouring the other, Gumb creates a patchwork dermal envelope' (8), a hybrid comparable to the bloody mask produced by Lecter out of the face of a prison guard. The interweaving of grotesque physicality and psychological monstrosity harks back to William Hope Hodgson's *The House on the Borderland* [1908], where the icon of the greedy animal par excellence symbolically mirrors extreme mental imbalance. The text, itself a hybrid commingling of horror, science fiction, historical allegory and the psychological thriller, features semi-human pig-like creatures whose deformities mirror the out-of-body hallucinatory experiences of the narrator. Hybrids of this kind help us give a tangibly aberrant form to the otherwise amorphous monstrosity of psychological processes.

The gastronomic theme so prominent in the Lecter saga also pervades Michel Faber's *Under the Skin*, a grotesque allegory orchestrated on the basis of the strategy of inversion. Furry, four-legged beasts become humans, and human beings in turn become clumsy and bizarre animals, or *vodsel*. The beast-eating earthling, accordingly, is ideated as flesh available for prodigal consumption by otherworldly creatures supposedly endowed with superior intellectual and gustatory powers. However, the ultimate monster is neither the *human* nor the *vodsel* but the hybrid being constructed through technosurgery, Isserley, who uncomfortably combines features of both species and whose function is to pass off as a female *vodsel*, capture male *vodsel* by giving them lifts in her customized vehicle and then convey them to the farm where they will be 'shaved, castrated, fattened, intestinally modified, chemically purified' (2001:97) to prepare them for ingestion by humans. Having had half of her 'backbone amputated' (127), a spurious chin put in place, her teats removed from her abdomen and replaced with melon-like breasts, and her 'genitals . . . buried forever inside a mass of ugly scar tissue caused by the amputation of her tail' (186), Isserley is painfully aware of her monstrosity, of the shock and repugnance felt by members of her original species in her presence.

The mouth, posited by Bakhtin as pivotal to the production of grotesque effects, has also frequently been employed as a symbol of voracious sexuality and has, accordingly, been conventionally associated with female eroticism on the basis of woman's objectification as a predatory monster. The most obvious examples of the collusion of femininity and monstrosity are proffered by ancient mythology and its unruly hosts of harpies, gorgons, termagants and maenads, amongst other ominous creatures. Especially intriguing are sirens and mermaids, namely hybrids with the torsos of women and the lower halves of birds or fish, since these have symbolized for millennia the fatal attraction of dark femininity. As Meri Lao observes, as 'feminine divinities who are also part of the animal order', sirens and their close relations posit the threat of 'a double nature' holding 'prerogatives of both their components; irrational entities, eternally provocative and disturbing' (1999:11). Homer's account of the sirens luring Ulysses towards death by means of their irresistible song has resonated over the centuries in the writings of William Shakespeare, Friedrich de la Motte-Fouque, Hans Christian Andersen, James Joyce, W. B. Yeats, T. S. Eliot and Oscar Wilde; in the paintings of Hieronimus Bosch, Peter Paul Rubens, David Delamare, Arnold Bocklin, J. W. Waterhouse, Lord Leighton, Aubrey Beardsley, Edvard Munch and René Magritte; in Hollywood movies such as *Million Dollar Mermaid* (1952) and *Splash* (1984); and in advertisements for products as diverse as mineral water, beer, blue jeans, vacuum cleaners and water-resistant wigs.

A contemporary interpretation of the female hybrid related to the figure of the classic mermaid is supplied by Nancy A. Collins (see also **Chapter 1**), in 'Catfish Gal Blues'. The Catfish Gals have 'the upper parts of women and from the waist down are big ole channel cats' (1999:216). The story revolves around the platonically amorous liaison between the blues player Hop and a catfish gal who rewards him with coins and other 'goodies' (222) buried at the bottom of the Mississippi river in exchange for his guitar-playing. Like her marine predecessors, Collins's hybrid combines monstrous and seductive features: 'her upper lip was extremely wide, with the familiar whiskers growing out of them, and she had slits instead of a nose'. At the same time, she is endowed with an irresistibly 'dreamy look' and moves with exceptional grace, 'like a dolphin walking on its tail' (220). The elusive, phantasmic and ultimately fugitive nature of hybrid entities such as the ones described by Lao and Collins brings to mind some of the most memorable figures depicted by Surrealist artists and, specifically, their tendency to seem to materialize and disappear simultaneously. The paintings of Salvador Dalí, Remedios Varo, Robert Delvaux, René Magritte and Francis Bacon, among many others, offer kaleidoscopic galleries of hybrids whose proclivity to mutate within the picture's very frame echoes the fluidity of legendary water creatures. In Bacon, for example, solid bodies tend to fade and dissolve as, in Tom Lubbock's words, 'one part of the flesh melds and sucks into another part, while others suddenly vanish away or cut off into the void' (Lubbock 1998).

Although female hybrids have been mercilessly demonized by mythology as receptacles of darkly enticing and irrational energies, those figures have also, at times, been employed as a means of throwing into relief the murky underside of enlightened reason itself. Euripides's tragedy *The Bacchae* (5th century BC) underscores this point. Dionysus's female worshippers are construed by Greek culture as disruptive due to their combination of opposing drives that render them both loving and bestial, nurturing and aggressive, just as the god himself is described as simultaneously terrifying and gentle. However, the most dele- teriously disruptive forces are ultimately seen to reside not with the maenads but with the champion of rationality and order, the Theban ruler Pentheus who, in repressing the Dionysian cult, stifles his own humanity and paves the way to his own violent death. Pentheus himself is thus made bestial by hubris, arrogance and religious intolerance. His ordeal shows that, while a willing and gradual surrender to instinctual drives is likely to yield salutary and cathartic effects, resistance is conducive to a sudden collapse of defences and ultimately to insanity.

A present-day variation on this theme is supplied by Eric Van Lustbader's 'An Exaltation of the Termagants', likewise concerned with the latent monstrosity of the apparently self-possessed male self. The story traces the protagonist's nightmarish journey through a series of terrifying locations, guided by female fantasy characters who, regardless of their somatic features, are all rendered somewhat monstrous by their hybrid personalities and grotesque surroundings. In the closing pages, we discover that all these imaginary creatures ensue from the protagonist's aversion to his disabled sister, the 'monster' that has haunted him since childhood. Women, the tale intimates, become monstrous termagants when petrifying fears induced by cultural taboos, such as the ones surrounding disability, are projected onto them. Like Pentheus, Van Lustbader's character allows his desire for control to degenerate into a self-destructive passion. As his sister warns him, annihilating what he loathes most intensely will inevitably amount to self-annihilation: 'The part you had to face . . . couldn't be killed – not without killing yourself, anyway' (1999:199).

In the context of modern narratives of darkness, one of the most overt examples of the interweaving of gender issues and the hybrid/grotesque is supplied by Angela Carter's *The Passion of New Eve* (1982). Here, as Lucie Armitt observes, 'Eve/lyn the central protagonist and Tristessa, his/her idealized "other", come together as mirrored doubles. Thus we find a multiple hybridiza- tion of the female grotesque, trapped . . . within the structures of a fantastic monstrosity' (1996:163–4). The novel teems with images of composite and varyingly distorted bodies that faithfully encapsulate Bakhtin's association of carnivalesque transgression with 'a wild anatomical fantasy' (1984:345). The Mother is a patchwork body combining human and animal attributes: her neck is a 'bull-like pillar' and she flaunts, sow-like, multiple tiers of nipples (Carter 1982:59). Eve/lyn her/himself is obviously hybrid due to her/his anatomical and psychological transsexuality, while Tristessa is half human and half cinematic projection. While the Mother's composite nature carries palpably grotesque connotations, Tristessa's is more elusive. A ghostly, virtually incor- poreal presence whose skin is coterminous with the screen upon which beams of light and 'strands of silver' (127) are projected, Tristessa nonetheless possesses the uncanny solidity of a simulacrum: the construct so unreal that it paradoxically becomes more real than the real. Indeed, the character epitomizes the hybridization not only of gender boundaries but also of the dividing-line between the actual and the simulated. Eve/lyn, relatedly, is consistently involved in games wherein reality is conceived of as a by-product of textuality: s/he develops an infatuation with Tristessa via the screen and it is through the mediation of celluloid that her psychosexual transmutation is sustained. Moreover, the novel can be read as an allegorical record of American life as inextricably interwoven with what Jean Baudrillard terms 'the passion for images' (1988:56). In Baudrillard's text, as in the title of Carter's novel, passion ushers in a semiotic dance of ambivalence which, as testified by the word's Christian import, connotes a hybrid compound of extreme pain and ecstatic pleasure.

No creature is exempt from the prospect of degeneration into a monster. Patrick McGrath, Anne Rice and Angela Carter apply this notion to the angelic realm by emphasizing the most eminently corporeal, and indeed least palatable, attributes of their particular fictional angels. McGrath strips the angel of all vestiges of idealized purity and incorporeal grace by emphasizing not only the creature's bodiliness but also, more specifically, its susceptibility to endless corruption, decay and disease. Indeed, the short story 'The Angel' systematically debunks conventional notions of spirituality by means of an uncanny defamiliarization of the supernatural body:

> There was, first of all, the smell: a wave of unspeakable foulness was released with the removal of the corset . . . Harry's [the angel's] flesh had rotted off his lower ribs and belly, and the clotted skin still clinging to the ribs and hipbones that bordered the hole was in a state of gelatinous putrescence. In the hole I caught the faint gleam of his spine, and amid an indistinct bundle of piping the forms of shadowy organs . . . He should have been dead, and I suppose I must have whispered as much, for I heard him say that he could not die. (1995:17)

In Rice's *Vittorio, The Vampire*, angels are likewise portrayed as vulnerable creatures in spite of their amazing talents. Though 'monumentally solid', they have a 'wide-eyed simplicity', and beneath the glorious plumage of their wings one can detect 'shoulders . . . sloped like those of a young boy' (Rice 2000:205–6). Above all, faced with fundamental questions about God's plans, they pathetically concede: 'We are only angels' (215) – 'We don't know!' (285).

In Carter's *Nights at the Circus* (this text is also examined in **Chapter 3**), the winged heroine Fevvers is repeatedly compared to an angel and, on at least one occasion, specifically to Azrael, the angel of death (1984:77). Her preternatural connotations are consistently thrown into relief but this narrative strategy of mythologization does not etherealize the character.

It actually reinforces Fevvers's corporeality to grotesque extremes. Throughout the novel, she is portrayed as an uncanny compound of glamour and vulgarity, glory and grossness, feminine charm and masculine bulk, magnetism and down-to-earthness. A 'being on the borderline of the species', an 'ambivalent body' (81), Carter's angel incarnates the uncanny in the guise of the hybrid/grotesque by simultaneously triggering the sensation of 'enchantment' and a feeling of 'revulsion' (69). Analogously paradoxical reactions are elicited by the vast collection of threshold creatures that populate the novel: the mouthless Toussaint, the inert Sleeping Beauty, the bisexual Albert/Albertina, the Human Chicken impersonated by the anti-hero Walser, clowns whose grotesque countenance obscures the barrier between the face and the mask, shamans promoting the dissolution of the individual self and the collapse of distinctions between humans and animals.

Throughout history, hybrid and grotesque entities have proved immensely adaptable vehicles for the articulation of enduring cultural anxieties, and have been rendered manageable by the translation of their troubling anatomies into *curiosities*. Their exploitation as fairground material, typified by the cases of the Sicilian Fairy Caroline Crachami (1815–24) and the Elephant Man Joseph Merrick (1862–90) in Victorian England, attests to their domestication as sources of amusement. Nevertheless, those creatures return to haunt the imagination, their insistent resurgence mirroring the pervasiveness of fear as an existential condition and of dark textuality as its narrative constellation. We are time and again drawn back to the oxymorons of the monster as an entertaining threat, or as a frightening recreation, in just the same way as we continue revisiting narratives of darkness as protean media through which omnipresent, yet inchoate, fears come to be transmuted into apprehensible shapes, however fleeting these might be.

—15—
𝕿𝖍𝖊 𝕬𝖇𝖏𝖊𝖈𝖙

THE MONSTER MAY BE IDEATED as a hideous enemy, as a tantalizing playmate, as a baffling admixture of the familiar and the unknown. Yet, the Gothic vision proposes that what is ultimately most intractably monstrous about our encounters with darkness is their exposure of troubling leftovers which come across as horrifying due to their stubborn materiality and terrifying due to our inability to comprehend their scope. These remainders consist of the debris floating in the wake of abortive socializing processes and elicit sensations of anxiety insofar as they cannot be conclusively accommodated either in the realm of normality or in that of abnormality. Embedded in the flow of fear that unrelentingly courses through human life, those evasive residues point to the persistence of heterogeneous fragments of experience which the encultured adult world is powerless to clarify and incorporate into its sign systems. They teeter at the point of cleavage between the prelinguistic realm of infancy and the symbolic order without being definitively assimilable by either. They bear witness to the elusiveness of all meaning. This perspective is exhaustively documented by the psychoanalytic theories of Julia Kristeva.

Kristeva uses the concept of horror to describe the ways in which we revolt violently against aspects of our being which society deems unacceptable. In order to be admitted into the symbolic order, the subject must differentiate itself from others by shedding everything which culture perceives as unclean, disorderly, asocial or antisocial. This process is termed *abjection*, and all the putatively improper stuff which the subject aims at casting off constitutes the *abject*. This is not a definable object for we can only identify it as something alien which calls our existence as independent creatures into question: '*Abjection* is something that disgusts you, for example, you see something rotting and you want to vomit – it is an extremely strong feeling that is at once somatic and symbolic, which is above all a revolt against an external menace from which one wants to distance oneself, but of which one has the impression that it may menace us from the inside' (Hoffman Baruch 1996:118). Especially threatening are those borderline parts of the physiological apparatus through which abject materials pass and the materials themselves: blood, semen, urine, faeces, tears, milk, sweat. These question the body's self-containedness, for they are neither totally contained within the organism nor fully external to it. The most common objects of repugnance cited by Kristeva as likely candidates for abjection are filth, waste, dung and food items (for example, the skin on the surface of milk) which tend to induce nausea. Kristeva also points out that abomination, defilement and the unclean have often been associated with the feminine and the maternal. In the Old Testament the consumption of milk is prohibited because milk is linked with the physical and symbolically incestuous relationship between mother and child. The connection between the abject and the female body will be considered later in this chapter.

The problematic materials and physical regions associated with the phenomenon of abjection do not carry merely somatic connotations. In fact, they replicate, at the level of the flesh-and-bone organism, anxieties concerning the protection of a culture's boundaries that pervade the body politic in its entirety. As Mary Douglas points out,

> Any structure of ideas is vulnerable at its margins. We should expect the
> orifices of the body to symbolize its specially vulnerable points. Matter issuing
> from them is marginal stuff of the most obvious kind. Spittle, blood, milk,
> urine, faeces or tears by simply issuing forth have traversed the boundary of
> the body. . . . The mistake is to treat bodily margins in isolation from all other
> margins. There is no reason to assume any primacy for the individual's attitude
> to his own bodily and emotional experience, any more than for his cultural and
> social experience. (1966:121)

In other words, the vulnerability and relative instability of liminal aspects of the organism mirror salient characteristics of all putative lines of demarcation. Cultural practices and customs designed to delimit the physical self could therefore be read as symbolic attempts to protect a whole culture from alien incursions.

Douglas also emphasizes that the fear of pollution, so central to the dynamics of abjection, does not emanate from any one specific category of being but rather from threshold states. Food-related prohibitions, such as the ones upon which the Jewish concept of *kosher* is founded, issue from an aversion to animals that elude neat compartmentalization: 'To be holy is to be whole, to be one; holiness is unity, integrity, perfection of the individual and of the kind. The dietary rules merely develop the metaphor of holiness on the same lines' (54). Thus, cleansing rituals are construed as a means of securing the wholeness/holiness of both singular bodies and communities against the menace posed by transitional beings and the connotations of confusion, impurity and disarray which they inevitably carry. Over the centuries, leprous, polluted and decaying anatomies have been subjected to severe censorship for the same reason: they threaten the margins of the supposedly taintless body and of the legitimate cultural order which rests upon it.

The corpse is a particularly disturbing manifestation of the abject, not simply because it signifies death but also because it reminds us of what our material bodies are destined to become and, in a sense, *already* are. The lifeless body, prone to corruption and decay, is just the culmination of processes of physical transformation and deterioration which the living organism experiences on a daily basis. In other words, what bothers us about the corpse is not its association with death as such: our reaction to a dead body prepared for a funeral is likely to be very different from our reaction to a carcass on the verge of putrefaction. The carcass reminds us of what we 'permanently thrust aside in order to live': it 'is death infecting life' (Kristeva 1982:3–4). The Gothic vision consistently returns to the coexistence of life and death as a major topos in the orchestration of monstrosity. Indeed, as Noel Carroll points out,

> Many monsters of the horror genre are interstitial and/or contradictory in
> terms of being both living and dead: ghosts, zombies, vampires, mummies, the
> Frankenstein monster, Melmoth the Wanderer, and so on. Near relatives to
> these are monstrous entities that conflate the animate and the inanimate:
> haunted houses, with malevolent wills of their own, robots, and the car in
> King's *Christine.* (1990:32)

The blurring of the dividing-line between life and death plays a pivotal role in Clive Barker's 'Confessions of a (Pornographer's) Shroud' (*Books of Blood, vol. 3*). Brutally killed in the wake of his unwitting complicity with the porn industry, Ronnie Glass retains a mysterious energy that enables him to animate the shroud in which the pathologists have wrapped him, turn the 'sullen linen into a semblance of life' (1999a, Vol. 3:95), give it a quasi-human form and use it to take revenge on his murderer. As death takes on the power to simulate life, the very notion of aliveness becomes nebulous: abject-like, the shroud is concurrently a body and not a body, an animate entity and a spectre, reality and illusion.

Although we are trained to believe that the expulsion of the abject is the precondition of our coming into being as autonomous subjects, our mastery of the abject is ineluctably incomplete insofar as its ghostly presence relentlessly threatens to engulf and disintegrate our identities and our boundaries. It is a black hole on the edge of identity into which we may implode anytime. The subject that tirelessly endeavours to shed the abject is 'on a journey, during the night, the end of which keeps receding' (Kristeva 1982:8). No less problematic is the fact that the abject is simultaneously repulsive and attractive. It elicits feelings of visceral repugnance insofar as it is associated with the murky and the undifferentiated; yet, in its penchant for challenging conventional symbolic categories, it also points to an alternative dimension wherein, were we exempted from the process of abjection, we could live out a pleasing fantasy of plenitude and not be expected to sever the self from the Other.

Many of the monsters presented by narratives of darkness could be regarded as manifestations of the abject. From Mary Shelley's *Frankenstein* [1818], through R. L. Stevenson's *The Strange Case of Dr Jekyll and Mr Hyde* [1886], to Peter Straub's *Ghost Story* [1979], contact with alien forms inevitably engenders sensations of nausea and physical disorientation. However, those same forms are uncannily fascinating, either because, as Enfield says of Hyde, they defy description and hence invite the imagination to wander, or because they are erotically enticing at the same time as they elicit disgust. In *Ghost Story*, Don becomes aware of his shock of repulsion while making love to the monster Alma Mobley. Comparable emotions are experienced by the monstrous protagonist's lovers in Clive Barker's 'Jacqueline Ess, Her Will and Testament' (*Books of Blood*, *vol. 2*). Vassi describes her nocturnal metamorphoses in a tone that evokes sensory loathing and attraction at once:

> Her very fabric was on the move, her muscle, her hair, the down on her cheek moving to the dictates of some internal tide. Her lips bloomed from her bone, boiling up into a slavering tower of skin; her hair swirled around her head as though she were lying in water; the substance of her cheeks formed furrows and ridges like the ritual scars on a warrior; inflamed and throbbing patterns of tissue, swelling up and changing again as a pattern formed. The fluxion was a terror to me, and I must have made some noise . . . That was, you can understand, a pivotal experience. (1999a, *vol. 2*:66)

Later he adds: 'She was (is) sublime . . . I lived in a permanent ecstasy of her' (68).

The abject does not merely oscillate between the opposed poles of hideousness and attractiveness but actually embodies both at one and the same time. It closely resembles the phenomenon of fear as a condition that continually interweaves paralyzing and vitalizing potentialities. Fear does not affect us systematically, through the alternation of clearly demarcated moments of pain occasioned by the recognition that we are in its grip, and equally well-defined moments of pleasure resulting from the hope that we might extricate ourselves from it. In fact, negative and positive feelings coexist at all times. If we are unrelentingly haunted and incapacitated by dread, the awareness of its omnipresence is also a gateway to a more comprehensive understanding of what and where we are and hence the prelude to a willingness to embrace darkness as a potential source of illumination. We cannot even begin to know ourselves unless we are prepared to acknowledge the extent to which fear relentlessly shapes us. The abject exhibits analogous traits by bringing together shifting signifiers of pleasure and pain in a hybrid constellation.

A. L. Barker's *The Gooseboy* [1987] supplies a graphic incarnation of precisely such a hybrid in the description of the character to whom the title refers:

> One side of his face, the left side, was no age. It was no face. Just a piece of raw meat like the meat on butchers' hooks, purple over the bone and dried up, the sort of cut you wouldn't buy. He had something that passed for an eye, though I couldn't pass it, and a puckered-up slit like a drawstring purse. All that was bad enough, but it stopped on a line from his forehead to his chin; no merging, no blending, one skin-cell dead and rotten, the next one to it living and sweating. The right side was all right, eye, nose, mouth perfectly formed – they used to call that sort of lip a Cupid's Bow till Cupid went out of fashion – half a perfect face. (1999: 71)

The notion that the collusion of the repulsive and the seductive around which abjection revolves has the power to awaken both the body and the psyche, as attested to by the dynamics of fear itself, is corroborated by the deformed boy's ability to revive, and allow an outlet for, desires and passions hitherto relegated to the most shadowy recesses of the female protagonist's being. Reflecting upon a totally unexpected sexual encounter with the physically deformed character, the aging Dulcie, having thus far sublimated her frustration behind a stereotypical facade of hard-nosed efficiency, admits to having grasped for the first time in her life the meaning of erotic *jouissance*: 'I was fully conscious that I'd never get another moment of glory like this one. No need to remind myself to make the most of it: you don't quantify at a time like that' (95).

Chet Williamson's 'Excerpts from the *Records of the New Zodiac* and the Diaries of Henry Watson Fairfax' offers an intriguing variation on the theme of abjection by positing human flesh itself as the ultimate manifestation of the abject: a liminal, concurrently repugnant and appealing entity to be possessed and consumed in order to prove one's power in the symbolic order. (Cannibalism is also discussed in **Chapters 11, 12** and **14**.) The New Zodiac is an exclusive club for the mega-rich comprising twelve 'Charter Members', each associated with one of the stellar signs, in the midst of which capitalist competitiveness escalates to preposterously macabre extremes. A club dinner is held 'on the final Saturday evening of every month', all arrangements made by 'that month's host' (1999:154). Striving to outshine their associates by means of increasingly outlandish menus and wines, the twelve characters soon fall prey to a diabolical passion. The imperative to excel erases all other considerations. Culinary superiority is not merely conveyed by the degree of sophistication with which the various dishes are prepared and garnished but, more importantly, by ensuring that each recipe contains the flesh of a person or persons closely associated with a member of the club. A financial enemy, a collaborator, a team of lawyers, a mistress and a daughter are among the sacrificial victims alluded to by the *Records*. The narrator, Capricorn, stages a final meal – he is the sole host and guest. The other eleven members, 'victims of their own hunger and the things that hunger brought' (163–4), provide the menu.

Hors d'oeuvres à la Aquarius	*Pisces jardinière*
Potage queue de Aries	*Taurus rôti*
Gemini paté	*Cancer à la crème*
Leo d'agneau – mint sauce	*Roast suckling Virgo*
Libra Parmentière	*Scorpio à la casserole*
Sagittarius de lait farci au marrons	

The consumption of human flesh is here equated to the shedding of varyingly intimate attachments as abject marginalia whose destruction is supposed to guarantee the unchallenged omnipotence of the symbolic subject.

As mentioned earlier, Western culture has repeatedly constructed the female body as a principal manifestation of the abject due to its fluid, sprawling and leaky nature, demonized it as an unsavoury subversion of aesthetic ideals of unity and integrity, and accordingly subjected it to regimenting strategies intended to frame its boundlessness. As Lynda Nead observes, 'the female body is defined as lacking containment and issuing filth and pollution from its faltering outlines and broken surfaces' and it is in an effort to enclose it within clear-cut boundaries that mainstream male artists have sought to 'perform a kind of magical regulation of the female body' (1992:7) by translating it into a 'hermetically sealed' (8) icon of purity and beauty. Of the various aspects of feminine corporeality that tend to elicit negative responses, fat is indubitably the most insistently stigmatized, for it represents 'excess, surplus matter. It is a false boundary . . . and needs to be stripped away' (10). Thus, like the abject, fat signals a liminal region between the self and the non-self. It is perceived at once as part of the organism and as extraneous to it, as the outermost edge of the physical being and as an illusory frame.

These ideas are vividly dramatized by Margaret Atwood's *Lady Oracle* [1976] and it is with an assessment of this dark narrative, intimately bound up with the Gothic vision, that the present chapter closes. The novel employs recursively the image of the fat body as a symbol upon which both physical and psychological experiences of abjection converge. Just as the Kristevan abject is never conclusively expelled, so fat, even once it has been shed in order to construct a bounded self, continues to surround Joan, Atwood's heroine, 'like a mist, like a phantom moon' (1982:214). The defiance of culturally prescribed borders which the excessive body denotes is replicated throughout the narrative by the disruption of the humanist myth of a self-contained identity by a proliferation of split subjectivities, alter egos and plural masks: 'hadn't my life always been double?', Joan wonders. 'There was always that shadowy twin, thin when I was fat, fat when I was thin, myself in silvery negative, with dark teeth and shiny black pupils glowing in the black sunlight of that other world. . . . But not twin even, for I was more than double, I was triple, multiple, and now I could see that there was more than one life to come, there were many' (246). Concurrently, she is haunted by nightmares revolving around a grotesque 'Fat Lady', seen walking the tightrope amidst the roar of 'insulting songs' (102) or ice-skating gracefully until the crowd, outraged by her bizarre countenance, go 'for the harpoon gun' (274).

Moreover, the personalities which Joan alternately adopts and discards echo the rhythms of abjection as a process in which, as we have seen, life and death drives uncannily coalesce. Indeed, the heroine is ideated as a subject required to kill off certain facets of her being, primarily the obese and mother-dominated child, in order to secure the survival of other identity constructs. Most significantly, Joan moves in and out of two contrasting authorial personas, the writer of Costume Gothics and the writer of female hermetic poetry, murdering one every time she assumes the other. Creative activity itself is construed as a process that unfolds on the borderline between life and death. In the process, we do not witness a smooth transition from one configuration of selfhood to another but rather abrupt discontinuities and a dizzying oscillation between disparate subject positions none of which may be definitively destroyed or asserted. As Elizabeth Bronfen points out, in 'her repeated attempt to vanish and reemerge as someone else', Joan is eventually 'forced to acknowledge the eternal return of the same' (1992:416). In this respect, her plight evokes the agonies of the budding subject, struggling to eliminate the abject only to be confronted, time and again, with its stubborn resurgence.

Furthermore, *Lady Oracle* posits the Gothic vision itself as the ultimate embodiment of the abject. Gothicity is a liminal phenomenon insofar as it concurrently elicits repulsion and fascination: it is presented on the one hand, as objectionable, due to its insistent return to the theme of female oppression, yet attractive on the other, not merely because it allows for escapist flights into alternative dream worlds but also by virtue of its allegorical function as social critique. Marginalizing the Gothic as a second-rate genre pandering to the paltry fantasies of naive female readers does not amount to emancipating women from reductive role models since it actually effaces its value as a cogent, albeit formulaic, commentary on eminently real power relations revolving around issues of sexuality and gender. The Gothic, therefore, may be dismissed as an undesirable appendage to the laws of the symbolic, yet its tales of horror, terror and fear articulate the sins of the symbolic itself: Joan's ordeal does not, after all, differ substantially from the tribulations of her fictional heroines (Charlotte, Penelope, Felicia) or indeed from those of the Lady of Shallott, to which the novel consistently refers. We may choose to cast the Gothic vision off in much the same way as we endeavour to disavow the abject. However, the Gothic is no less adept than the abject at resurfacing in myriad forms as the major discursive field wherein fear's affects, terror and horror ceaselessly interplay.

Ultimately, the abject owes its enduring power to its inherent ambivalence. On the one hand, it stands for ambiguous substances and experiences that threaten our corporeal and psychological integrity and must be rejected if we are to function as socialized subjects. On the other hand, by surviving even the most drastic purification rituals and tenaciously returning to haunt us, the abject alerts us to the existence of forces that transcend the strictures of the symbolic. Though deeply disturbing, it nonetheless holds tantalizing prospects for the extension of the self and of its culturally imposed boundaries. Furthermore, it is worth contemplating the possibility that by constantly requiring us to kill parts of ourselves in order to be, the process of abjection may provide therapeutic opportunities for rehearsing death. In its ambiguity, that process bears affinities with the dynamics of fear. Indeed, both phenomena resist conclusive assimilation to dominant signifying structures by allowing the abhorrent and the alluring to meet and merge in mutual suffusion, thus eliciting at once sensations of revulsion and elation. By communing with the fearful and the abject, rather than devoting ourselves to their annihilation, we may develop unexpectedly capacious sensibilities, insofar as their persistent evocation of paradoxical affects is likely to expand the territories of both our vigilant consciousness and our dormant unconscious fantasies.

Epilogue

NARRATIVES OF DARKNESS informed by the Gothic vision evince an arguably unparalleled versatility to supply images through which the anxieties of successive epochs may be communicated. Many-chambered caves wherein the irrational often reigns supreme, they insistently erode the agendas of the Enlightenment by making the rule of reason no more than the icing on the cake of civilization. They cultivate an anti-humanist ethos that throws into relief our isolation and puniness in the face of both external threats and inner goblins. Above all, they compel us to confront the sources and affects of fear as an endemic condition, capable of numbing the intellect and the senses and, concurrently, of strengthening consciousness by making us recognize levels of reality which social conventions tend to occlude, generally for the purpose of anaesthetizing fear's very ubiquity. Icons and fantasies of inversion, transgression, decay and excess play an important part in this vision. Far from constituting sporadic occurrences or flitting traces in the corridors of perception, these images and imaginings pervade consciousness and are able to bring it to life even as they appear to paralyse it: they invigorate our mental and sensory capacities by stressing that human identities are neither coherent nor abiding but rather transient effects of performance. The subject's putative stability is a product of the repetition of stylized acts. Even at its most luminous, the self is dimmed by eerie shadows.

The discourse of darkness mirrors the dynamics of fear by virtue of its pervasiveness, propensity to assume a plurality of forms, and paradoxical status as a dimension which we deem overpowering and yet seek, consciously or unconsciously, in an effort to fathom the inexplicable. Dark places, as locations upon which light fails or refuses to shine, both literally and figuratively, exemplify this state of affairs. They are not, unproblematically, demonic netherworlds and accursed haunts which we strive to avoid. Indeed, while frightened adults often resemble small children running away screaming from a magic-lantern show, they are also pretty much like children peeping from behind the curtains at the scary scenes on the television screen. While sites of darkness may repel us, they simultaneously map a challenging territory which we deliberately look for and travel through, albeit in a tentative and meandering fashion. We do so in the hope that they may provide some answers, however provisional, to questions regarding our place in the universe and our world's place in a sprawling galaxy of other, visible and invisible, worlds. (See **Chapter 1**.)

Confronting fear as an ongoing condition which no known culture, economy or creed is conclusively capable of exorcizing, often entails attempts to ascertain the temporal connotations of frightening sensations and events. Are there specific times, either in an individual's or in a society's history, when disabling anxieties are likely to be felt more acutely? If so, could such times be defined on the basis of distinctive and recursive characteristics? It seems that the emergence of the unwelcome does not automatically coincide with a definable set of circumstances. We are hardly ever in a position to predict with absolute accuracy what feelings and responses, dread included, will be generated by a given situation. This is confirmed by the fact that times of sorrow and times of joy are equally capable of bringing us face to face with the mind's darkest idols. Furthermore, the phenomenon of fear is not universal but contingent on historical and ideological contexts. While it is important to recognize that virtually all angles of the Gothic vision serve to alert us to the existence of inscrutable forces, it is also crucial to acknowledge that they do so in a protean variety of ways, and that the fictional configurations they spawn are largely influenced by the cultural circumstances of their construction and reception. By extension, one ought to observe that the experience of painfully disconcerting emotions is immensely variable. If there is a constant in its narrative articulation over time, it is that, just as fear itself is endemic, so dark narratives are an enduring aspect of human creativity whose exuberant vitality is attested to by their tendency to exceed generic classification.

At the same time as we feel compelled to explore tenebrous regions in an effort to unravel the enigma of our place in the world, we feel drawn to bleak moments of horror and terror by a longing to negotiate the temporal boundaries of our existence and, ultimately, the ineluctability of its destination: death. Dark times, in their multifarious manifestations, are metaphorical anticipations of the sepulchral gloom associated with physical dissolution: a source of dread, but also an invitation to confront the prospect of our annihilation and hence a means of reinforcing the sense of being alive. (See **Chapter 2**.) The facet being disclosed by fear that may be regarded simultaneously as the most intriguing and the most distressing, is the human psyche's own inherent darkness. All psyches are to some extent dark because all individuals host, in varying degrees, thoughts, fantasies and desires of which they are only dimly aware or plainly unaware. The relationship between such thoughts, fantasies and desires and the phenomenon of fear is twofold. On the one hand, submerged psychic contents are themselves a source of apprehension insofar as their surfacing (however partial or haphazard this may be), impels us to stare at the darkest Beyond – the stranger within our very selves. On the other hand, by acknowledging those psychic contents, we may at least begin to develop strategies for dealing with troubling emotions and for enabling our anxieties to feed, rather than stunt, our creative and imaginative faculties: for example, through storytelling. (See **Chapter 3**.)

Misleadingly associated, primarily by the guardians of enlightened common sense, with an irrational and infantile behaviour concomitant with inarticulateness, dumbstruck silence or else the inconsequential babble of lunatics and visionaries, fear actually has a language. It would perhaps be more accurate, in fact, to say that it speaks and writes through a polyphony of codes. This is eloquently documented by narrative articulations of spectrality and haunting. The forms of dread induced by these phenomena entail complex and, by and large, unsettling dialogues between the self and the non-self, presence and absence, being and its negation, what we see and what we think or wish to believe we see. These exchanges require the elaboration of vocabularies and tropes that often exceed the limits of everyday discourse. Their most salient attribute is a constant oscillation between alternative levels of meaning and interpretation. The rhetoric of fear as exemplified by the Gothic vision, with its emphasis on dark fantasy, the supernatural and the ghostly, encompasses a wide range of both verbal and visual languages, image repertoires, performative acts and stylistic devices. The rhetorical principle of ambiguity plays a vital role. Logical distinctions are blurred and the dividing line between sense and nonsense is obfuscated within a pervasive atmosphere of suspense and undecidability. (See **Chapter 4**.)

The ghost, as an emblematic incarnation of the inexplicably frightening, does not constitute a monolithic category. In fact, there are many spectral forms, for ghostliness is no less prismatic than fear itself. What the spectre almost invariably marks is an absence, a lacuna in the fabric of reality, a non-space which we feel attracted towards for the very reason that it can be neither found nor charted. Ultimately, we haunt that non-place no less than it haunts us. Despite this recurrent component of the language of spectral fear, it is nevertheless crucial to realize that phantasms are not invariable and timeless, since they actually mirror specific cultural preoccupations – as vampires, hybrids and legion other monsters also do. Suspended between fiction and social reality, capable of participating in both and yet never conclusively accommodated by either, preternatural entities epitomize the spirit of ambiguity which the discourse of fear unrelentingly fosters. Their duplicitous status owes much to their ability to evoke simultaneously sensations of terror and horror. Indeed, they embody the proclivity, insistently exhibited by the Gothic, to challenge conventional distinctions between those two affects by positing them as interacting aspects of the experience of fear. Creatures that subvert or invert the laws of nature throw the collusion of terror and horror into relief by producing feelings of disorientation through the juxtaposition of the incorporeal and the material. Indefinite and impalpable manifestations of alien worlds are consistently interwoven with starkly tangible and spine-chilling occurrences. (See **Chapter 5**.)

The concurrently terrifying and horrifying sensations associated with menacing forms and with the reactions they elicit in their victims also characterize several scenes of haunting. The physical circumstances of our encounters with a dark Other both terrify and horrify us by alternately dissolving the solidity and form of landscape and architecture alike into amorphous sources of psychosomatic displacement, and giving palpable shape to the most stubbornly inchoate apprehensions of the mysterious. In so doing, they conjure up a para-digmatically Gothic world of uncertainty and paranoia in which neither ethical nor aesthetic standards are sacrosanct. Ghost-infested settings proffer invita-tions to enter secreted portions of reality in which everyday certainties are spookily suspended or mockingly flouted. They are frequently traps and prisons, no doubt, but they are also alluring venues wherein the unknown's compelling powers may be grappled with. (See **Chapter 6**.)

Spatial, temporal and psychological darknesses tend to manifest themselves narratively by means of a complex rhetoric in which the ambiguity and open-endedness of both identity and meaning are repeatedly foregrounded. The interplay of terror and horror within the dialectic of fear contributes in crucial ways to that rhetoric, and shows that feelings of disorientation conveyed by both tangible and intangible phenomena are, at once, both a constant in our patterns of perception and cognition and historically situated events. Accord-ingly, narratives inspired by a Gothic sensibility include many genres and subgenres which tend to become more or less prominent in relation to changing cultural scenarios. In its variety, dark textuality replicates the operations of fear itself. It is as a corollary of fear's ubiquitousness that its affects take mul-tifarious guises and express themselves through a broad range of languages, codes and texts. If dread were a unified experience, tied to clearly identifiable situations and occurrences, it would perhaps be possible to delimit the sphere of its fictional manifestations. However, this is not the case. Fear is sprawling and multi-faceted, and its representations consequently display kaleidoscopic mobility. The openendedness of such constellations is borne out by the ambiva-lent status of the verbal and visual images supplied by dark fiction. Both underscore the impossibility of differentiating neatly between terror as a response to the indefinitely frightening and horror as a response to the physi-cally repulsive. Indeed, both the written word and the visual image partake concurrently of the immaterial and the embodied. (See **Chapter 7**.)

On the one hand, the experience of fear is encoded through words: disem-bodied signs that symbolize reality, arbitrarily and conventionally, and cannot be treated as physical objects. Furthermore, fear often makes itself felt most gratingly through elusive visions that lack clear dimensions and contours. On the other hand, both words and visions are powerfully material; they are capable of evoking intensely physical sensations and reactions. The materiality of images makes it possible to conceive of texts as bodies in their own right. Indeed, a textual identity, the character and makeup of a narrative, could be said to coincide with its bodily configuration. In the specific realm of dark writing, a particularly interesting case is offered by narratives whose material construction echoes the messages they articulate. Gothic figures of fragmentation, disorder and excess are frequently mirrored by textual bodies that reject organic unity in favour of a multiplicity of viewpoints and styles, pastiche, collage and quilting. These provide a representational correlative for the polymorphousness of fear itself. At the same time, they comment on the aspirations and preoccupations of particular societal and epistemic formations, for fragmented and disunified stories reflect the monstrous and spectral forms which cultures ideate in order to express their unease in the face of an unquantifiable Other. Often the splintered textual corpus represents, no less pointedly than its themes do, an ominous creature laden with political, economic, racial and sexual connotations. (See **Chapter 8.**)

Whilst the Gothic text/body may give rhetorical expression to collective anxieties, it may also be a vehicle for voicing individual fears springing not merely from the dread of pain and obliteration but also from a desire to understand the source of the creative impulse. Many authors have talked about the possible reasons behind their commitment to dark writing in terms of both broadly cultural and specifically personal phobias. Whereas it would be somewhat preposterous to argue that all those who write dark narratives do so in order to give public expression to private experiences, it would seem that storytelling geared towards the articulation of some of the murkiest aspects of human existence does serve a therapeutic function. Taking fear into the domains of fictional writing, or indeed into those of cinema and other visual and performance arts, is a way of metamorphosing its destructive energies into productivity, of countering the threat of dissolution by creating alternative worlds wherein the birth, growth and self-perpetuation of scariness could be traced. These fictional enterprises do not actually eliminate fear. In fact, they often underscore its stark inevitability: no sooner is one source of fear grasped than another reveals itself. To this extent, the Gothic vision could be considered a form of therapy insofar as it helps both authors and readers realize that the dark Other is not a limit but rather a threshold continually asking to be crossed and recrossed. (See **Chapter 9.**)

The narrative orchestration of fear is largely concerned with the confrontation of borders and, more or less overtly, with strategies for trespassing the frames of language and subjectivity alike. Even writers who put themselves into their tales quasi-autobiographically are never wholly in control of either their words or their selves. Quite regardless of whether or not they end up scaring themselves while seeking to scare their audiences, by entering the narrative they become akin to fictional characters and must therefore ultimately doubt their own reality. What is most beneficial about this process is its invitation to face up to the constructed nature of the subject and of its fashioning by the symbolic order. No less unsettling, yet potentially salutary, is the recognition that ostensibly extraordinary events and phenomena often stem from utterly ordinary, even banal, circumstances. This makes the dark tale an inconclusive game whose climax is hard to foresee. Especially daunting are those narratives in which an apparently insignificant or only marginally meaningful move sets off a chain of appalling events with no clear logical outcome, governed almost against sense and reason by an indomitable principle of ineluctability. Wrestling with the random tides of chance and contingency may eventually lead to an acknowledgement of the provisional character of both texts and selves. Tales of Gothic darkness insistently posit storytelling and identity as forever unfinished processes, only precariously adjusted to a universe where the shadows tend to lengthen well before twilight.

The proposition that the articulation and confrontation of fear are concurrently individual and collective experiences is most explicitly demonstrated by stories that investigate darkness with particular reference to familial conflicts wherein the representatives of different generations can be seen both as individuals haunted by private obsessions and as embodiments of broader cultural ordeals. Narratives spanning early Gothic fiction to the present keep returning to the themes of the doomed family/community, dynastic enmity and trans-generational curses as lenses through which to view the disabling preoccupations, secrets and lies that beset both the individual's development and enculturement, and the processes through which whole societies mould and perpetuate themselves. The geographical and architectural settings in which familial and societal traumas are enacted often simulate symbolically the predicaments of their inhabitants. What is especially daunting about such locations is the fact that their figurative power does not consist of a single set of attributes and does not spring from the repetition of invariable motifs. The fears coursing through families as microcosms of entire cultures assert themselves equally imposingly in aristocratic castles, Victorian mansions and contemporary suburbs. (See **Chapter 10.**)

The child has time and again been employed as the figure through which societies endeavour to domesticate their darkest fears. In both classic and recent forms of Gothicity, children are relentlessly persecuted, victimized, abandoned and released into unknown dangers by adults anxious to protect themselves. Children become the scapegoats whose sacrifice is supposed to heal the older generations' wounds and expiate society's sins. (See **Chapter 11.**) The victimization of the young is often warranted by the claim that children are not the innocent creatures that Romanticism made them out to be but actually dark and latently monstrous beings. It has often been argued, for example, that the games played by children are not simply instrumental to their socialization but are also ways of subverting adult morality though the creation of parallel universes, with mores of their own, in which violence plays a conspicuous part. It has also been shown that children are inherently aggressive, that they harbour cannibalistic drives and are capable of perpetrating appalling acts of sexual abuse. The child's demonic inclinations are highlighted by a number of narratives that present the young as the Other: a menacing entity at odds with the norms erected by the adult world so as to define and regiment people's identities at all levels – gender, sexuality, race, ethnicity, class. (See **Chapter 12**.)

Moreover, while children are demonized and sacrificed in the interests of the preservation of normality and order, their predicaments are open to two contrasting readings. On the one hand, one may feel some sympathy for defenceless young people at the mercy of crude, brutal or plainly indifferent parents and guardians. On the other hand, one is often reminded, both in ostensibly serious and in parodic fashions, that kids themselves are callous, self-centred and shallow. What should be emphasized is that at the same time as adults exploit the curiosity and naive adventurousness of children to keep their own nightmares at bay, children themselves confront the dark in their own terms in a struggle to understand and name fear. This often entails a willingness to commune, in fantasy and play, with scary creatures and intimations of danger. It is unlikely that children would derive much solace from the notion that darkness should not be dreaded because it is in darkness that their bodies have been conceived and have developed. Little comfort, likewise, is to be gleaned from the assertion that the bogeyman taunting the young from a corner of the bedroom at night is merely a heap of discarded clothes. In order not to be driven to lunacy by the tongue of darkness licking hungrily at the walls of their apparently safe homes, children need to enter an imaginative dialogue with their potential adversaries. They need to give them shapes and labels if they are to grasp, however hazily, abstract concepts such as death. Without subscribing to the idea that children themselves are monstrous, it could be argued that one of the reasons they treasure monsters (as toys, cartoons, characters in books) is that the vampire, the werewolf, the Mad Doctor, the Wild Things, dinosaurs and digimons, to mention but a few, signify death: death is what happens when the monsters come and get you.

The theme of monstrosity supplies a provisional exit point for the exploration of the Gothic vision conveyed by dark fiction. This is for three principal reasons. First, the resilience exhibited throughout history by aberrant creatures as incarnations of deep-seated anxieties and as appropriate vehicles for the narrative constellation of fear echoes the ongoing resurgence of dark writing itself. We return to monsters with the same assiduous longing that drives us to give fear imaginative shapes, plots and settings. Second, just as dark stories are not timeless by virtue of their adoption of recursive formulae and themes but actually rework continuously those elements according to changing ideological and historical circumstances, so monsters alter over time and space to give specific formulation to contingent structures of fear. This is clearly evinced by the evolution of vampire figures, varyingly adopted to voice legion anxieties to do with physical, moral, political and sexual violation. (See **Chapter 13.**) Third, in distorting the putatively normal body by recourse to a plethora of hybrid and grotesque forms, the discourse of monstrosity colludes with the Gothic vision by radically challenging the unity and permanence of both individual and collective identities. (See **Chapter 14.**) Ultimately, it is fear itself that most tenaciously resists compartmentalization, for its sources are not univocally categorizable as obnoxious and repulsive. In fact, they partake of the monstrous logic of abjection (See **Chapter 15**), whereby what disgusts us most potently is also capable of inducing strong feelings of fascination and desire. It is by relentlessly interweaving the repellently odious and the tantalizingly attractive that fear may help us stretch the limits of both our daytime consciousness and our night-time visions.

References

Primary Sources

Note that where two dates are supplied, the first refers to the original date of publication and the second to the edition used in the preparation of the book.

Ackroyd, P. (1985) *Hawksmoor*, London: Hamish Hamilton.

Aldiss, B. [1991] (1992) *Dracula Unbound*, New York: Harper.

Andersen, H. C. (1989) *Tales from Hans Andersen*, London: André Deutsch.

Anscombe, R. [1994] (1995) *The Secret Life of Lazlo, Count Dracula*, London: Bloomsbury.

Atwood, M. [1976] (1982) *Lady Oracle*, London: Virago.

Austen, J. [1818] (1984) *Northanger Abbey*, H.Ehrenpreis (ed.), Harmondsworth: Penguin.

Aycliffe, J. (1996) *The Lost*, London: HarperCollins.

Ballard, J. G. [1973] (1995) *Crash*, London: Vintage.

Barker, A. L. [1987] (1999) *The Gooseboy*, London: Virago.

Barker, C. [1984] (1999a) *Books of Blood, vols.1–3*, London: Little, Brown & Co.

Barker, C. [1987] (1999b) *Weaveworld*, Glasgow: HarperCollins.

Baudelaire, C. [1857] (1961) *Les Fleurs du mal*, A. Adam (ed.), Paris: Garnier.

Baudelaire, C. (1993) *The Flowers of Evil*, trans. J. McGowan, Oxford: Oxford University Press.

Baum, F. [1900] (1978) *The Wonderful Wizard of Oz*, New York: Ballantine.

Baum, F. [1910] (1979) *The Emerald City*, New York: Ballantine.

Beckford, W. [1786] (1986) *Vathek*, in *Three Gothic Novels*, P. Fairclough (ed.), London: Penguin.

Bierce, A. (1964) *Ghost and Horror Stories of Ambrose Bierce*, E. F. Bleiler (ed.), New York: Dover.

Blackwood, A. (1973) *Best Ghost Stories of Algernon Blackwood*, E. F. Bleiler (ed.), New York: Dover.

Blatty, W. P. (1999) 'Elsewhere', in A. Sarrantonio (ed.), *999*, London: Hodder & Stoughton.

Braddon, M. E. [1867] (1992) 'The Cold Embrace', in R. Dalby (ed.), *The Virago Book of Victorian Short Stories*, London: Virago.

Brite, P. Z. [1992] (1994a) *Lost Souls*, London: Penguin.

Brite, P. Z. [1993] (1994b) *Drawing Blood*, London: Penguin.

Brite, P. Z. (1997) *Exquisite Corpse*, London: Phoenix.

Brite, P. Z. (1999) *Self-made Man*, London: Orion.

Brock, P. (2000) *Indiana Gothic*, London: Hodder & Stoughton.

Brockden Brown, C. [1798] (1991) *Wieland and Memoirs of Carwin the Biloquist*, J. Fliegelman (ed.), Harmondsworth: Penguin.

Brontë, C. [1847] (1981) *Jane Eyre*, Q. D. Leavis (ed.), London: Penguin.

Brontë, E. [1847] (1969) *Wuthering Heights*, D. Daiches (ed.), Harmondsworth: Penguin.

Broughton, R. [1873] (1992) 'The Truth, the Whole Truth, and Nothing But the Truth', in R. Dalby (ed.), *The Virago Book of Victorian Short Stories*, London: Virago.

Bryers, P. (2000) *The Prayer of the Bone*, London: Bloomsbury.

Burke, J. L. (1997) *In the Electric Mist with Confederate Dead*, London: Orion.

Campbell, R. (1999) 'The Entertainment', in A. Sarrantonio (ed.), *999*, London: Hodder & Stoughton.

Carroll, L. [1865/1872] (1986) *Alice's Adventures in Wonderland* and *Through the Looking Glass*, Harmondsworth: Penguin.

Carter, A. (1982) *The Passion of New Eve*, London: Virago.

Carter, A. (1984) *Nights at the Circus*, London: Picador.

Carter, A. (1993) *The Bloody Chamber and Other Stories*, London: Penguin.

Carter, A. (1996) *Burning Your Boats: Collected Short Stories*, London: Vintage.

Charnas, S. McKee [1980] (1983) *The Vampire Tapestry*, London: Granada.

Coleridge, S. T. (1991) *Poems*, J. Beer (ed.), London: Everyman.

Collins, N. A. (1999) 'Catfish Gal Blues', in A. Sarrantonio (ed.), *999*, London: Hodder & Stoughton.

Collins, W. [1860] (1985) *The Woman in White*, J. Symons (ed.), London: Penguin.

Collodi, C. [1883] (1986) *The Adventures of Pinocchio*, trans. N. J. Perella, Berkeley: University of California Press.

Coover, R. [1991] (1997) *Pinocchio in Venice*, New York: Grove Press.

de Sade, Marquis (1991) *Justine, Philosophy in the Bedroom and Other Writings*, trans. R. Seaver and A. Wainhouse, London: Arrow.

Dickens, C. [1836-7] (1998) *The Pickwick Papers*, London: Everyman.

Dickens, C. [1843-8] (1994) *The Christmas Books*, London: Penguin.

du Maurier, D. [1938] (1992) *Rebecca*, London: Arrow.

du Maurier, D. (1973) *Don't Look Now and Other Stories*, London: Penguin.

Eliot, G. [1878] (1985) *The Lifted Veil*, London: Virago.

Ellis, B. Easton (1991) *American Psycho*, London: Picador.

Ellison, R. [1952] (1981) *Invisible Man*, New York: Vintage.

Euripides (1982) *The Bacchae*, trans. M. Cacoyannis, New York: New American Library.

Faber, M. (2001) *Under the Skin*, Edinburgh: Canongate.

Faulkner, W. [1930] (1996) *As I Lay Dying*, London: Vintage.

Fowler, C. (1995) *Roofworld*, London: Warner Books.

Fowler, C. (1997) *Disturbia*, London: Warner Books.

Freeman, M. [1920] (1992) 'Shadows on the Wall', in R. Dalby (ed.), *The Virago Book of Victorian Short Stories*, London: Virago.

Gaiman, N. (1999) *The Sandman: The Dream Hunters*, London: Titan Books.

Gardner, H. (ed.) (1999) *The Oxford Book of English Verse*, Oxford: Oxford University Press.

Gaskell, E. [1852] (1992) 'The Old Nurse's Story', in R. Dalby (ed.), *The Virago Book of Victorian Short Stories*, London: Virago.

Gibson, W. [1988] (1995) *Mona Lisa Overdrive*, London: HarperCollins.

Gilman, C. Perkins [1892] (1981) *The Yellow Wallpaper*, London: Virago.

Godwin, W. [1794] (1988) *Things As They Are, or, The Adventures of Caleb Williams*, M. Hindle (ed.), London: Penguin.

Goethe, J. W. [1808/1832] (1969) *Faust, Part I and Part II*, trans. P. Wayne, Harmondsworth: Penguin.

Goethe, J. W. (1998) *Complete Poems*, trans. J. Whaley, New York: Peter Lang.

Graves, R. [1955] (2000) *The Greek Myths, vol. 1*, London: Folio Society.

Grimm, J. L. C. and W. C. Grimm [1822] (2000) *The Fairy Tales of the Brothers Grimm*, trans. Mrs E. Lucas, London: Folio Society.

Harris, T. (1990) *The Silence of the Lambs*, London: Arrow.

Hautala, R. (1999) 'Knocking', in A. Sarrantonio (ed.), *999*, London: Hodder & Stoughton.

Hawthorne, N. [1850] (1978) *The Scarlet Letter*, New York: Knopf.

Herbert, J. (1975) *The Fog*, London: New English Library.

Hill, S. [1983] (1998) *The Woman in Black*, London: Vintage.

Hill, S. [1993] (1999) *Mrs de Winter*, London: Vintage.

Hodgson, W. Hope [1908] (1996) *The House on the Borderland*, London: New English Library.

Høeg, P. (1994) *Miss Smilla's Feeling for Snow*, London: Flamingo.

Hoffmann, E. T. A. (1992) *The Golden Pot and Other Tales*, trans. R. Robertson, Oxford: Oxford University Press.

Hogg, J. [1824] (1947) *Private Memoirs and Confessions of a Justified Sinner*, London: Cresset Press.

Holland, T. (1996) *The Vampyre*, London: Warner Books.

Irving, W. (2000) *The Legend of Sleepy Hollow and Other Stories*, W. L. Hedges (ed.), London: Penguin.

Jackson, S. [1959] (1984) *The Haunting of Hill House*, New York: Viking.

James, H. (1962-64) *The Complete Tales of Henry James*, L. Edel (ed.), London: Everyman.

James, H. (1992) *The Turn of the Screw and Other Stories*, T. J. Lustig (ed.), Oxford: Oxford University Press.

James, M. R. (1998) *Casting the Runes and Other Ghost Stories*, M. Cox (ed.), Oxford: Oxford University Press.

Keats, J. (1988) *Poems*, J. Barnard (ed.), London: Penguin.

King, S. (1977) *Salem's Lot*, London: New English Library.

King, S. [1977] (1978) *The Shining*, London: New English Library.

King, S. [1987] (1988) *Misery*, London: New English Library.

King, S. [1996] (1999a) *The Green Mile*, London: Orion.

King, S. (1999b) *Bag of Bones*, London: Hodder & Stoughton.

Koontz, D. [1999] (2000) *False Memory*, New York: Doubleday.

Lamb, W. (2000) *I Know This Much Is True*, London: HarperCollins.

Lansdale, J. R. (1990) 'Mad Dog Summer', in A. Sarrantonio (ed.), *999*, London: Hodder & Stoughton.

Le Fanu, J. Sheridan (1964) *Best Ghost Stories of Sheridan Le Fanu*, E. F. Bleiler (ed.), New York: Dover.

Lewis, M. [1796] (1998) *The Monk*, C. Maclachlan (ed.), London: Penguin.

Ligotti, T. (1999) 'The Shadow, the Darkness', in A. Sarrantonio (ed.), *999*, London: Hodder & Stoughton.

Lovecraft, H. P. [1928] (1997) 'The Dunwich Horror', in *Crawling Chaos*, C. Wilson (ed.), London: Creation Books.

McGrath, P. (1995) 'The Angel', London: Penguin.

McKiernan, D. L. (1999) 'Darkness', in A. Sarrantonio (ed.), *999*, London: Hodder & Stoughton.

Mahy, M. (1999) *The Haunting*, London: Puffin.

Maturin, C. [1820] (1989) *Melmoth the Wanderer: A Tale*, D. Grant (ed.), Oxford: Oxford University Press.

Morrison, T. (1987) *Beloved*, New York: Knopf.

Newman, K. [1992] (1993) *Anno Dracula*, New York: Carroll & Graf.

Newman, K. (1999) 'Amerikanski Dead at the Moscow Morgue', in A.Sarrantonio (ed.), *999*, London: Hodder & Stoughton.

Oates, J. C. (1999) 'The Ruins of Contracoeur', in A. Sarrantonio (ed.), *999*, London: Hodder & Stoughton.

O'Brien, J. F. [1859] (1994) 'What Was It?', in *Fantasmi Irlandesi*, Milan: Newton Compton.

Peacock, T. Love [1817–18/1831](1982) *Nightmare Abbey* and *Crotchet Castle*, R. Wright (ed.), Harmondsworth: Penguin.

Peake, M. [1946–59] (1992) *The Gormenghast Trilogy*, London: Vintage.

Perrault, C. [1697] (2000) *The Fairy Tales of Charles Perrault*, trans. R. Samber, London: The Folio Society.

Poe, E. Allan (1986) *The Fall of the House of Usher and Other Writings*, D. Galloway (ed.), London: Penguin.

Polidori, J. [1819] (1966) *The Vampyre*, in *Three Gothic Novels*, E. F. Bleiler (ed.), New York: Dover.

Pyper, A. (2001) *Lost Girls*, London: Pan Books.

Radcliffe, A. [1794] (1998) *The Mysteries of Udolpho*, B. Dobree (ed.), Oxford: Oxford University Press.

Repchuck, C., C. Keen, G. Cowan, K. Wootton and C. Wallace (1999) *Spooky Stories*, Bath: Mustard.

Rhys, J. [1966] (1968) *Wide Sargasso Sea*, Harmondsworth: Penguin.

Rice, A. [1976] (1994a) *Interview with the Vampire*, London: Warner Books.

Rice, A. [1985] (1994b) *The Vampire Lestat*, London: Warner Books.

Rice, A. [1988] (1994c) *The Queen of the Damned*, London: Warner Books.

Rice, A. [1990] (1991) *The Witching Hour*, London: Penguin.

Rice, A. [1992] (1993) *The Tale of the Body Thief*, London: Penguin.

Rice, A. [1993] (1994d) *Lasher*, London: Penguin.

Rice, A. [1994] (1995) *Taltos*, London: Arrow.

Rice, A. (1995) *Memnoch the Devil*, London: Chatto & Windus.

Rice, A. (1998) *The Vampire Armand*, London: Chatto & Windus.

Rice, A. (2000) *Vittorio, the Vampire*, London: Arrow.

Rowling, J. K. (1997) *Harry Potter and the Philosopher's Stone*, London: Bloomsbury.

Rowling, J. K. (1998) *Harry Potter and the Chamber of Secrets*, London: Bloomsbury.

Rowling, J. K. (1999) *Harry Potter and the Prisoner of Azkaban*, London: Bloomsbury.

Rowling, J. K. (2000) *Harry Potter and the Goblet of Fire*, London: Bloomsbury.

Ryman, G. (1999) *Was*, London: Flamingo.

Rymer, J. M. [1845–7] (1970) *Varney the Vampire*, New York: Arno Press.

Saberhagen, F. [1975] (1980) *The Dracula Tape*, New York: Ace.

Schnitzler, A. [1926] (1999) *Dream Story*, trans. J. M. Q. Davies, London: Penguin.

Sendak, M. (1963) *Where the Wild Things Are*, London: Red Fox.

Shakespeare, W. (1988) *The Oxford Shakespeare*, S. Wells and G. Taylor (eds.), Oxford: Oxford University Press.

Shelley, M. [1818] (1987) *Frankenstein*, M. K. Joseph (ed.), Oxford: Oxford University Press.

Siddons, A. Rivers [1978] (1995) *The House Next Door*, New York: Harper.

Stevenson, R. L. [1886] (1979) *The Strange Case of Dr Jekyll and Mr Hyde and Other Stories*, Harmondsworth: Penguin.

Stoker [1897] (1993) *Dracula*, Ware: Wordsworth Classics.

Straub, P. [1979] (1994) *Ghost Story*, New York: Harper.

Straub, P. (2000) *Mr X*, London: HarperCollins.

Tennant, E. (1990) *Two Women of London*, London: Faber & Faber.

Van Lustbader, E. (1999) 'An Exaltation of the Termagants', in A. Sarrantonio (ed.), *999*, London: Hodder & Stoughton.

Walpole, H. [1764] (1996) *The Castle of Otranto*, W. S. Lewis (ed.), Oxford: Oxford University Press.

Williamson, C. (1999) 'Excerpts from the *Records of the New Zodiac* and the Diaries of Henry Watson Fairfax', in A. Sarrantonio (ed.), *999*, London: Hodder & Stoughton.

Wilson, F. P. (1999) 'Good Friday', in A. Sarrantonio (ed.), *999*, London: Hodder & Stoughton.

Winterson, J. [1987] (1988) *The Passion*, London: Penguin.

Yarbro, C. Quinn (1999) *Blood Roses: A Novel of St Germain*, New York: Tor.

Yarbro, C. Quinn (2000) *Come Twilight: A Novel of St Germain*, New York: Tor.

Secondary Sources

Abraham, N. (1987) 'Notes on the phantom: a complement to Freud's meta-psychology', *Critical Inquiry* 13:287–92.

Adorno, T. and M. Horkheimer (1986) *Dialectic of Enlightenment*, trans. J. Cumming, London: Verso.

Aguirre, M. (1990) *The Closed Space: Horror Fiction and Western Symbolism*, Manchester: Manchester University Press.

Aikin, A. and J. Aikin (1773) 'On the pleasure derived from objects of terror', in *Miscellaneous Pieces in Prose*, London: Fortune.

Armitt, L. (1996) *Theorizing the Fantastic*, London: Arnold.

Auerbach, N. (1995) *Our Vampires, Ourselves*, Chicago: University of Chicago Press.

Bachelard, G. (1994) *The Poetics of Space*, trans. M. Jolas, Boston: Beacon Press.

Bakhtin, M. (1984) *Rabelais and His World*, trans. H. Iswolsky, Bloomington: Indiana University Press.

Baltrusaitis, J. (1977) *Il Medioevo fantastico*, Milan: Mondadori.

Barker, C. (1986) 'On horror and subversion', in T. Underwood and C. Miller (eds.), *Kingdom of Fear*, London: New English Library.

Barker, C. (1987a) An Interview with Nigel Floyd, *Samhain* No.4, July. Also available on
http://www.btinternet.com/revelations/bloodbarker.html

Barker, C. (1987b) Transcript of talk held at UCLA on 25 February 1987. Available on http://www.btinternet.com/revelations/bloodbarker.html

Barthes, R. (1973) *Mythologies*, trans. A. Lavers, London: Cape.

Barthes, R. (1990) *The Pleasure of the Text*, trans. R. Miller, Oxford: Blackwell.

Barthes, R. (1996) *Sade/Fourier/Loyola*, trans. R. Miller, Baltimore: Johns Hopkins University Press.

Bataille, G. (1987) *Eroticism*, trans. M. Dalwood, London: Marion Boyars.

Bateson, G. (1972) *Steps to an Ecology of Mind*, Chicago: University of Chicago Press.

Baudrillard, J. (1988) *America*, London: Verso.

Baudrillard, J. (1991) 'Two essays: 2. Ballard's *Crash*', *Science Fiction Studies*, vol.18, part 3, November.

Bell, M. 'Woman in the Jamesian Eye': www4.ncsu.edu:8030/-malsgaa/woman_in_the_jamesian_eye.htm

Bettelheim, B. (1991) *The Uses of Enchantment*, Harmondsworth: Penguin.

Birkett, D. (1998) 'I'm Barbie, buy me', *Guardian Weekend*, 28 November.

Blanchot, M. (1982) 'The two versions of the imaginary', in *The Space of Literature*, trans. A. Smock, Lincoln: Nebraska University Press.

Bloch, R. (1998) 'On horror writers', in C. Bloom (ed.) (1998), *Gothic Horror*, London: Macmillan.

Bloom, C. (1998) 'Introduction' to C. Bloom (ed.), *Gothic Horror*, London: Macmillan.

Bonaparte, M. (1949) *Life and Works of Edgar Allan Poe*, trans. J. Rodker, London: Imago.

Borges, J. L. (1970) 'Partial Magic in the *Quixote*', in *Labyrinths*, trans. J. E. Irby, Harmondsworth: Penguin.

Botting, F. (1996) *Gothic*, London: Routledge.

Branham, R. (1983) 'Fantasy and ineffability: fiction at the limits of language', *Extrapolation*, 24:66–79.

Briggs, J. (1977) *Night Visitors*, London: Faber & Faber.

Brite, P. Z. (1998) Interview with Dmetri Kakmi http://www.geocities.com/Vienna/Strasse/6443/interview.html

Bronfen, E. (1992) *Over Her Dead Body*, Manchester: Manchester University Press.

Brooks, P. (1976) *The Melodramatic Imagination*, Baltimore: Yale University Press.

Brown, R. (1999) 'Spookier than thou: charting the goth inversion' http://www.thestranger.com/1999-07-29/art.html

Burke, E. [1757] (1987) *A Philosophical Enquiry into the Origin of Our Ideas of the Sublime and the Beautiful*, J. T. Boulton (ed.), Oxford: Blackwell.

Calvino, I. (1980) *Una Pietra Sopra*, Turin: Giulio Einaudi.

Campbell, J. (1988) *The Power of Myth*, New York: Doubleday.

Campbell, R. (2000) 'Welcome to my haunted domain', British Fantasy Society http://www.herebedragons.co.uk/campbell/main.htm

Carro, V. (1999) 'Fun with Fortunato', *The World of Interiors*, December.

Carroll, N. (1990) *The Philosophy of Horror, or Paradoxes of the Heart*, London: Routledge.

Carter, A. (1979) *The Sadeian Woman*, London: Virago.

Cecil, D. (1948) *Early Victorian Novelists*, Harmondsworth: Pelican.

Chodorow, N. (1978) *The Reproduction of Mothering*, Berkeley: University of California Press.

Clark, K. (1995) *The Gothic Revival*, London: Thames & Hudson.

Clery, E. J. (1999) *The Rise of Supernatural Fiction 1762–1800*, Cambridge: Cambridge University Press.

Davenport-Hines, R. (1998) *Gothic: Four Hundred Years of Excess, Horror, Evil and Ruin*, London: Fourth Estate.

Day, W. P. (1985) *In the Circles of Fear and Desire*, Chicago: University of Chicago Press.

Deserts of the Dead
    http://www.geocities.com/narniagate'DesertsoftheDead.html

Dijkstra, B. (1986) *Idols of Perversity*, Oxford: Oxford University Press.

Donovan, A. (1987) *Alice and Dorothy: Reflections from Two Worlds*, in J. O'Beirbe Milner and L. Floyd Morcock Milner (eds.), *Webs and Wardrobes*, Lanham, MD: University of America.

Douglas, M. (1966) *Purity and Danger*, London: Routledge & Kegan Paul.

Eliade, M. (1952) *Images et symboles*, Paris: Gallimard.

Eliot, T. S. (1999) *Selected Essays*, London: Faber.

Farrington, K. (2000) *The History of Supernatural*, London: Chancellor Press.

Felman, S. (1982) 'Turning the screw of interpretation', in S. Felman (ed.), *Literature and Psychoanalysis: The Question of Reading Otherwise*, Baltimore: Johns Hopkins University Press.

'Female roles in the fairy tales of Charles Perrault'
    http://iabramson.web.wesleyan.edu/perrault.htm

Ferguson Ellis, K. (1989) *The Contested Castle*, Urbana: University of Illinois Press.

Francis, A. C. (1998) 'On *The Vampire Tapestry*', in C. Bloom (ed.), *Gothic Horror*, London: Macmillan.

Franklin, M. (1998) 'Beckford', in M. Mulvey-Roberts (ed.), *The Handbook to Gothic Literature*, London: Macmillan.

Franklin, M. (1998) 'Orientalism', in M. Mulvey-Roberts (ed.), *The Handbook to Gothic Literature*, London: Macmillan.

Freud, S. (1908) 'Creative writers and day-dreaming', *The Standard Edition of the Complete Works of Sigmund Freud*, vol.9, trans. J. Strachey, London: Hogarth Press and the Institute of Psychoanalysis.

Freud, S. (1919) 'The uncanny', *The Standard Edition of the Complete Works of Sigmund Freud*, vol.17, trans. J. Strachey, London: Hogarth Press and the Institute of Psychoanalysis.

Freud, S. (1920) 'Beyond the pleasure principle', *The Standard Edition of the Complete Works of Sigmund Freud*, vol.17, trans. J. Strachey, London:

Hogarth Press and the Institute of Psychoanalysis.

Gassier, P. and J. Wilson (1971) *The Life and Complete Work of Goya*, New York: Norton.

Gay, P. (1984) *The Bourgeois Experience: Victoria to Freud, vol. 1: Education of the Senses*, Oxford: Oxford University Press.

Gelder, R. (1994) *Reading the Vampire*, London: Routledge.

Giddens, A. (1982) *Modernity and Self-Identity: Self and Society in the Late Modern Age*, New York: Simon & Schuster.

Gifford, D. (1976) *James Hogg*, Edinburgh: The Ramsay Head Press.

Gilbert, S. and S. Gubar (1984) *The Madwoman in the Attic: The Woman Writer and the Nineteenth-Century Literary Imagination*, New Haven: Yale University Press.

Gilead, S. (1991) 'Magic abjured: closure in children's fantasy fiction', *PMLA*, 10:277–93.

Goodall, J. (1996) 'General Adaptation Syndrome: hypochondrias of the fin de siècle', in H. Grace (ed.) *Aesthesia and the Economy of the Senses*, Nepean: PAD Publications, University of Western Sydney.

Gordon, A. (1997) *Ghostly Matters*, Minneapolis: University of Minnesota Press.

Goth Primer:
  http://www.sfgoth.com/primer

Grantz, D., 'I am safe'
  http://poedecoder.com.essays.safe

Grunenberg, C. (1997) 'Unsolved mysteries', in C. Grunenberg (ed.), *Gothic*, Cambridge, MA: MIT Press.

Halberstam, J. (1995) *Skin Shows: Gothic Horror and the Technology of Monsters*, Durham, NC: Duke University Press.

Handwerk, G. (1990) 'Of Caleb's guilt and Godwin's truth: ideology and ethics in *Caleb Williams*'
  http://muse.jhu.edu/demo/elh/60.4handwerk.html

Hannaham, J. (1997) 'Bela Lugosi's dead and I don't feel so good either', in C. Grunenberg (ed.), *Gothic*, Cambridge, MA: MIT Press.

Hearn, L. (1900) 'Nightmare-touch', in C. Bloom (ed.) (1998), *Gothic Horror*, London: Macmillan.

Heilman, R. (1947) 'The Freudian reading of *The Turn of the Screw*', *Modern Language Notes* 62:433–45.

Helman, C. (1992) *The Body of Frankenstein's Monster*, New York: Norton.

Hindle, M. (1988) Introduction to *Things As They Are, or, the Adventures of Caleb Williams*, London: Penguin.

Hoffman Baruch, E. (1996) 'Feminism and psychoanalysis', in *Julia Kristeva: Interviews*, R. Mitchell Guberman (ed.), New York: Columbia University Press.

Horner, A. (1998) 'Heroine', in M. Mulvey-Roberts (ed.), *The Handbook to*

Gothic Literature, London: Macmillan.

Hughes, R. (1991) *The Shock of the New*, London: Thames & Hudson.

Hume, K. (1984) *Fantasy and Mimesis*, New York: Methuen.

Hume, R. (1969) 'Gothic versus Romantic', *PMLA* 84.

Hyland, P. (1990) '*Vathek*, heaven and hell', in K. W. Graham (ed.), *Vathek and the Escape from Time: Bicentenary Revaluations*, New York: AMS Press; cited in http://www.engl.virginia.edu/-enec981/Group/liz.death.html

Jackson, R. (1981) *Fantasy: The Literature of Subversion*, London: Methuen.

Kant, I. [1790] (1987) *The Critique of Judgment*, trans. W. S. Pluhar, Indianapolis: Hackett Publishing.

Kayser, W. (1981) *The Grotesque in Art and Literature*, New York: Columbia University Press.

Kennedy, J. G. (1987) *Poe, Death and the Life of Writing*, New Haven: Yale University Press.

Kilgour, M. (1990) *From Communion to Cannibalism*, Princeton: Princeton University Press.

King, S. (1993) *Danse Macabre*, London: Warner Books.

Klein, M. (1988) *The Selected Melanie Klein*, J. Mitchell (ed.), London: Routledge.

Koontz, D. (1999) '*False Memory* As I Remember It' http://www.amazon.com/exec/obidos/tg/feature/-/22115/104-5094060-0292451

Koppelman, D. (1999) 'Aesthetic realism and Picasso's *Guernica*: for Life': http://www.aestheticrealism.org/GUERNICA_dk.htm

Kosofsky Sedgwick, E. (1985) 'Toward the Gothic: terrorism and homosexual panic', in *Between Men: English Literature and Male Homosexual Desire*, New York: Columbia University Press.

Kristeva, J. (1982) *Powers of Horror*, trans. L. Roudiez, New York: Columbia University Press.

Krutch, J. Wood (1926) *Edgar Allan Poe: A Study in Genius*, New York : Knopf.

Lacan, J. (1972) 'Seminar on "La lettre volée"', trans. J. Mehlman, *Yale French Studies*, 48.

Lacan, J. (1977) *Écrits: A Selection*, trans. A. Sheridan, London: Tavistock Publications.

Lacan, J. (1982) 'Desire and the interpretation of desire in *Hamlet*', in S. Felman (ed.), *Literature and Psychoanalysis: The Question of Reading Otherwise*, Baltimore: Johns Hopkins University Press.

Lao, M. (1999) *Sirens: Symbols of Seduction*, trans. J. Oliphant, Rochester, VT: Park Street Press.

Lechte, J. (1990) *Julia Kristeva*, London: Routledge.

Light, A. (1984) 'Returning to Manderley: romance fiction, female sexuality and class', *Feminist Review,* 16:7-23.

'Love, Death, and Stephen King'
    http://www.amazon.com/exec/obidos/tg/feature/-/5604/002-1741305-
    0266637

Lovecraft, H. P. (1973) *Supernatural Horror in Literature*, New York: Dover.

Lubbock, T. (1998) 'Francis Bacon: the man who put the pain into painting',
    Independent, 2 October:
    http://www.francis-bacon.cx/articles/10_98.html

Lustig, T. J. (1992) Introduction to *The Turn of the Screw and Other Stories*,
    T. J. Lustig (ed.) Oxford: Oxford University Press.

Lyotard, J.-F. (1984) *The Postmodern Condition: A Report on Knowledge*, trans.
    G. Bennington and B. Massumi, Manchester: Manchester University Press.

McCracken, S. (1998) *Pulp: Reading Popular Fiction*, Manchester: Manchester
    University Press.

McGrath, M. (2000) 'The witching hour', *Guardian*, 28 October.

Mackenzie, S. (1999) 'Fear, be my friend', *Guardian Weekend*, 23 October.

Marigny, J. (1994) *Vampires: The World of the Undead*, trans. L. Frankel,
    London: Thames & Hudson.

Menegaldo, G. (1996) 'Gothic convention and modernity in J. R. Campbell's
    short fiction', in V. Sage and A. L. Smith (eds.), *Modern Gothic*, London:
    Macmillan.

Mettler, P. (1995) *Making the Invisible Visible*, Munsterschwarzach Abtei:
    Benedikt Press.

Miles, R. (1998) 'Nathaniel Hawthorne', in M. Mulvey-Roberts (ed.), *The
    Handbook to Gothic Literature*, London: Macmillan.

Miller, A. (1981) *The Drama of the Gifted Child*, trans. R. Ward, New York: Basic
    Books.

Miller, A. (1983) *For Your Own Good*, New York: Basic Books.

Monahan, J. (1999) 'Chilled to the bone', *Guardian*, Guardian Education,
    7 December.

Moonstone, R. (1995) 'The Origins of Hallowe'en':
    http://www.northvermont12.com/halloween/origins.html

Moretti, F. (1997) *Signs Taken for Wonders*, London: Verso.

Morris, D. B. (1985) 'Gothic sublimity', *New Literary History* 16.

Mulvey-Roberts, M. (1998) 'Introduction' to M. Mulvey-Roberts (ed.), *The
    Handbook to Gothic Literature*, London: Macmillan.

Nardin, J. (1978) '*The Turn of the Screw*: the Victorian background', *Mosaic*
    12:131-42.

Nash, W. (1990) *The Language of Popular Fiction*, London: Routledge.

Nead, L. (1992) *The Female Nude: Art, Obscenity and Sexuality*, London:
    Routledge.

Newman, J. (1998) 'On *The Haunting of Hill House*', in C. Bloom (ed.), *Gothic
    Horror*, London: Macmillan.

Nietzsche, F. (1990) *Beyond Good and Evil*, trans. R. J. Hollingdale, Harmondsworth: Penguin.

Nordau, M. [1892] (1993) *Degeneration*, Lincoln: University of Nebraska Press.

Olson, P. F. on Algernon Blackwood:
http://www.horrornet.com/rootsof.htm

Palfrey, D. H. (1995) 'The Day of the Dead':
http://www.mexicoconnect.com/mex_/muertos.html

Poe, E. Allan (1845) 'The imp of the perverse', *Graham's Magazine*.

Porter, A., 'A brief history of the gothic movement 1970s to 1990s':
http://www.gothics.org/subculture/origin.html

'Psychology of sexuality in fairy tales':
http://shise.web.wesleyan.edu/LandofFaery.psycho.html

Punter, D. (1996) *The Literature of Terror*, vol.1, New York: Longman.

Punter, D. (1998) 'Terror', in M. Mulvey-Roberts (ed.), *The Handbook to Gothic Literature*, London: Macmillan.

Radcliffe, A. (1826) 'On the supernatural in poetry', *New Monthly Magazine, 7*.

Ramsland, K. (1994) *The Vampire Companion*, London: Little, Brown & Co.

Rance, N. (1993) 'Fiends in the cellar: Daphne du Maurier and the infernal world of popular fiction', in C. Bloom (ed.), *Creepers*, London: Pluto Press.

Robinson, W. J. (1922) *Married Life and Happiness*, New York: Eugenics Publishing.

Rushdie, S. (1992) *The Wizard of Oz*, London: BFI Publishing.

Sacks, O. (1986) *The Man Who Mistook His Wife for a Hat*, London: Picador.

Sage, V. (1998) 'Gothic Revival', in M. Mulvey-Roberts (ed.), *The Handbook to Gothic Literature*, London: Macmillan.

Sage, V. and A. L. Smith (1996) 'Introduction' to V. Sage and A. L. Smith (eds), *Modern Gothic*, London: Macmillan.

Said, E. (1988) 'Crisis (in orientalism)', in D. Lodge (ed.), *Modern Criticism and Theory*, London: Longman.

Salon Interview with Stephen King:
http://www.salon.com/books/int/1998/09/cov_si_24int2.html

Schneede, U. M. (1988) *Edvard Munch: The Early Masterpieces*, trans. A. Heritage and P. Kremmel, Munich: Schirmer/Mosel.

Seifert, L. C. (1996) *Fairy Tales, Sexuality, and Gender in France 1690-1715*, New York: Cambridge University Press.

Skal, D. (1990) *Hollywood Gothic*, London: Andre Deutsch.

Smith, A. L. (1993) 'A word kept back in *The Turn of the Screw*', in C. Bloom (ed.), *Creepers*, London: Pluto Press.

Snyder, L. A. (1999) An Interview with Nancy A. Collins:
www.sfsite.com/darkplanet/nonfic/NancyC.html

Stallybrass, P. and A. White (1986) *The Politics and Poetics of Transgression*, London, Methuen.

Straub, P. (1999) 'Introduction' to P. Z. Brite, *Self-Made Man*, London: Orion.

Straub, P. On *Mr X*
http://pluto.spaceports.com/mot/Straub.htm

Summers, M. (1938) *The Gothic Quest: A History of the Gothic Novel*, London: Fortune.

Summers, M. (1960) *The Vampire: His Kith and Kin*, Hyde Park, NY: University Books.

'Teaching gender roles: fairy tales and beyond'
http://iabramson.web.wesleyan.edu/project.htm

Thiher, A. (1987) *Words in Reflection*, Chicago: University of Chicago Press.

Todorov, T. (1975) *The Fantastic: A Structural Approach to a Literary Genre*, trans. R. Howard, Ithaca, NY: Cornell University Press.

Tolkien, J. R. R. (1966) 'Tree and Leaf', in *The Tolkien Reader*, New York: Ballantine.

Toth, C. (1997) 'Like cancer in the system', in C. Grunenberg (ed.), *Gothic*, Cambridge, MA: MIT Press.

Twitchell, J. B. (1988) *Dreadful Pleasures*, Oxford: Oxford University Press.

Uglow, J. (1992) Introduction to *The Virago Book of Victorian Short Stories*, London: Virago.

Varma, D. P. (1988) *The Gothic Flame*, Lanham, MD: Scarecrow Press.

Vico, G. [1725] (1968) *The New Science*, trans. T. Goddard and M. H. Fisch, Ithaca, NY: Cornell University Press.

Victorian Web:

Flaxman, R. L.
http://landow.stg.brown.edu/victorian/tech/wrdpaint.html

Landow, G. P.
http://landow.stg.brown.edu/victorian/tech/radcliffe.html

Warner, M. (1995) *From the Beast to the Blonde*, London: Vintage.

Warner, M. (2000) *No Go the Bogeyman*, London: Vintage.

Williams, A. (1995) *Art of Darkness*, Chicago: University of Chicago Press.

Wilson, E. (1934) 'The ambiguity of Henry James', *Hound and Horn*, 7:385–406.

Winnicott, C., R. Shepherd and M. Davis (eds.) (1989), *D. W. Winnicott: Psycho-Analytic Explorations*, London: Karnac Books.

Wisker, G. (1993) 'At home all was blood and feathers: the werewolf in the kitchen – Angela Carter and horror', in C. Bloom (ed.), *Creepers*, London: Pluto Press.

'Women and the Gothic', in *Sublime Anxiety*:
www.lib.virginia.edu/exhibits/gothic/women.html

Ziegler, R. (1993) 'Incorporation and rebirth in *The Silence of the Lambs*', *Notes on Contemporary Literature*, March.

Zipes, J. (1991) *Fairy Tales and the Art of Subversion*, New York: Routledge.

Zipes, J. (1997) *Happily Ever After*, New York and London: Routledge.

Filmography

American Psycho (2000) Dir. Mary Hannon

Blade (1998) Dir. Stephen Norrington

The Blair Witch Project (1999) Dirs Daniel Myrick and Eduardo de Sanchez

Bram Stoker's Dracula (1973) Dir. Dan Curtis

Bram Stoker's Dracula (1992) Dir. Francis Ford Coppola

Cape Fear (1991) Dir. Martin Scorsese

Dracula (1931) Dir. Tod Browning

Dracula (1979) Dir. John Badham

The Exorcist (1973) Dir. William Friedkin

Eyes Wide Shut (1999) Dir. Stanley Kubrick

Halloween (1978) Dir. John Carpenter

The Hand That Rocks the Cradle (1992) Dir. Peter Hanson

The Haunting (1963) Dir. Robert Wise

The Haunting (1999) Dir. Jan de Bont

Horror of Dracula (1958) Dir. Terence Fisher

John Carpenter's Vampires (1998) Dir. John Carpenter

The Lost Boys (1987) Dir. Joel Schumacher

Million Dollar Mermaid (1952) Dir. Mervyn LeRoy

Near Dark (1987) Dir. Kathryn Bigelow

Nightmare on Elm Street (1984) Dir. Wes Craven

Nosferatu (1922) Dir. F. W. Murnau

Nosferatu the Vampire (1979) Dir. Werner Herzog

Omen (1976) Dir. Richard Donner

The Piano (1993) Dir. Jane Campion

Quills (2000) Dir. Philip Kaufman

Rosemary's Baby (1968) Dir. Roman Polansky

Scary Movie (2000) Dir. Keenan Ivory Wayans

Scream (1996) Dir. Wes Craven

Shadow of the Vampire (2000) Dir. E. Elias Merhige

The Shining (1980) Dir. Stanley Kubrick

The Silence of the Lambs (1991) Dir. Jonathan Demme

Sleepy Hollow (1999) Dir. Tim Burton

Splash (1984) Dir. Ron Howard

Vampire's Kiss (1989) Dir. Robert Bierman

What Lies Beneath (2000) Dir. Robert Zemeckis

The Wizard of Oz (1939) Dirs George Kukor, Richard Thorpe, King Vidor, Victor Fleming

Index